Politics: A Beginner's Guide to Western Political Philosophy

Matt Smith

ATHENA PRESS
LONDON

Politics: A Beginner's Guide to Western Political Philosophy
Copyright © Matt Smith 2010

ISBN 978 1 84748 705 6

Previously published by the author with Athena Press:
Bridge: Adding Precision and Pre-emption to Two-over-one and Acol (2008)

First published 2010 by
ATHENA PRESS
Queen's House, 2 Holly Road
Twickenham TW1 4EG
United Kingdom

Printed for Athena Press

Acknowledgements

My sincere thanks to all the Internet sources that I have unashamedly used. In fact, it is intentional in that I hope that I will draw attention to the vast wealth of information that is now available on the Internet for anyone interested in politics and political philosophy.

Clearly, in a book of this nature, there are no claims to originality in terms of the ideas of political philosophy that have been included. It is more a question of finding academic sources that are able to express original ideas in a form that is readily comprehensible to a reader new to political philosophy.

I am of course fully aware of the possible inaccuracies of Wikipedia but would argue that this is not a major problem in the context of this book.

My only claim to originality is in terms of the overall presentation and style. I hope that it will encourage and interest the new reader to continue so that the objectives for the book are met.

My thanks to Ruth Evans, Adam Hall, Phil Harrison and John Schiffeler for commenting on the readability and suitability of the text as an introductory book.

To Fran

for her love, patience and never-ending support

Sources

Extracts from *What Is Good?* London, Phoenix, 2007, reproduced
with the kind permission of Professor A C Grayling

An extract from comments on the post-2008 US election scene by
Jonathan Clarke and co-writer Dr Amy Zalman reproduced with
their kind permission

A quote by Adam Posen from *International Finance*, October 1998,
reproduced with the kind permission of the Peterson Institute for
International Economics

Quotes from Murray Rothbard's arguments against protectionism
reproduced with the kind permission of the Ludwig von Mises
Institute

Quotes by Chantal Mouffe on agonism reproduced with her kind
permission

Theda Skocpol's ideas in *Diminished Democracy* reproduced with
her kind permission

G William Domhoff's ideas on the 'Government Class'
reproduced with his kind permission

Quotes from 'Feminists on Power' reproduced with the kind
permission of Professor Amy R Allen

Quotes from *Imperfect Garden* by Todorov reproduced with the kind permission of Mike Schwartz

Quotes from *The Power Elite* reproduced with the kind permission of Nik Mills

Contents

Foreword

The purpose of this book is to provide a clear and readable introduction to Western political philosophy, a beginner's guide in fact.

It should appeal to those in the UK and USA who recognise the importance of philosophy and are:

- interested in acquiring an understanding and overview of the key ideas
- wanting to try to develop and refine their personal political beliefs
- looking to be stimulated to read more widely and discover how to readily access interesting and relevant material, especially on the Internet.

It is not the intention to promote any particular mix of ideas and values, but to help you to develop and refine the particular political philosophy that works for you, so you may more confidently express and explain it to others. I can assure you that I have tried to be non-judgemental when dealing with controversial political and religious ideas.

The first part of the book will move to a point where the reader can begin to understand the political philosophy behind the way they vote.

The second part will introduce further philosophical ideas and examine broader issues of political controversy that are of current concern in the world today.

The approach used is one that the author has successfully employed and developed while teaching students at undergraduate and postgraduate levels over a period of thirty years in universities.

I am aware of the difficulties of using -isms (for example,

theism), which regroups the thoughts of individual authors under generic labels. However, I would argue that this is of great benefit at an introductory level where it is essential for the author and reader to have at hand a common language, even if at first it only gives a superficial understanding. This, together with self-confidence, is the best precursor for more in-depth study.

The economic collapse of 2008 together with the elections of a new American president in November 2008 and a new UK Prime Minister in May 2010 makes this an appropriate time to publish, given the rethinking that it will occasion.

Part One

Philosophy Underlying UK/USA Politics

1

Political Philosophy

Human nature, always ready to offend even where laws exist.

Thucydides

A natural repugnance to seeing any sentient being, especially our fellow man, perish or suffer.

Rousseau

The sleep of reason brings forth monsters.

Francisco de Goya

Reason can wrestle terror, and overthrow it at last.

Euripides

I start by letting you know that there are summaries at the end of each chapter. I tell you this now as many readers like to read the summary first, as it may aid understanding if you know how things will develop. If you have not done this before, try it now.

If you visit www.google.com and search for 'politics', a whole world of information will open up for you. You will be welcomed into, among others, Wikipedia (a free encyclopaedia), Wikiquote (a free online compendium of sourced quotations), the political sites of the world's newspapers and TV channels, political blogs such as The Huffington Post or Guido Fawkes (of varying quality but fascinating), www.politics.co.uk (an Internet site which claims to be 'politically neutral'), the American Political Science Association and Institute, a site which will take you into a world of political references. Finally, Richard Kimber's Political Science

Resources is an extensive collection of over 3,200 links to the major political and governmental sites around the world.

And this is just the tip of the iceberg. Thus, part of my aim is to guide you through this minefield of highly subjective information and disinformation.

The purpose in writing this book is to show you how to eventually make good use of all of this information by providing a clear and readable introduction to Western political philosophy, although some brief reference will have to be made to Eastern thought when considering Islam.

In writing this book I am thinking of someone of any religious or political opinion who nevertheless recognises the importance of Western political philosophy and is interested in acquiring an understanding and overview of the key ideas, and wanting to try to develop and refine their personal political beliefs.

It is not the intention to promote any particular mix of ideas and values, but to help you to develop and refine the particular political philosophy that works for you, so you may more confidently express and explain it to others.

> If you can't say it clearly, you don't understand it yourself.
>
> John Searle, from Wikiquote

I am conscious in saying this that I am setting myself a hard task and no doubt you will spot areas before the conclusion where I give my own views away.

I would argue that this is a particularly opportune moment to produce this book as 'The party is definitely over. And the present decade has acquired its permanent character as a historical pivot defined by the nightmares of 9/11 and the panic of 2008–09.' (Andersen, April 2009)

It is a good time now as the world is in a period of profound change. This may be the end of the world as we have known it, but in the medium- to long-term future that might not turn out to be a bad thing, and it definitely is not the end of the world.

> It is simply not sustainable to have an economy where, in one year, forty per cent of our corporate profits came from a financial

sector that was based on inflated home prices, maxed-out credit cards, over-leveraged banks, and overvalued assets.

President Obama, April 2009

On reflection, how many of us have to admit that we pretended not to see the economic crash coming? From the beginning of the eighties until the start of the crash in the US, my local daily, the *Monterey Herald* is keen to inform me:

- the median price of a new home has increased by 400 per cent
- the size of the average new house has increased by fifty per cent
- the share of disposable income that we spent on a mortgage and consumer debt has risen by thirty-five per cent
- the amount of our disposable income that we saved has fallen from eleven to one per cent
- obesity has increased from fifteen to thirty-three per cent.

These figures are rough estimates but nevertheless they confirm the accurate caricature of Homer Simpson as the typical American: childish, irresponsible, wilfully oblivious, fat and happy. The situation in the UK has been very similar.

> The centre-left consensus that has shaped Britain since Labour swept to power under Blair in 1997 is disintegrating, and the New Labour project that created it – the potent mix of idealism and pragmatism, of social-democratic aspirations and fiscal conservatism, of commitment to equality and opportunity – needs a radical overhaul.

Mayer, 2009

Many can now see that the current crisis has been brought about by over two decades of self-destructive financial excess and a serious over-dependence on debt and fossil fuels.

This year [2009] Britain is likely to incur a fiscal deficit of more than twelve per cent of national income … If notionally a government were to try to balance the deficit by cutting expenditure, about one third of public expenditure would need to be cut; a government that tried to balance the books by raising taxation would need to increase all taxes by one third. Of course these are impossible figures, but they indicate the scale of cuts in spending and rises in taxation that will be needed.

Rees-Mogg, 2009

A major reason for the election of President Obama was his realisation that the US was entering a period of ideological flux.

Ronald Reagan changed the trajectory of America … He tapped into what people were feeling … [He] transformed American politics and set the agenda for a long time … In political terms, we may be in one of those moments where we can get a seismic shift in how the country views itself and our future.

President Obama, 2009

Similarly, the May 2010 General Election in the UK produced a 'hung' parliament, meaning that the electorate was not willing to give outright power to any one party. The outcome has been a coalition between the Conservatives and the Liberal Democrats.

'There are times perhaps once every thirty years when there is a sea change in politics … there is a shift in what the public wants and … approves of.' Thus did Jim Callaghan famously identify the tide of popular sentiment that would deliver three election victories to Margaret Thatcher.

Three decades have passed … and … forces no less strong … have delivered another extraordinary result. [The 2010 General Election] delivered as thorough a kicking as could have been delivered to the political class.

d'Ancona, 2010

So now is an excellent time to join the debate. The familiar polarisation of left and right is losing its salience and China has emerged as a booming member of the global order, socialist now in name only. Ideological autopilots are being turned off and many people are reverting to their pragmatic, common-sense selves.

We cannot rule out the possibility of new ideologies with mass mobilising potential that are capable of legitimising new regimes, benevolent or authoritarian.

So let us go back to the net for some definitions. For political science, Wikipedia suggests it is 'concerned with the theory and practice of politics and the description and analysis of political systems and political behaviour. It is often described as the study of politics defined as "who gets what, when and how".'

Then the Internet Encyclopaedia of Philosophy suggests political philosophy 'has its beginnings in ethics: in questions such as what kind of life is the good life for human beings. Since people are by nature sociable – there being few proper anchorites who turn from society to live alone – the question follows as to what kind of life is proper for a person among people.'

And the difference between the two is that 'Political science predominantly deals with existing states of affairs, and insofar as it is possible to be amoral in its descriptions, it seeks a positive analysis of social affairs … Political philosophy generates visions of the good social life: of what ought to be the ruling set of values and institutions that combine men and women together.'

That seems clear in that we are concerned with thinking about what it means to lead a good life. There will not be full agreement on this, but so long as you are reasonably clear as to what you are trying to do to lead a good life, and provide coherent arguments to support your views, then you have a political philosophy.

Western political philosophy can be traced back to its inception in Athens in fifth-century BC where the Greek philosophers were the first to argue that we are all political animals:

> If the earlier forms of society are natural, so is the state, for it is the end of them, and the nature of a thing is its end. For what each thing is when fully developed, we call its nature … Hence it is evident that the state is a creation of nature, and that man is by nature a political animal.

Aristotle c. 330 BC

Thus the question is raised of whether or not it is possible to wield power over people wisely. According to Aristotle, the goal toward which humanity develops, beginning with families, and then villages, is life in a *polis*, a city. To him 'man is by nature a political animal' means that human society tends to develop towards the goal of city life.

The eighteenth- and nineteenth-century writers did not accept Aristotle's view that the *polis* was the final stage; they thought there were more stages than he knew about. Adam Smith, for example, argued that a 'commercial society' was the final stage, but Marx stated that the 'commercial society' Smith described had developed into the specific form of 'capitalism', and the dynamic of capitalism would in turn give rise to another, and final, stage, 'socialism'.

Before we develop the idea of political philosophy in more depth, a brief look at some etymology (the study of the history of words) should prove helpful. Reading N S Gill's article 'A Little Etymology' (About.com:Ancient/ClassicalHistory) would also clear the air.

In classical Greek there were two words for 'rule' or 'government', namely *kratos* and *arche*.

Kratos means might, power, dominion or sway; *arche* sometimes means a beginning or origin (archaeology is the study of origins), but sometimes it means supreme power or sovereignty.

From *kratos* we derive various words that end in '-cracy' such as democracy and aristocracy. From *arche* we derive various words that end in '-archy' such as monarchy and anarchy.

Monos in Greek meant 'one' or 'single'. *Demos* meant 'the people'. *Aristos* meant 'the best'; *oligos* meant 'few'.

Another political word is 'tyranny', from *turannos* meaning 'lord' or 'master', or someone who had seized monarchy by force.

Another is 'despot' – that meant the master of slaves, or a monarch who treats his subjects like slaves.

Write down one under the other:

- first line 'monarchy, tyranny or despotism'
- second line 'aristocracy or oligarchy'
- third line 'democracy'.

The words in the first line apply to governments headed by a single person – 'tyranny' and 'despotism' imply an unfavourable judgment; 'monarchy' is the neutral term, meaning literally rule by a single person.

The words in the second line apply to government by a relatively small number: 'oligarchy' means literally rule by the few, but it was used generally to express disapproval; 'aristocracy' means 'rule by the best', who will be few.

'Democracy' in the third line means rule by the people.

From the start, political philosophy has been concerned with the issues arising from three fundamental questions. To have a political philosophy you must have reasoned answers to these questions.

The three questions (Dalton, 1991) are:

1   What are the essential characteristics of human nature, and does how your view of what they are influence your vision of a good society?

2   What is the right relationship between an individual and society?

3   In what ways may human nature and society change, and how does this happen?

These questions will be explained simply in part one of the book and returned to in more detail in the second part, where the role of 'the social' and 'power' in political philosophy will be further developed.

To start you thinking about these questions at this point, I would like you to carry out a small exercise. I have listed below a number of statements that are related to the questions. Please write in pencil 'A' if you agree or 'D' if you disagree with each statement. If some of them do not mean much to you, go by intuition. Do not worry at this stage, as you can revise your decisions at any time as we go along.

- Social unity and harmony are desirable and achievable.
- Human nature is innately sinful, aggressive and violent.

21

- Legitimate political authority comes from the individual.

- Human beings are fundamentally unequal.

- An enduring and universal system of ethical and moral values is not possible.

- Radical change should be achieved by gradual evolutionary means.

You will also notice some quotations at the start of every chapter. They are not necessarily linked to the chapter, but do provide interesting and opposing thoughts that will help you to think over the questions above as you go along.

When you think you understand the chapter, another idea is to make additional notes in pencil on the summary page.

Summary

A vast amount of free information on politics and political philosophy is available, but skill is required in its interpretation.

Now is an excellent time to join the debate. The familiar polarisation of left and right is losing its salience and China has emerged as a booming member of the global order, socialist now in name only. Ideological autopilots are being turned off and many people are reverting to their pragmatic, common-sense selves.

Political science predominantly deals with existing states of affairs, and insofar as it is possible to be amoral in its descriptions, it seeks a positive analysis of social affairs... Political philosophy generates visions of the good social life, namely, of what ought to be the ruling set of values and institutions that combine men and women together.

Political philosophy concerns itself with three fundamental questions:

1   What are the essential characteristics of human nature, and how does your view of what these are influence your vision of a good society?

2   What is the right relationship between an individual and society?

3   In what ways may human nature and society change, and how does this happen?

- -

Reader's Notes:

2

-isms and Reality

A just law is a man-made law that squares with the moral law.

Martin Luther King

Once a man has authority, he must be obeyed … whether just or not so just … there is nothing so disastrous as anarchy.

Creon in *Antigone*

The purpose of this chapter is to help you to begin to understand:

- the process by which you try to understand reality through the interrelationship of fact, theory, and value
- the part played by -isms in this process, starting with -isms in general, e.g. plagiarism, surrealism in this chapter, continuing with political -isms e.g. socialism, conservatism in the next chapter.

Can one have a political philosophy without first having a general philosophy?

Clearly they would need to be intrinsically linked and logically consistent with each other.

Developing your own general philosophy is important because it helps you to sort out and make sense of your own ideas so that you can begin to understand the so-called reality of the world around you and your place in it.

This all sounds somewhat abstract, so let us try to simplify and explain via some examples.

First of all, how are fact, theory and value interrelated with each other and reality?

Imagine that we all view the world through our own pair of spectacles with unique lenses, which represent what seems to us to be the most acceptable mix, or interrelationship, of ideas, facts and values.

We value some things more than others – say, family before career; we find some theories provide more acceptable answers than others – say, evolutionism rather than creationism; and some facts lead us to come to some conclusions rather than others – say, independent reports on car reliability.

As society changes the mix changes, but we always finish up with the one we are most comfortable with. There are contradictions and things we cannot really explain, but it is for most of the time the best we can do. For most of us the mix changed quite rapidly when we were young, but as we got older it changed less frequently.

Some of us are more adamant than others that our mix is preferable and we will as a consequence be more reluctant to change. This is commendable if we can give logical arguments to support why our mix is the best one for us. Some of us feel the mix is right but would like to be clearer in our minds as to why this is the case. If you fall into this latter category, then this book should be very helpful.

There are therefore at any one moment in time thousands of facts, ideas and values floating around in the minds of people and grouped together in a multitude of different ways.

It is pretty safe to assume, however, that although every person will have their own unique mix, there will be some who will have more in common than others – for example, members of the Republican Party, Conservative Party or of the Catholic Church.

So how do we explain how different people are relatively content with a different mix of lenses to perceive reality?

Imagine a TV debate on unemployment where two eminent professors have been asked to explain what unemployment is, what causes it and how best to combat it. Assume that both professors are equally intelligent, have the same debating skills and that the only difference between them is their contrasting political philosophies, one being an American capitalist and the other a Chinese Marxist.

Do not worry at this stage if you are not clear as to the differences between capitalism and Marxism – that comes later. The key point is that in the political arena they will have widely varying values. Outside of the political arena, they may of course share certain similarities and tastes for example, being both happily married with four children and being vegetarians. They will, however, have completely opposing views on unemployment. As a result of their differing political positions, they will favour different theories to explain things and use the same facts to support different conclusions.

Having listened to the debate, what conclusions are open to you?

If both present their respective cases with equal skill and profundity of thought, surely it becomes a matter of which case you find the more preferable or acceptable given your own mix of facts, theories and values that influence your thinking. Every individual has their own unique mix which is a product of nature and nurture, the way you have interacted with your environment as you have grown up.

The more you have a good understanding of your own mix, the more you will able to consider issues logically and dispassionately. If you find this difficult – and most do – you can maintain your intellectual honesty by making your value positions clear.

To reach a conclusion on the debate in terms of one view being better than the other would require substantial global evidence as to:

- the relative importance of the questions being addressed by each view
- the quality of the responses to those questions
- a sound understanding and awareness of one's own value positions.

Secondly, let us clarify what exactly is meant by an -ism.

Imagine asking a representative sample of the population to select those ideas and values which they felt best demonstrated the key political ideas and values of Margaret Thatcher or Ronald Reagan when they were in power. Ideas and values that might be included might be, for example, privatisation, the importance of monetary policy and the value of the importance of competition. This collection of ideas and values might come to be called Thatcherism or Reaganism over time if as a body of ideas and values they are felt to be important. At this point an -ism is born.

Please note that no judgments are implied here vis-à-vis the merits or demerits of Thatcherism and Reaganism.

Readers should note that at the time of writing, Margaret Thatcher was the most recent UK politician to be elevated to an -ism; Blairism has been occasionally mentioned but never consolidated.

An -ism therefore is a collection or mix of ideas and values that exist at a certain moment in time and represent something that people feel is significant and important.

We use -isms to help us to perceive the real world. The lens in our spectacles will contain many -isms, each one being given our own personal level of priority.

Let us explore this concept of an -ism in more detail.

First, some -isms are more important and enduring than others; this is mainly to do with their socio-political significance.

For example, it is possible to divide the population into those with and without ginger hair, but so far this has not been seen to be of sufficient social significance for gingerism to emerge. In contrast, divisions based on ethnicity and gender produce both racism and sexism, around which controversy has existed throughout much of time.

Luddism, however, was doomed to a short existence. Although one could sympathise with the short-term economic hardship that occasioned the riots and machine-breaking when the new technology was introduced, it was clear that in the longer term there would be more employment created by the new technology.

Second, an -ism should be seen as dynamic rather than static, as some ideas within the package may come or go over time, or others may assume greater importance. For example, racism is perhaps today more concerned with what is seen as unfair competition over jobs as a result of immigration than colour of skin. Some might argue that there are certain core values that are immutable.

Third, some -isms can of course overlap and contain other -isms. Thatcherism and Reaganism, for example, contain individualism, capitalism, nationalism, monetarism, conservatism and liberalism, just to name a few! There can be a fine line between the ending of one -ism and the start of another. For example, if private ownership is gradually increased in an economy, at which point do you cease to talk of communism and begin to talk of capitalism? In other words you are thinking along a 'dimension'.

Fourth, some -isms may not just overlap and contain other -isms, they may contradict and be in competition with one another. It is quite feasible for some bits to be included and others lost. Thatcherism, as we have already mentioned, is among others, a careful blend of liberalism and conservatism, two -isms, which we will see, only partially sit together.

Fifth, -isms must be seen as society- or culture-specific. To give an obvious example, the ideas and values which collectively represent capitalism would be different in North Korea and Cuba from the USA or the UK.

Finally, there can be moral and value judgments within an -ism that can be contentious. For example, anti-Semitism represents the ideas and values of those who dislike Jews and would wish to discriminate against them.

Summary

We try to make sense of reality through the interrelationship of fact, theory and value.

An -ism is a way of thinking and seeing things which sees certain ideas and values at a particular time as more important than others.

An -ism lasts as long as it has significance.

An -ism is dynamic and overlaps with and contains other -isms. They can compete with one another, are society- and culture-specific, and can contain moral judgments and values that are contentious.

▪ ▬ ▬ ▬ ▬ ▬ ▬ ▬ ▬ ▬ ▬ ▬ ▬ ▬ ▬ ▬ ▬ ▬ ▪

Reader's Notes:

3

From -isms to Ideology

It seems that I am wiser than he is, to this small extent that I do
not think that I know what I do not know.

Socrates

Man is the measure of all things.

Protagoras

This chapter will try to explain:

- which -isms are the concern of political philosophy and
  which are not
- the relationship between an -ism and an ideology.

Readers will probably feel quite confident in asserting that
Thatcherism/Reaganism is a political -ism but will be less
confident in explaining why. Let us try to address this.

In Chapter 1 it was suggested that Western political philosophy is concerned with the issues arising from three fundamental
questions:

1   What are the essential characteristics of human nature,
    and how does one's view of what these are influence
    one's vision of a good society?

2   What is the right relationship between an individual and
    society?

3   In what ways may human nature and society change, and
    how does this happen?

Let us try to relate these questions to Thatcherism and Reaganism, again remembering that this is purely for illustrative purposes.

Thatcherism/Reaganism sees people as self-interested individuals, i.e. if given an opportunity they will try to use it to their own advantage. Success breeds self-respect. It is therefore crucial for people to be given equal opportunity and encouragement to advance themselves in competitive situations.

This implies minimal interference from government and trade unions in the market. The importance of supply-side economics is stressed, i.e. to prosper you must supply the right goods and services at the right time, at the right quality and at the right price.

An organisation such as the EU (the 'Common Market') is useful if it increases opportunities, but not if it reduces individual rights and increases the power of the state.

Change occurs as resources (land, labour, capital and enterprise) move to more profitable areas, such as financial services and hypermarkets, and away from less profitable areas. This will generate short-term hardships, but the profits generated by this will finance the growth from which everyone to a greater or lesser degree will eventually benefit. You cannot have winners without losers.

Hopefully you will now feel able to explain why Thatcherism/Reaganism is a political -ism, irrespective of whether or not you sympathise with the mix of theory and values that it extols.

An -ism becomes an -ism of political philosophy when the ideas and values are concerned with achieving power over people by coercion or persuasion.

As an -ism it is available to help you think through your own political philosophy, as are other political -isms such as Marxism, republicanism and conservatism. As you read more you will become more drawn to some than others, or bits of some rather than others.

Some people find one -ism so appealing to them that instead of just using it as a mix of ideas and values to help them make sense of things, they adopt it and it becomes the way to interpret things and decide how they should act and behave.

An -ism becomes an ideology when you decide to use it in this way to interpret the way you perceive reality. It is important to realise that it now becomes more than just a body of knowledge available to you to help you make decisions. It becomes the body of knowledge by which you decide what is right and wrong.

This is not necessarily a problem if you have clearly thought it through and it gives you a clear sense of purpose and understanding in life. It can give you an important sense of conviction.

However, you must never forget the aspects of an ideology outlined earlier and in particular their dynamism, cultural specificity, value assumptions, and possible inner contradictions.

To try to illustrate this more simply, imagine the situation in Germany at the time of the rise to power of Hitler. He realised that if you want to persuade people to see things your way, and give you the power you require to pursue your own policies, you must present them with an appropriate ideological view, which they will take on board. Nazism gave the German people back their self-esteem and others to blame for their current plight. Goebbels, Hitler's propaganda chief, allegedly said words to the effect that if the Jews had not existed, they would have had to be invented.

Ask yourselves how likely it would be that if you had lived in Germany at the time you might have worn 'Nazism spectacles' for a while and felt that it gave you an ideology, a vision of reality which offered you a way forward. If you are honest, how far would the massive attempt at indoctrination, coercion and fear also have given you a push?

This last example has clearly been chosen as a warning never to stop testing and reviewing your own pair of ideological spectacles to ensure that they really are your own choice.

Summary

An -ism becomes an -ism of political philosophy when the ideas and values are concerned with achieving power over people by coercion or persuasion.

An -ism becomes an ideology when you decide to use it to interpret the way you perceive reality.

The embracement of an ideology must always be accompanied by an awareness of its nature and a degree of certainty that it really is commensurate with your own values.

A political -ism is the key building block of this book.

- -

Reader's Notes:

4

Dimensional -isms

Access to power, then, must be confined to men who are not in love with it, who lust for it.

Plato

Moderation and the mean are always best … Men who are in this position are most ready to listen to reason … the best form for political society is one where power is vested in the middle class.

Aristotle

This chapter will introduce you to the idea of two opposing -isms on the same dimension from one opposite to another.

The first dimension of capitalism/socialism should be seen as an economic scale. At one extreme you will have total communism and socialism, with full public ownership of all resources, and at the other end full competition and private ownership. At the halfway point on the line between the two extremes there will be fifty per cent public and fifty per cent private ownership.

The second dimension of authoritarianism and libertarianism should be seen as a social scale.

Libertarianism is in fact the antonym of authoritarianism and is a term used by a broad spectrum of political philosophies that prioritise individual liberty and seek to minimise or even abolish the state. Here we will take that meaning of libertarianism that is best described as political individualism.

Although this may sound somewhat daunting at this moment, it will hopefully be much clearer by the end of the chapter.

The descriptive summaries of the -isms in this next section have been taken from Wikipedia. This is for two reasons. They are as good as any. This is not an academic book on Marxism, for example; all I am trying to do is find you an accessible source which will give you the basic ideas. Secondly, they encourage you to access the site and all the free information to be found on political philosophy.

So please access Wikipedia and try to see how I have sourced this section. It is perfectly OK to do this so long as you admit to it and do not pretend they are your own words as this is plagiarism. Why spend five sentences trying to explain something if you have discovered someone who does the job perfectly in one. If this, of course, were a PhD thesis, every word that was not original would have to be referenced right down to the actual page.

Others' Internet sources will be given throughout this book and in the bibliography at the end. I will always acknowledge my use of the net.

CAPITALISM/SOCIALISM

Hopefully most of you have some awareness of a book by William Golding entitled *The Lord of the Flies* or you may have seen the film version. Briefly the book/film depicts what happens to a group of schoolchildren when their plane crashes and they are the only survivors on a remote island with little chance of quick rescue.

They divide into two groups: one decides to proceed on the principle of mutual cooperation and the other to favour competition, the survival of the fittest and the 'will to power' (achievement, ambition, the striving to reach the highest possible position in life, which Nietzsche believed to be the main driving force in man).

Try to imagine a line or dimension which starts at one end with maximum cooperation and ends at the other with maximum competition. Along the line there is a gradation with equal cooperation and competition at the halfway point.

It would follow that at the cooperative end everything would be publicly owned and at the competitive end it would be privately owned.

Think for a moment as to where on this continuum you would most like the society you live in to be. Clearly you are not going to be allowed to say 'at the competitive end if I am rich', and if such a thought never passed your mind please accept my apologies. You must imagine that you could be placed in a society anywhere on the continuum.

Most people, I would suggest, will not state a preference for a society towards the two extremes, although there are famous political and economic writers who advocate these positions. Of these we will consider Adam Smith and Karl Marx, two famous advocates of capitalism and socialism respectively, and the ones you will most likely have heard of.

Sir Keith Joseph, a minister with the Thatcher government, was so enamoured of Adam Smith that he made his book *The Wealth of Nations*, published in 1776, prescribed reading for all his civil servants.

Smith was an eccentric but benevolent intellectual, comically absent-minded, with peculiar habits of speech and gait and a smile of 'inexpressible benignity'. My wife thought that I was describing myself when she first read the paragraph and said she agreed with every word apart from 'intellectual'.

However, he is also regarded as the founding father of economic philosophy and the first advocate of a free market system. So what exactly were the key ideas in his book?

There are three main concepts that Smith expands upon in his work, that form the foundation of free market economics:

- freedom of trade
- pursuit of self-interest
- division of labour.

To understand them fully we need briefly to look back historically at the economic development of Western European society.

The idea of economic development, i.e. increased government concern and action to increase general economic welfare, did not exist in feudal times in the UK.

R H Tawney captured this frame of mind when he wrote:

Rapid economic change as a fact, and continuous economic progress as an ideal, are the notes, not of the history of the West, but of little more than the last four centuries ... [prior to that] the common man looked to the good days of the past, not to the possibilities of the future, for a standard of conduct and criterion of the present; accepted the world, with plague, pestilence and famine, as heaven had made it; and were incurious as to the arts by which restless spirits would improve on nature, if not actually suspicious of them as smelling of complicity with malign powers.

Tawney, 2006

Feudalism began to decline after its zenith in the thirteenth century. With the decline of feudalism and the rise of the nation state came increased government concern regarding general economic welfare. Government-led efforts to increase wealth through exports became an explicit goal under a set of beliefs referred to as mercantilism.

It was once thought that the wealth of a nation consisted in money (gold and silver). Governments tried to make their countries wealthy by prohibiting export of gold and silver (they had in mind the need to have gold and silver available to buy arms and soldiers in time of war; money could be translated fairly quickly into military power). However, merchants found this inconvenient, because they needed to send gold and silver abroad to pay for what they were importing, and they persuaded governments instead to attend to 'the balance of trade' (the relation between imports and exports), claiming that what makes a country rich is to export much and import little, since exports bring money into the country and imports send it out. Hence governments adopted policies favouring exports and hindering imports, encouraging local production ('protectionism' in modern terms, and the subject of a later chapter).

In 1776, Adam Smith published *The Wealth of Nations*, where he argues that the progress of human well-being has been due and will continue to be due primarily to free exchange, which makes the possible division of labour, and that government cannot hasten this natural process. The chief function of government is to protect freedom of exchange by upholding justice, i.e. property rights.

He criticised the concept of mercantilism in that he felt that the regulatory and monopolistic practices characteristic of mercantilism limited a country's economic growth. He argued that governments should not particularly favour exports or hinder imports, and should allow individuals to get on with making money in the way that seems best to them, for they know their own business best, and the wealth of the country consists in their wealth.

He believed that the best way to increase the wealth of a nation was through the reduction of barriers that hindered growth. To Smith, government intervention in the economy was such a barrier. He argued that the economic system was world-wide, and as such should not be burdened by political or national barriers. Tariffs on traded goods should be eliminated; free trade should be the norm.

Contrary to popular belief, Smith never proposed a complete ban on government involvement in the economy. He was an advocate of limited government intervention, arguing that a government's role should be limited to national defence, internal security, and the provision of reasonable laws and fair courts in which private disputes could be peacefully adjudicated.

Under Smith's model, government involvement in any area other than those stated above would have a negative impact on economic growth. This is because economic growth is determined by the needs of a free market and the entrepreneurial nature of private persons. If there is a shortage of a product its price will rise, and so stimulate producers to produce more, while at the same time attracting new persons into that line of produc-tion. If there is an excess supply of a product, prices will fall and producers will focus their energy and money in other areas where there is a shortage or where there is a need which no one has yet satisfied (thereby creating a new market).

Smith argued that this system would be regulated by the self-interest of each individual capitalist. He believed that each individual knows his own interest better than anyone, especially the government. In Smith's model, the sum total of individual interests will maximise the general welfare and liberty of all.

Care must be taken here in that *The Wealth of Nations* is sometimes misrepresented as an argument that all will be well if people are allowed to follow merely self-interest. Smith did in fact write an earlier book (1759) entitled *The Theory of Moral Sentiments*, where he attached great importance to justice and other moral virtues that limit the pursuit of self-interest.

He begins the book:

> How selfish so ever man may be supposed, there are evidently some principles in his nature, which interest him in the fortune of others, and render their happiness necessary to him, though he derives nothing from it except the pleasure of seeing it.

In Smith's theory the immediate standard of right and wrong consists in the feelings of human beings. In making moral judgments we need make no reference to God but can follow our feelings or propensities which include:

- sympathy, a disposition to experience certain feelings when we see another person in a certain situation

- a tendency to want others to feel towards us in a way that harmonises with our feelings about ourselves

- a disposition to want to be worthy of the approval of others.

Finally, we look at Smith's ideas on the division of labour.

In the first sentence of *The Wealth of Nations*, Smith foresaw the essence of industrialism by asserting that division of labour represents a qualitative increase in productivity, and it was in fact the dynamic engine of economic progress.

His example was the making of pins. He argued that the specialisation and concentration of the workers on their single sub-tasks often leads to greater skill and greater productivity on their particular sub-tasks than would be achieved by the same number of workers each carrying out the original broad task. For example, pin makers were organised with one making the head of the pin, and another one the body, each using different equipment.

However, in a further chapter of the same book, Smith criticises the division of labour, saying it leads to a 'mental mutilation' in workers; they become ignorant and insular, as their working lives are confined to a single repetitive task. The contradiction has led to some debate over Smith's opinion of the division of labour.

In complete contrast to this view of capitalist economic development came the ideas of Karl Marx.

In 1867, Karl Marx published *Das Kapital*, a work that systematically and historically analysed the capitalist system. His theories would provide much of the arguments that have opposed development models based on capitalism and the laissez-faire system.

Marx lived at a time when capitalism was at its prime and was spreading throughout the world. Members of the capitalist class had become masters of both the social and political spheres. Their power was the fruit of the industrial revolution and of the many political and military battles that the capitalist class had waged against the nobility. The capitalists had joined with the working class to wrestle power away from the nobility. The first great battle, labelled the French Revolution, was fought in 1789 in France. In 1848, once again beginning in Paris, the capitalists staged a new revolution with the help of the working class. As a result of these victorious revolutions, the capitalists obtained political control.

According to Marx, this allowed the capitalist class to create a government that would allow it to exploit the working people. Thus, for Marx, the government was nothing more than a tool of the capitalist class.

Marx believed that just as the bourgeoisie (the capitalist middle class) had relied on revolutionary movements to wrestle power from the nobility, so, too, could the working class, called the proletariat, eventually overthrow the bourgeoisie. For Marx, the eventual fall of the bourgeoisie was not only desirable, it was also inevitable.

He reached this conclusion based on his economic theory of labour. Specifically, he developed the doctrine of surplus value. At the heart of the doctrine was the conclusion that the worker was being exploited. The worker received only a fraction of the value of the product that his labour produced. The capitalist class kept the remainder. This theft eventually led to an economic crisis caused by overproduction, where the vast majority of the population could not afford to consume the products that the owners of capital produced. The capitalist's answer to this problem was the continual creation of new markets.

Marx saw capitalism as a historical necessity because it was the most productive and flexible economic system in human history. It could move capital and labour to meet demand faster than any of the previous systems that it had replaced. Marx, however, refused to accept capitalism as the ultimate mode of production or economic system.

He believed the system was plagued with internal contradictions that would inevitably lead to its destruction and replacement by a more advanced system.

According to Marx, the relations of production (the way people interact in a particular economic system) create different economic classes. For example, under the feudal economic system, two classes existed: the nobility and the peasantry. The dominant class, the nobility, created a system to maintain its position. Religion, government, laws and morals reflected the needs of the dominant class and were used to perpetuate its position of power. As capitalism emerged, a new dominant class, the bourgeoisie, began to appear. The nobles and the bourgeoisie eventually clashed and the latter was victorious.

Marx believed that the advent of capitalism set in motion its own final downfall. He reasoned as follows: The capitalist system cannot exist without workers. As more factories are built, more people will be forced to work in them. Thus, under capitalism, the army of workers will continually expand. With the expansion of capitalism around the world comes the global creation of a working class.

This system is ruthless, however. In order to survive, capitalists must continually strive to out-produce one another. But not all capitalists will be able to compete. Capital will become concentrated in fewer hands. The bourgeoisie that are unable to compete will be forced to join the working class or perish. This process will continue until one day the proletariat masses will be able to take control of the system by overthrowing the bourgeoisie, resulting in a classless society. No new class will arise because class arises from economic differences, and capitalism will have eliminated these differences by making everyone a proletariat.

Since the concepts of state, religion, morality and laws were mechanisms to maintain class differences, they, too, will disappear. Government will not be eliminated immediately. A limited form of government (a proletariat dictatorship) will be put in place to prevent a possible attack by any surviving bourgeoisie. This dictatorship will eventually become useless, and when it does, it will 'wither away'. At this point, socialism will have been achieved.

For Marx, economic development was tied to class struggle. Economic development could only be achieved as a class; individual achievement was not emphasised. Trust in the government and cooperation with its goals was also viewed as betrayals of the class struggle. The government's involvement in social reform was nothing more than an attempt by the bourgeoisie to appease the workers and thereby force them to abandon the struggle. Since the government reflects the will of the dominant class, it would never enact any law benefiting the subservient class.

Indeed, Marx viewed politics as a mechanism created by the bourgeoisie to confuse the workers and divide them. Political divisions fuel nationalism that, in turn, misleads workers from one country into believing that the workers of another country are enemies. Marx would argue, for example, that there is no difference between the class relations in Mexico and those in the United States. Workers in both countries are being exploited.

To summarise (Gieben, 2006):

1   Marx rejects the notion of 'the individual' at the basis of liberal political theory. He views man as a social being, and social classes as the key political actors.

2   He focuses on the economic 'base' as decisively determining the political and social 'superstructure', thus rejecting the liberal separation of the narrow political sphere from the wider operation of the market and economic forces in civil society.

3   He denies that the state can ever be a neutral force, impartially arbitrating social conflicts; on the contrary,

he thinks it plays a central role in the maintenance of class-divided societies, and must, over the long term, protect the interests of the economically dominant class.

4   Formal equality in both legal and political rights means little in the face of inequalities of wealth and power.

5   Freedom, for Marx, entails 'the complete democratisation of society as well as the state; it can only be established with the destruction of social classes and ultimately the abolition of class power in all its forms'.

So there you have it, two contrasting philosophies as to how a society should develop. Do not worry if you cannot absorb all of the detail. The main thing is to grasp that here are two opposite views and to begin to think about which view you feel most comfortable with. Remember the example given in the first chapter with regard to the two professors: it is not a question of 'better' or 'best'.

So where do you think you stand on the capitalism/socialism dimension? Imagine for the moment placing a cross on a horizontal line as to where you would prefer to be on the dimension.

AUTHORITARIANISM/INDIVIDUALISM

Authoritarianism describes a form of government characterised by an emphasis on the authority of the state.

Its main characteristics (Vestal, 1999) are:

- highly concentrated and centralised power structures, in which political power is generated and maintained by a repressive system that excludes potential challengers and uses political parties and mass organisations to mobilise people around the goals of the government

- the principles of:
  - rule of men, not rule of law
  - rigged elections

- all important political decisions made by unelected officials behind closed doors (e.g. democratic centralism)
- a bureaucracy operated quite independently of rules, the supervision of elected officials, or concerns of the constituencies they purportedly serve

- the informal and unregulated exercise of political power
- leadership that is self-appointed and even if elected cannot be displaced by citizens' free choice among competitors
- no guarantee of civil liberties or tolerance for meaningful opposition
- weakening of civil society
- no freedom to create a broad range of groups, organisations and political parties to compete for power or question the decisions of rulers, with instead an attempt to impose controls on virtually all elements of society
- political stability maintained by:
  - control over and support of the military to provide security to the system and control of society
  - a pervasive bureaucracy staffed by the regime
  - control of internal opposition and dissent
  - creation of allegiance through the various means of socialisation.

While both authoritarianism and totalitarianism are forms of autocracy, totalitarianism is generally considered to be an extreme version of authoritarianism. Totalitarian dictators develop a charismatic mystique and a mass-based, pseudo-democratic interdependence with their followers via the conscious manipulation of a prophetic image. Three classic examples are Hitler, Stalin and Mussolini.

The utilisation of power for personal aggrandisement is more evident among authoritarians than totalitarians. Lacking the binding appeal of ideology, authoritarians support their rule by a

mixture of instilling fear and granting rewards to loyal collabora-
tors. Thus, compared to totalitarian systems, authoritarian
systems may also:

- leave a larger sphere for private life
- lack a guiding ideology
- tolerate some pluralism in social organisation
- lack the power to mobilise the whole population in
  pursuit of national goals
- exercise their power within relatively predictable limits.

Some democracies may be considered authoritarian. An illiberal
democracy like Singapore, as an example, is distinguished from
liberal democracy in that illiberal democracies lack some democratic features, such as:

- the rule of law
- an independent judiciary
- separation of powers
- civilian control of the military
- freedom of speech and assembly
- freedom from censorship.

The central characteristic of an illiberal democracy is that
institutional political processes are skewed in favour of the
incumbent regime. Opposition may be dealt with by means of:

- onerous regulations on political organisations in civil
  society
- unfair electoral processes (such as barriers to ballot access
  or extensive gerrymandering)
- manipulation of the media (either by ignoring or distort-
  ing opposition, or by biased coverage of opposition, often
  in a state-owned press).

Conservatives who do not believe in the strength of the individual will favour authoritarian regimes.

The position of conservatism on matters of morality is relatively simple; they believe in the existence of common values fixed by the society in which they live.

> The repression of curiosity and the submission of reason to faith is a more effective ... means of fixing the mind of men ... therefore it suits society better than free enquiry.
>
> Louis de Bonald, 2006

Conservatives see man as imperfect, therefore, only a force greater than man's can constrain him to behave virtuously. It is not too difficult to see how some conservatives may therefore favour an authoritarian theocratic state.

At the opposite end of the dimension we find individualism/libertarianism.

Individualism argues that the individual human being is a self-sufficient entity. The individualist cherishes independence, the expression of desires and personal wills. It can be traced back to Stoicism (Valantasis, 2008) that presents man as aspiring to the ideal of a self-sufficient being. Take care here in that today the word 'stoic' has come to mean 'unemotional' or 'indifferent to pain'. The Stoics did not seek to extinguish emotions; rather they sought to transform them by a resolute *askēsis* (practice, training or exercise, the renunciation of worldly pursuits to achieve higher intellectual goals), which enables a person to develop clear judgment and inner calm. Logic, reflection and concentration were the methods of such self-discipline.

The black sheep of individualism is of course the Marquis de Sade, but this sadistic variant is not indispensable to the doctrine.

In political philosophy, the individualist theory of government holds that the state should protect the liberty of individuals to act as they wish, as long they do not infringe on the liberties of others.

This contrasts with authoritarian political theories, where, rather than leaving individuals to pursue their own ends, the state ensures that the individual serves the whole society.

The term has also been used to describe 'individual initiative' and 'freedom of the individual'. This theory is described well by 'laissez-faire', which means in French 'let [the people] do' [for themselves what they know how to do]. This term is commonly associated with a free market system in economics, where individuals and businesses own and control the majority of factors of production. Government interferences are kept to a minimum.

Individualists are chiefly concerned with protecting individual autonomy against obligations imposed by social institutions (such as the state).

For some political individualists, who hold a view known as 'methodological individualism', the word 'society' can never refer to anything more than a very large collection of individuals.

Society does not have an existence above or beyond these individuals, and thus cannot be properly said to carry out actions, since actions require intentionality, which in turn requires an agent, and society as a whole cannot be properly said to possess agency; only individuals can be agents.

The same holds for the government. Under this view, a government is composed of individuals; despite the point that democratic governments are elected by popular vote, the fact remains that all of the activities of government are carried out by means of the intentions and actions of individuals.

Individualism has two basic objections to authoritarianism:

- it stifles individuality and diversity by insisting upon a common social identity, whether it's nationalism or racialism, etc.

- it is linked to significant state intervention (statism) and the diminution of freedom when political authority is used to advance goals.

The key ideas of individualism are put forward by Friedrich Hayek (2007) in his book *The Road to Serfdom*, published in 1944 and translated into approximately twenty languages. Hayek believed that all forms of collectivism could only be maintained eventually by some kind of central authority. Hayek claimed that socialism required central economic planning and that such planning in turn had a risk of leading towards political systems where the state organises all aspects of public and private life, i.e. totalitarianism.

Totalitarian regimes or movements, he argued, maintain their power by means of an official all-embracing ideology supported by the use of propaganda disseminated through the state-controlled mass media. This is backed up by a single party controlling the state, restricting free speech, and using mass observation techniques and terror to control the people.

Hayek also argued that while, in centrally planned economies, an individual or a select group of individuals must determine the distribution of resources, these planners will never have enough information to carry out this allocation reliably. The efficient exchange and use of resources, Hayek claimed, can be maintained only through the price mechanism in free markets. In an article, 'The Use of Knowledge in Society' (2004), Hayek argued that the price mechanism serves to share and synchronise local and personal knowledge, allowing society's members to achieve diverse, complicated ends through a 'self-organising system of voluntary cooperation'.

In Hayek's view, the central role of the state should be to maintain the rule of law, with as little arbitrary intervention as possible.

As you did with capitalism and socialism, try to place yourself along the dimension of individualism and authoritarianism.

Again, do not be too surprised if you are more central than towards the extremes.

If you are wondering where we are on this dimension in the UK or USA at the time of writing, all will be revealed in the next chapter.

Summary

A dimensional -ism is one where you have two opposing philosophies in the same dimension.

According to Smith, the government should play a limited role in the economy. He believed that economic growth depended on the free market and the entrepreneurial spirit of private persons.

According to Marx, government was a tool used by capitalists to perpetuate their power. From a Marxist perspective, development is a process of class struggle.

According to Marx, capitalism's inherent contradictions would eventually cause its downfall. Marxism views government-led social reform and nationalism as mechanisms to perpetuate exploitative development.

Authoritarianism describes a form of government that is characterised by highly concentrated and centralised power structures, in which political power is generated and maintained by a repressive system that excludes potential challengers and uses political parties and mass organisations to mobilise people around the goals of the government.

Individualist theory of government holds that the state should protect the liberty of individuals to act as they wish, as long as they do not infringe on the liberties of others. Hayek's *The Road to Serfdom* argues that the efficient exchange and use of resources can be maintained only through the price mechanism in free markets. In Hayek's view, the central role of the state should be to maintain the rule of law, with as little arbitrary intervention as possible.

- -

Reader's Notes:

5

-isms and How One Votes

> All associations are instituted for the purpose of attaining some good, for all men do all their acts with a view to achieving something, which is, in their view, a good.
>
> Aristotle

> We have wished ... for a disaster or for a social change to come and bomb us into the Stone Age.
>
> Brand

So now let us see if we can use these ideas to help you see the philosophy behind how you vote. The problem, of course, is that an attempt now has to be made to relate -isms to the modern political parties in the UK and USA and what they purport to stand for.

We will concentrate on the two main political parties in each country, Labour and Conservative, and Republican and Democrat.

Hopefully you can grasp that the particular 'pair of ideological spectacles' which best represent a political party will change over time. So we need to try and disentangle:

- where you stand
- the national picture
- the modern parties today as compared with where they were in the recent past.

We will start with your views because, once I have revealed the positions of the main parties to you, they are bound to influence you if you regularly vote. You are probably already guessing, but try not to.

A simple diagram will help to clarify the key points.

This information has been taken from the Internet site 'the Political Compass' (www.politicalcompass.org) and their ideas and text are fully acknowledged.

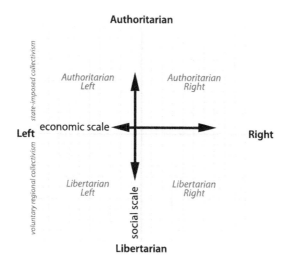

Imagine that the horizontal line represents the dimension of socialism and capitalism – the Economic Scale – and the vertical line the dimension of authoritarianism and libertarianism/individualism – the social scale.

Ask yourself where on each line you would place your own position as viewed through your personal -ism or ideological spectacles, assuming that there are no other -isms to be taken into account.

To make sure you understand the task, if you place yourself where the two lines intersect, you are saying that you prefer a world where the forces of socialism, capitalism and authoritarianism, individualism are equal.

If you would prefer more emphasis on competition and the private sector, the point you select will be increasingly 'right' of centre and hence the concept of being 'right-wing' as opposed to 'left-wing'.

If you would prefer more freedom for the individual and less government central control, the point you select will be increasingly below centre.

Please place a cross at the intersection of the two points; for example, if you want total socialism and authoritarianism you would put a cross at the top left corner (extreme 'left-wing') and if you want the complete opposite, capitalism and individualism (extreme 'right-wing'), you put a cross in the bottom right corner.

If you have access to the net, go to the Political Compass site where you can take a three-minute test which will place you on the dimensions (www.politicalcompass.org/test).

I still suggest you do both exercises in the order suggested if you can, as you can then compare the two results. If they are not the same, have a think about why this might be the case, as logically they should be.

Do not read on until you have placed a cross.

Now for some predictions and comments. (See chart below.)

For the UK (US readers please do not omit this section):

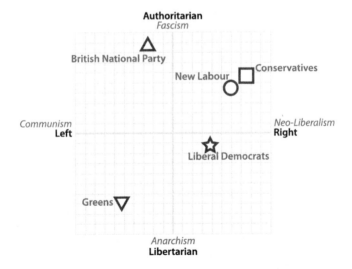

LABOUR

If you are a Labour moderniser or Blairite, your cross will more likely be in the top right of the diagram. If, however, you are a member of the Socialist Labour Party your cross will be on the left.

CONSERVATIVE

If your cross is in the top right quarter, you are most likely to be a Conservative voter. The more progressive you are, the further down and towards the centre of the sector your cross will be.

LIBERAL DEMOCRAT

If your cross is centre right, you are likely to have voted Liberal Democrat, showing a markedly greater concern for civil liberties.

OTHERS

Note that the difference between the BNP and the Greens on the economic scale is not great, but there's a huge gap on the social scale.

Next, a few words about popular political terms.

Once you accept that left and right are merely measures of economic position, the 'extreme right' refers to an extreme economic position that may be practised by social authoritarians (top right) or social libertarians (bottom right).

Similarly, the 'extreme left' identifies a strong degree of state economic control, which may also be accompanied by libertarian (bottom right) or authoritarian (top left) social policies.

It is muddled thinking to describe the likes of the British National Party simply as 'extreme right'. The truth is that on issues like health, transport, housing, protectionism and global-isation, their economics are left of Labour, let alone the Conservatives. It is in areas like police power, military power, school discipline, law and order, race and nationalism that the BNP's real extremism – as authoritarianism – is clear.

With mainstream social democratic parties adopting, reluc-tantly or enthusiastically, the new economic orthodoxy (neoliberalism), much of their old economic baggage has been taken over by National Socialism. Since the rise of Nazism, which called itself 'National Socialism', the term has been used in

Europe and North America almost exclusively by political parties with combined authoritarian, racial and nationalist views.

Election debates between mainstream parties are increasingly about managerial competence rather than any clash of vision and economic direction. 'More style than substance' is a popular way of describing it.

In the chart below, you can see the three largest UK parties and the positions that they have occupied in recent years, up to and including 2008.

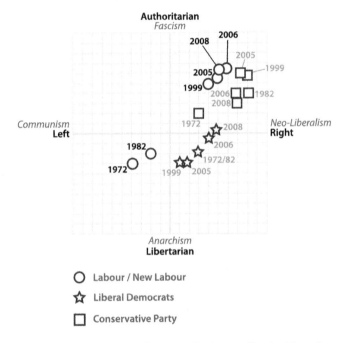

We see that New Labour, for example, is actually significantly to the right of the 1972 pre-Thatcher Conservative Party. If your cross is on the left side of the diagram, e.g. as in 1972 and 1982, you are likely to be a traditional Labour voter who regretted the removal of Clause IV:

> To secure for the workers by hand or by brain the full fruits of their industry and the most equitable distribution thereof that may be possible upon the basis of the common ownership of the means of production, distribution and exchange, and the best obtainable system of popular administration and control of each industry or service.

The change under Gordon Brown's leadership is largely one of style rather than substance. A circle for 2009 would, I suggest, show movement to the centre on the economic scale and movement towards authoritarianism on the social scale. However, it would appear from the election manifesto of 2010 that it will please the Labour Party further down the social scale.

As the centre of political gravity has moved generally rightwards, the Liberal Democrats, who have held the most consistent ground, now occupy similar economic ground to the other parties, while maintaining a markedly greater concern for civil liberties, as evidenced by their position on the social scale! As Gordon Brown resigned after the General Election, we will have to await the result of the leadership contest to see which way the Labour Party will move in opposition.

Although David Cameron is popularly perceived as 'less right-wing' than other recent Tory leaders, his real difference is on the social rather than the economic scale, where in the election run-up he increasingly attacked Labour's 'control state' with sweeping powers to intrude into people's private lives. A square on the graph for 2009 would have moved even further away from authoritarianism. As the Prime Minister is in a Conservative/Liberal Democrat coalition, the move will clearly be even further towards the centre, much to the annoyance of the 'neo-Thatcherites'.

In 2008/2009, there has been more and more mention from politicians that 'right' and 'left' are no longer meaningful terms. To the contrary, they are as meaningful as ever, providing that it is understood that they are simply defining economic positions.

For the USA (UK readers please do not omit this section):

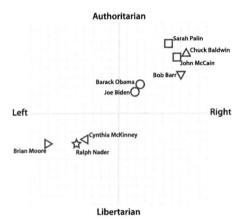

- Bob Barr, Libertarian Party
- Chuck Baldwin, Constitution Party
- Cynthia McKinney, Green Party
- Ralph Nader, Independent
- Brian Moore, Socialist Party

Here predictions are somewhat easier as most US readers should be in the top right corner with the Republicans (square) and Democrats (circle), the latter being in a more centrist position. I say 'should' as I wonder how many US readers will place their cross in a more central position and be surprised to be so authoritarian and capitalist.

When examining the chart, it is important to note that although most of the candidates seem quite different, in substance they occupy a relatively restricted area within the universal political spectrum.

Democracies with a system of proportional representation give expression to a wide range of political views. While Cynthia McKinney and Ralph Nader are depicted on the extreme left in an American context, they would simply be mainstream social democrats within the wider political landscape of Europe.

Similarly, Obama is popularly perceived as a leftist in the

United States while elsewhere in the West his record is that of a moderate conservative.

Sarah Palin's detractors popularly describe her as an extreme right-winger. In reality, she has some protectionist leanings. Her comparatively extreme positions are on the social rather than the economic scale.

It is important for readers to consider both sections on the UK and USA, otherwise important points in this first half of the book will be missed.

In my opinion, most Americans do not realise how far the arena in which US politics operates is to the right in economic terms and authoritarian in social terms. Hopefully US readers can now see those in the UK are somewhat bemused by Obama being attacked as a socialist/communist by his opponents; it is all very relative. The Republican opposition to universal health care is also difficult to comprehend, as the rest of Europe has known nothing else for many years. It has been the case in the UK since the end of World War Two.

This next chart shows most of the candidates from the Primaries. Observant readers will notice shifts in the positions of Biden, Obama and McCain. The move by McCain to the top right is of course as a result of the insistence of the GOP (Grand Old Party, alternative name for Republican Party) on the acceptance of Palin instead of Lieberman.

57

To help UK readers:

- Mike Gravel, Democratic Party, late switch to Libertarian Party
- Dennis Kucinich, Democratic Party (left wing).

Where does this all leave us in both the UK and USA after the election of Obama in the USA, the economic collapse of 2008 and the new Conservative/Liberal Democrat coalition in the UK?

The government of Britain since World War Two can be conveniently divided into five periods.

From May 1945 to 1979, although the Tories were in control for most of the time, Britain was much closer to socialism than capitalism. From every Prime Minister, from Attlee to Heath, came an acceptance of the authority of the state to manage the economy, to prevent the social evil of unemployment, to provide health care and to own great tracts of British industry.

This Keynesian model collapsed in the economic crisis of the seventies when high unemployment and inflation co-existed, rendering demand management techniques apparently unworkable.

From 1979 to 1997, Thatcher challenged the old model and replaced it with one that liberated economic markets and challenged the authoritarian power of the state, (a similar policy was adopted by Reagan). It was claimed that the policy brought prosperity to millions of ordinary Britons through, for example, the sale of council houses (publicly owned houses that were rented) and privatisation (the opportunity to buy shares in a nationalised company that was placed in private ownership, e.g. British Telecom or British Gas).

The arrival of Blair (1997–2007) led to the development of what he called 'the third way' which pulled the Conservative Party more into the centre and the Labour Party to the economic right.

With the accession of Gordon Brown (2007–2010), there was evidence of a move back towards authoritarianism and socialism. There were initially contradictory signals from the Brown government in that on the one hand he was injecting billions of pounds into the economy – signs of a return to the failed policy of the seventies, i.e. massive central intervention financed by unsustainable levels of debt. On the other hand there was an intention to part-privatise the Royal Mail, a continuation of Blair's 'third way'. This latter policy was, however, shelved in June 2009.

During the run up to the election, Brown made a number of speeches stressing the importance of liberty and the individual, indicating a clear positioning down the social scale for the election manifesto. He also took steps to play down his control-freak image.

David Cameron (2010–?), the Conservative party leader, has moved his party much further along the social scale, stressing in speeches, in the election run-up, that: 'A Conservative government would constantly ask two essential questions: Does this action enhance personal freedom and does it advance political accountability?' He has partially allied his thinking to Blond's (2010) ideas on a new left conservatism that is attractive to the poor.

In May 2010, David Cameron became Prime Minister, with a 'hung' parliament, i.e. no party with overall control. A coalition has been formed with the Liberal Democrats, bringing him into an even more centrist position.

In the USA, economic theory came together with Reaganism and Thatcherism in the eighties. Both introduced supply-side economic policies that rejected Keynesian demand management theory.

For non-economists, supply-siders argue that all efforts should be on producing the right goods at the right price, even if this has severe social consequences, while resources move from unprofitable to profitable production. The money supply is controlled to combat inflation, so excess demand for money will drive interest rates up. This is accompanied by deregulation, with substantial tax cuts paid for by reductions in government expenditure.

Demand-side policies argue that the government can control the economy by managing the level of demand in the economy. In the current recession there would be a need for large increases in government expenditure and tax cuts to stimulate demand for goods and services and hence levels of employment, the massive debt that is built up being eventually paid back by increased taxation revenue (income and sales) and less expenditure on unemployment, etc.

Reaganism/Thatcherism worked in the eighties. In the USA the Republicans persisted with an authoritarian and increasingly neoliberal approach (much influenced by Reaganism) while the Democrats moved into Blairite territory.

The Obama government, from early indications, seems to be moving economically to the left and following the Brown tactic of trying to spend one's way out of recession by rejecting the supply-side approach of Thatcher and Reagan, and going back to the demand-side management approach. The plans for health care and job creation will bring about considerable movement on the social scale if Obama can steer them fully through.

Goldberg has written a controversial book entitled *Liberal Fascism* (2008) where he suggests that fascism and left-wing philosophy are inextricably linked so that liberal (or left-wing) fascism (the top left square) will be the prevailing -ism of the next decade. The following is a précis of his key ideas.

Goldberg sees many similarities between Obama, Clinton, Blair and fascism.

- The cult of unity and the charismatic leader. Fascism mastered the control of the crowd to project an aura of unity, equality and common purpose, made possible by the cult of personality, the faith that a great leader would arise from among us.

- Slogans for centrists and moderates that belie a utopian vision for rule by benevolent masters. Italian fascism and German National Socialism were both sold as a third way; 'neither right nor left' was a central fascist slogan.

- The desire to find a moral equivalent of war that will bind the individual to the state. Roosevelt's New Deal was hailed initially by Mussolini as a great fascist under-taking, with Obama styling himself after FDR. Clinton (2008) has insisted that Americans 'have to start thinking and believing that there is not really any such thing as someone else's child'.

- The politically correct increasing micromanagement of daily life. CCTV cameras initially introduced for security reasons now increasingly police everything, and bans are being introduced on diverse goods. Hitler proclaimed that nutrition was not a private matter and advocated compulsory vegetarianism and research into organic foods.

Goldberg warns us that the liberal fascists will aim to save us by controlling everything we do from the moment we are born.

However, when historians look back on Obama's presidency, they may well judge him most on whether he managed to bring the emerging powers into the world order and unite them behind Western values, or at least achieve a workable compromise.

By the time Obama leaves office, assuming he serves two terms, it will be 2017, and countries like China, India and Brazil will surely have taken larger roles in the world economy. At the moment, none of them are in the G8 club, and only China has a spot on the UN Security Council. If America cannot find a way to bring China and India into the existing global power structure, they will start drifting away to form their own clubs.

It is not just institutional. China and the Islamic world are especially nervous about Western values. The financial crisis, coupled with the shredding of America's reputation over the past eight years, has given weight to those people who argue that Western capitalism and democracy are flawed, old models. The new president will have to resell what America stands for.

You may be interested to know that since World War Two the tendency has been for both government expenditure and taxation to increase continually. It perhaps then is more accurate to say that of the parties historically, the Republican and Conservative Party are most concerned to keep these rates of increase down.

If you are wondering why both expenditure and taxation have continued to increase, you should remember that US/UK populations are both increasing and ageing, so that an increasing percentage of the population is getting older.

If you combine this with the fact that at the other end of the scale more and more youngsters are entering the workforce later, it does not take much to see that a decreasing working population is increasingly being called upon to provide for an increasing non-working population.

Just to illustrate the effect of an aging population, David Willets (2010) states that spending on the elderly in the UK is predicted to rise from 20% of GDP today to 27% in 2060. This is the equivalent of an extra £60 billion of public money, at a time when the government will be desperate to make cuts.

All political parties are faced with this scenario that clearly impacts upon their policies and can create instability.

In an era of constraints the one thing that helps above all, of course, is an increase in the rate of economic growth. We now return to two dimensional/competing sets of -isms as to how best to achieve this.

Just to ensure that you have grasped the argument for growth, let me give you a very simple example.

Think of the total of our wealth as a country as a large cake. The faster the economy grows, the bigger the cake gets, resulting in one of the following:

- everyone getting a bigger equal slice if the cake is communally owned and divided evenly

- some getting big slices, some getting small and some getting none at all if everything is privately owned, but nevertheless, overall the average slice of cake will have grown.

And here we are back on the island with *Lord of the Flies* and the vital question of which mix of -isms in the spectacles is most likely to increase the rate of economic growth.

Where you placed your cross indicates the mix that you believe to be most likely to achieve this. The party you vote for is the one whose manifesto policies seem most empathetic to that mix.

Summary

To help you see the philosophy behind how you vote, an attempt has to be made to relate -isms to the modern political parties in the UK and USA and what they purport to stand for.

If you are right of centre, you attach greater importance to capitalism as opposed to socialism.

If you are left of centre you attach greater importance to socialism as opposed to capitalism.

If you are below centre, you believe that the power of the individual should be increased at the expense of government.

Your preferred mix is what you believe will achieve the greater and steadier growth rate over time within the context of a desired society.

- -

Reader's Notes:

Part Two
Philosophy Underlying World Issues

6

Political and Social Philosophy

If you have to make a choice, to be feared is much safer than to be loved. For it is a good general rule about men or humanity that they are ungrateful, fickle, liars and deceivers, fearful of danger and greedy for gain.

Machiavelli

The free development of each is the condition for the free development of all.

Karl Marx

An ideal society would simply be an agglomeration of ... social atoms ... that means that there would be no interdependencies ... except at best any that might be freely undertaken, emerging from the individual self-interest of these atomic agents.

Simon Blackburn

By now you should have a good idea of the key -isms in the lenses in your personal pair of spectacles. The difference between a political and non-political -ism has been explained and you should be thinking about which, if any, political -isms are included and how they interact with the other -isms. If you are prepared to concede that an -ism has ideological status, then you will be working out the full implications of this.

Now in the second part of the book I will take a broader political look at some of the world's current controversial areas and help you to make sense of them through your developing political philosophy. To do this I need to introduce you to the idea of social theory in addition to political theory.

This next section has been largely taken from Professor Gerard Delanty's website.

While the origins of political theory go right back to ancient thought, social theory is more a product of the modern industrial era, sometimes called modernity.

Social theory aims to provide a general interpretation of the social forces at work in the making and development of modern industrial society. Social theory was both a product of modernity and at the same time an attempt to reflect critically on its problems.

Modern society was seen as existing in a state of tension between the potential for crisis, and as a promise of new freedoms.

> This tension between crisis and future possibility encapsulates both the spirit of modernity and the responses of social theorists to the predicament of modern society. On the one side, modernity offered the vision of a social order that has been variously understood in terms of human autonomy or freedom and, on the other, modern society has unleashed forces that have the tendency to destroy the future possibilities contained within it.
>
> Delanty, 2007

Social theory then tries to make sense of modern society in terms of this dual conflict. Where social theorists have differed, it has been in their responses to what has been often called the 'central conflict of modernity'.

The rise of social theory can be related to the emergence of the 'social' as a specific domain separate from the sphere of the state and the realm of the household or private sphere. Early social theory was a response to the rise of 'civil society' and the recognition that society was something produced by human action, as opposed to being part of the preordained nature of the world.

According to Talcott Parsons (1967), in *The Structure of Social Action*, first published in 1937, modern sociology is essentially an attempt to find an answer to the problem posed by Thomas Hobbes (1588–1697) and John Locke (1632–1704), namely how social order is possible. While Hobbes and Locke conceived of this in political terms as a social contract, social theory properly begins only with the recognition that society is a reality in itself.

Rousseau and Montesquieu are usually regarded as the founders of sociology. Rousseau's (1990) *The Social Contract*, first published in 1762, introduced the notion of the 'general will' as the symbolic basis of social subjectivity that he linked to the importance of citizenship. He articulated a notion of society that was a departure from the earlier contractarian philosophies of the liberal thinkers. For instance, in the earlier *Discourse on the Origin of Inequality* (2006) he argued that inequality is a product of society as opposed to being natural.

But there is no doubt that it was Montesquieu (1989) in 1748 in *The Spirit of the Laws* who advanced the first sociological conception of society. He demonstrated how social control operates through what he called social mores (tastes and conventions). One of his great themes was that of the variability of human societies and the importance of social context. This work had a lasting influence on social theory in the idea it articulated that societies have inner logics of development and that the social is always more than the sum of its parts.

Just in case you are still struggling with this idea of society as a reality in itself, sui generis, let me give you an example.

In the sociology of Emile Durkheim (Cotterrell, 1999), sui generis is used to illustrate his theories on social existence. Durkheim states that the main object of sociology is to study social facts. These social facts can only be explained by other social facts. They have a meaning of their own and cannot be reduced to psychological or biological factors. Social facts have a meaning of their own; they are 'sui generis'.

Durkheim states that when one takes an organisation and replaces some individuals with some others, the essence of the organisation does not necessarily change. It can happen, for example, that over the course of a few decades, the entire staff of an organisation is replaced, while the organisation retains its distinctive character.

Durkheim does not limit this thought to organisation, but extends it to the whole society. He maintains that society, as it was there before any living individual was born, is independent of all individuals. His sui generis (its closest English meaning in this sense being 'independent') society will furthermore continue its existence after the individual ceases to interact with it. He concedes, though, that the two-way reaction between the individual and society can change both individual and society in the process.

If you are starting to worry at this moment, let me pause to reassure you that this is a book on political philosophy and not sociology. However, it is important for you to appreciate that in modern times, social and political theory are very much intertwined.

Out of this intertwining of social and political theory emerged political sociology that looks at power and power relationships in society. If you remember at the start of the book when I introduced definitions of politics and political philosophy, I said we would look at the special place of power in part two of the book.

Now is the time for me to introduce you to the idea of a 'contested concept' and clearly it is opportune to consider 'power' as such.

I have already introduced the idea to you in a simple way at the start of the book, but not by name. Can you remember where? If you are thinking of the two professors taking opposite views on unemployment, well done.

Although we use the term 'power' frequently in our everyday lives and seem to have little trouble understanding what is meant by it, the concept has sparked widespread and seemingly intractable disagreements among philosophers and social and political theorists.

For example, the literature on power is marked by a deep disagreement over the basic definition of power.

Some theorists define power as getting someone else to do what you want them to do (power-over). For example, Max Weber defines power as 'the probability that one actor within a social relationship will be in a position to carry out his own will despite resistance' (1978, p.53).

Robert Dahl offers what he calls an 'intuitive idea of power' according to which 'A has power over B to the extent that he can get B to do something that B would not otherwise do' (1957, pp.202–03).

Finally, from the net, to gather interest in his book on *Power: Its Forms, Bases and Uses*, Dennis Wrong gives a selection of chapters to be read. From this the definition of power is 'the capacity of some persons to produce intended and foreseen effects on others' (1995 p.35).

Others define power more broadly as ability or a capacity to act (power-to).

Thomas Hobbes's definition of power as a person's 'present means … to obtain some future apparent Good' (1985 [1641], p.150) is a classic example of this understanding of power, as is Hannah Arendt's (1970) definition of power as 'the human ability not just to act but to act in concert'.

What accounts for the highly contested nature of the concept of power?

I will answer this question by considering feminist ideas. I do this for two main reasons. Firstly, feminism is a body of thought that clearly has ideas as to how power can operate to the disadvantage of women; and secondly, it will help you to see how conceptions of power can impact disadvantageously on different social groups.

This next section is a précis taken from the section on feminism in the Wikipedia website, written by Amy Allen. She starts by reminding us that Lukes has suggested that our conceptions of power are themselves shaped by power relations. As he puts it,

How we think about power may serve to reproduce and reinforce power structures and relations, or alternatively it may challenge and subvert them. It may contribute to their continued functioning, or it may unmask their principles of operation, whose effectiveness is increased by their being hidden from view. To the extent that this is so, conceptual and methodological questions are inescapably political and so what 'power' means is 'essentially contested'…

Lukes, 2005, p.63

The idea that conceptions of power are themselves shaped by power relations is behind the claim, made by many feminists, that the influential conception of power as power-over is itself a product of male domination. The basic distinction between power-over and power-to runs through and structures much of the feminist discussion of power.

With regard to power-over conceptions of power in feminism itself, there are two main strands.

Distributive Power

Those feminists who conceptualise power as a resource understand it as a positive social good that is currently unequally distributed among women and men. For feminists who understand power in this way, the goal is to redistribute this resource so that women will have power equal to men. Implicit in this view is the assumption that power is 'a kind of stuff that can be possessed by individuals in greater or lesser amounts' (Young, 1990, p.31).

For example, in *Justice, Gender and the Family*, Okin (1989) argues that the contemporary gender-structured family unjustly distributes the benefits and burdens of familial life among husbands and wives.

Power as Domination

Young argues against the distributive concept of power and sees power as domination.

First, she maintains that it is wrong to think of power as a kind of stuff that can be possessed.

Second, she claims that the distributive model tends to presuppose a dyadic (comprising two elements) and atomistic (not divisible) understanding of power. As a result, it fails to illuminate the broader social, institutional and structural contexts that shape individual relations of power.

Third, the distributive model conceives of power statically, as a pattern of distribution, whereas Young, following Foucault (1980), claims that power exists only in action, and thus must be understood dynamically, as existing in ongoing processes or interactions.

Finally, Young argues that the distributive model of power

tends to view domination as the concentration of power in the hands of a few. This is not appropriate for the forms that domination takes in contemporary industrial societies such as the United States. In her view, in contemporary industrial societies, power is widely dispersed and diffused (Young, 1990a, pp.32–33).

Young conceptualises power not as a resource or critical social good, but instead as a relation of domination. Power is not just seen only as power-over, but as a specific kind of power-over relation, namely one that is unjust and oppressive to those over whom power is used.

More recently, Young (1990b, pp.142–3) has argued that insufficient attention is being paid to the role that female embodiment plays in women's oppression.

In her essay, 'Throwing Like a Girl', Young concentrates on 'the situatedness of the woman's actual bodily movement and orientation to its surroundings and its world' (Young, 1990b, p.143).

She notes that girls and women often fail to use fully the spatial potential of their bodies (for example, they throw like girls), they try not to take up too much space, and they tend to approach physical activity tentatively and uncertainly (Young, 1990b, pp.145–147).

> At the root of those modalities, is the fact that the woman lives her body as object as well as subject. The source of this is that patriarchal society defines woman as object, as a mere body, and that in sexist society women are in fact frequently regarded by others as objects and mere bodies.
>
> Young, 1990b, p.155

And yet women are also subjects, and, thus, cannot think of themselves as mere bodily objects. As a result, woman 'cannot be in unity with herself' (Young, 1990b, p.155).

Similarly Carole Pateman's *The Sexual Contract* (1988) claims that gender difference is constituted by domination. As she puts it, 'The patriarchal construction of the difference between masculinity and femininity is the political difference between freedom and subjection' (Pateman, 1988, p.207).

She also claims that male domination is pervasive, and she explicitly appeals to a master/subject model to understand it. As she puts it, 'In modern civil society all men are deemed good enough to be women's masters' (Pateman, 1988, p.219).

In Pateman's view, the social contract that initiates civil society and provides for the legitimate exercise of political rights is also a sexual contract that establishes what she calls 'the law of male sex-right', securing male sexual access to and dominance over women.

Finally in terms of power-over, according to the traditional Marxist account of power, domination is understood on the model of class exploitation.

Here domination results from the capitalist appropriation of the surplus value that is produced by the workers. As many second-wave feminist critics of Marx have pointed out, however, Marx's categories are gender-blind. Marx ignores the ways in which class exploitation and gender subordination are inter-twined; because he focuses solely on economic production, Marx overlooks women's reproductive labour in the home and the exploitation of this labour in capitalist modes of production.

As a result of this gender-blindness, socialist feminists have argued that Marx's analysis of class domination must be sup-plemented with a radical feminist critique of patriarchy in order to yield a satisfactory account of women's oppression; the resulting theory is referred to as dual systems theory (Eisenstein 1979).

> Dual systems theory says that women's oppression arises from two distinct and relatively autonomous systems. The system of male domination, most often called 'patriarchy', produces the specific gender oppression of women; the system of the mode of production and class relations produces the class oppression and work alienation of most women.

> Young, 1990b, p.21

With regard to power-to conceptions of power Nancy Hartsock in her book *Money, Sex and Power: Toward a Feminist Historical Materialism* (1983) is concerned with:

(1) How relations of domination along lines of gender are constructed and maintained and

(2) Whether social understandings of domination itself have been distorted by men's domination of women.

Hartsock, 1983, p.1

She criticises theories of power in mainstream political science for presupposing a market model of economic relations – a model that understands the economy primarily in terms of exchange, which is how it appears from the perspective of the ruling class, rather than in terms of production, which is how it appears from the perspective of the worker. She also argues that power and domination have consistently been associated with masculinity.

Because power has been understood from the position of the socially dominant, the ruling class and men, the feminist task, according to Hartsock, is to re-conceptualise power from a specifically feminist standpoint, one that is rooted in women's life experience – specifically, their role in reproduction. Conceptualising power from this standpoint can, according to Hartsock, 'point beyond understandings of power as power over others' (1983, p.12).

Foucault has inspired much of the work on power. According to him, modern power subjects individuals, in both senses of the term; it creates them as subjects by subjecting them to power.

Several of the most prominent Foucaultian feminist analyses of power draw on his account of disciplinary power in order to critically analyse normative femininity. In *Discipline and Punish*, Foucault analyses the disciplinary practices that were developed in prisons, schools and factories in the eighteenth century, including minute regulations of bodily movements, obsessively detailed time schedules and surveillance techniques, and how these practices shape the bodies of prisoners, students and workers into docile bodies (1977, pp.135–169).

Drawing on and extending Foucault's account of disciplinary power, Bartky (1977) analyses the disciplinary practices that engender specifically feminine docile bodies, including dieting practices, limitations on gestures and mobility, and bodily ornamentation. She also expands Foucault's analysis of the

Panopticon, Jeremy Bentham's design for the ideal prison, a building whose spatial arrangement was designed to compel the inmate to surveil himself, thus becoming, as Foucault famously put it, 'the principle of his own subjection' (1977, p.203).

With respect to gendered disciplinary practices such as dieting, restricting one's movement so as to avoid taking up too much space, and keeping one's body properly hairless, attired, ornamented and made up, Bartky observes,

> It is women themselves who practise this discipline on and against their own bodies ... The woman who checks her make-up half a dozen times a day to see if her foundation has caked or her mascara run, who worries that the wind or rain may spoil her hairdo, who looks frequently to see if her stocking have bagged at the ankle, or who, feeling fat, monitors everything she eats, has become, just as surely as the inmate in the Panopticon, a self-policing subject, a self committed to relentless self-surveillance. This self-surveillance is a form of obedience to patriarchy.
>
> Bartky, 1990, p.80

Allen shows how many other feminists argue for a re-conceptualisation of power as a capacity or ability – specifically, the capacity to empower or transform oneself and others.

For example, Miller claims that 'women's examination of power ... can bring new understanding to the whole concept of power' (Miller, 1992, p.241). She defines power as 'the capacity to produce a change – that is, to move anything from point A or state A to point B or state B'.

She suggests that women perceive power differently.

> There is enormous validity in women's not wanting to use power as it is presently conceived and used. Rather, women may want to be powerful in ways that simultaneously enhance, rather than diminish, the power of others.
>
> Miller, 1992, pp.247–248

Similarly, Virginia Held argues that women's unique experiences as mothers and caregivers give the basis for new insights into power.

The capacity to give birth and to nurture and empower could be the basis for new and more humanly promising conceptions than the ones that now prevail of power, empowerment, and growth.

Held, 1993, p.137

Finally Allen draws attention to Hoagland (1988) who defines power as 'power-from-within' which she understands as:

...the power of ability, of choice and engagement. It is creative; and hence it is an affecting and transforming power but not a controlling power ... such a standpoint might allow us to put forward an understanding of power that points in more liberatory directions.

Hoagland, 1988, p.118

Power-from-within is a positive, life-affirming, and empowering force that stands in stark contrast to power understood as domination, control or imposing one's will on another.

I can assure you that I have only just begun to scratch the surface in terms of feminist thinking on power.

Which conception do you favour? Power as power-over (as a resource, as domination, as dual-systems theory) or power as power-to (as capacity for transformation, as empowerment, as power-from-within)?

What I suggest you take away from this is an awareness of the depth of thought that can go into a single 'contestable concept' and the difficulties of definition that can arise from this.

Wilma van der Veen is a very well-organised Canadian academic who gives notes for all her courses on her website. She suggests that from a sociological point of view there are three types of power:

- Influence: persuasion, convincing someone of your views. Types of influence include: public opinion manipulation, propaganda (releasing info), political correctness (thought control), censorship (withholding info), chilling dissent ('big brother')

- Coercion: force, use or threat of use of force, to include genocide
- Authority: socially legitimate/sanctioned, from Weber (1922) we have three types:

    - Traditional: custom, habit, past practice, e.g. kings and queens
    - Charismatic: personality characteristic of a leader, e.g. Martin Luther King
    - Legal rational/bureaucratic: power made legitimate by institutionalisation of rules, regulations, and policies, often codified into laws.

Here we are clearly talking about politics as being power over people to bring about desired ends and suggesting different types of power that can be used individually or collectively.

For example, Hitler, Stalin, Mao and Franco are examples of dictators who openly used all three types of power and there are still similar dictatorships in power today, such as Saudi Arabia and North Korea.

There is a view that all governments in fact use all three types of power, it is just that some are more covert about it. When we sit down to watch *Spooks* from the UK and *24* from the US, and see scenes of torture involving government officials, we may suspect that in reality this is true. It is largely a matter of degree. It is interesting that since the acknowledgement of 'enhanced interrogation' and 'rendition flights' in both the UK and the USA both TV series now emphasise the official condemnation of such practice.

Clearly the relationship between the state and power is a crucial one and once again there are a number of competing explanatory frameworks of the state and power that you need to be aware of.

This as a complex area but I shall try to give you an outline of it by describing the main areas of disagreement.

First, and probably the most familiar, is pluralism. This sees politics as a contest for power among competing interest groups.

A leading representative of this line of thought is Robert Dahl (1961) who argued that there are numerous competing groups who compete and compromise with each other as circumstances change.

The key features are (according to van der Veen):

- societal power is decentralised, widely shared, diffuse and fragmented, deriving from many sources

- society consists of many diverse groups and associations (e.g. business, labour, professional, religious) and constitutes a conglomeration of dissimilar and often conflicting interests, none of which plays a singularly dominant role; through a process of democratic competition the nature and direction of society are determined

- society is made up of a multitude of conflicting interest groups balanced by the state; groups are equally influential in their impact on government policy and major institutions

- it is assumed that there is a natural balance of power among various groups, that is preserved through bargaining and compromise, win some and lose some, give and take, and thus equilibrium is reached in group struggle

- the existence of a shared acceptance of a basic political framework, i.e. consensus of values, democratic traditions, procedures and principles.

With regard to the role of the state:

- society is a struggle of competing groups within an arena refereed by the state

- the state represents institutionalised power and authority

- the state is supreme guardian of representative democracy in modern society

- the state serves neither its own interests nor those of any single group or class

- the state can act as bargaining agent or mediator
- the primary task of the state is to balance the interests of a multitude of competing groups and represent the interests of society as a whole.

Given the importance of competition for power, Dahl attached great importance to democracy for which he suggested five criteria (1989).

- Effective participation – citizens must have adequate and equal opportunities to form their preference and place questions on the public agenda and express reasons for one outcome over the other.

- Voting equality at the decisive stage – each citizen must be assured his or her judgments will be counted as equal in weight to the judgments of others.

- Enlightened understanding – citizens must enjoy ample and equal opportunities for discovering and affirming what choice would best serve their interests.

- Control of the agenda – the demos or people must have the opportunity to decide what political matters actually are and what should be brought up for deliberation.

- Inclusiveness – equality must extend to all citizens within the state. Everyone has a legitimate stake within the political process.

On first reading, this might all sound very reasonable to you and perhaps you would like it to be, but are the claims for democracy and a neutral state sustainable?

How many of you have read *The Queen and I* by Sue Townsend?

She imagines a Britain where an unforgiving, newly elected anti-monarchy party decides that the entire royal family must learn to live like other Britons, or in their case, like desperately poor lower-class Britons on a hideous housing estate in a provincial city. Townsend has terrific fun imagining how they would cope: the Queen buckles down sturdily, mindful of stiff-upper-lip duty; Prince Philip goes to pieces and takes to his bed, and so on.

Imagine instead it is the Workers' Revolutionary Party who, as well as being anti-monarchists, are a Marxist party pledged to end privatisation in all its forms. Do you really believe such a party would be allowed to be elected or do you think the Queen and the military might appear on TV to say that fresh 'democratic elections' would be held after a brief military interregnum?

So let us study democracy in more detail. First a study of our electoral statistics is interesting in terms of what we understand by democracy. From the Internet you can obtain election statistics for the UK from 1918–2005.

General Election Results: 1918–2005: United Kingdom

Votes (millions) Share of Vote (%)

	Con	Lab	Lib
1918	38.4%	20.9%	25.9%
1922	38.2%	29.5%	28.9%
1923	37.9%	30.5%	29.6%
1924	47.2%	33.0%	17.6%
1929	38.2%	37.0%	23.4%
1931	60.7%	30.7%	6.8%
1935	53.5%	37.9%	6.5%
1945	39.7%	47.7%	9.0%
1950	43.3%	46.1%	9.1%
1951	48.0%	48.8%	2.6%
1955	49.6%	46.4%	2.7%
1959	49.4%	43.8%	5.9%
1964	43.3%	44.1%	11.2%
1966	41.9%	47.9%	8.5%
1970	46.4%	43.0%	7.5%
1974	37.8%	37.2%	19.3%
1974	35.7%	39.3%	18.3%
1979	43.9%	36.9%	13.8%

1983	42.4%	27.6%	25.4%
1987	42.2%	30.8%	22.6%
1992	41.9%	34.4%	17.8%
1997	30.7%	43.2%	16.8%
2001	31.7%	40.7%	18.3%
2005	32.4%	35.2%	22.0%

Candidate Seats Won

	Con	Lib	Lab
1918	382	57	163
1922	344	142	62
1923	258	191	158
1924	412	151	40
1929	260	287	59
1931	474	52	36
1935	429	154	21
1945	210	393	12
1950	297	315	9
1951	321	295	6
1955	344	277	6
1959	365	258	6
1964	303	317	9
1966	253	363	12
1970	330	287	6
1974	297	301	14
1974	276	319	13
1979	339	268	11
1983	397	209	23
1987	375	229	22
1992	336	271	20
1997	165	418	46
2001	166	412	52
2005	198	355	62

There are many interesting observations that can be made vis-à-vis democracy:

In terms of seats won, the Conservatives were the largest party on fourteen occasions, and Labour the largest on ten. In three elections the party with most seats failed to gain an overall majority. In 1923 the Conservatives gained 258 out of 615 seats; in 1929 Labour won 287 out of 615 seats and in February 1974 Labour gained 301 out of 635 seats.

On three occasions the party gaining most votes did not win the most seats. In 1929, the Conservatives polled the most votes but the Labour Party won the election with 27 more seats. In 1951 Labour polled most votes yet won 26 fewer seats than the Conservatives. In February 1974, the Conservatives polled 180,000 more votes than Labour but they won four fewer seats.

Since 1918, the Conservatives' best result in terms of seats won was in the 1931 election (474 seats). This was due to the formation of the National Government coalition between the Conservatives, Labour, the National Labour Organisation, and national parties. The Conservatives' best result in the post-war period was in 1983 when they won 397 seats. Correspondingly, this was Labour's worst post-war result in terms of seats (209) as well as share of the vote (27.6%).

Labour's 418 seats won in 1997 was their highest ever, while their highest vote share was recorded in 1951 (48.8%), an election they lost. The Conservatives' lowest vote share was in 1997 (30.7%).

The Liberal Party won 163 seats in the 1918 General Election, its best result in terms of seats won. Their highest share of the vote was in 1923 when they gained 29.6%, while their lowest was in 1951 (2.6%). Since 1945 the highest number of seats won by the (now) Liberal Democrats was 62 at the 2005 General Election, their best performance since 1923. In the 2010 General Election, the Conservatives obtained 36.1% of the vote and 306 seats. It should be noted that in 2005 Tony Blair for Labour had a comfortable working majority with 35.2% of the votes. David Cameron in 2010 has had to enter a coalition with the Liberal Democrats as the outcome was a 'hung' parliament, i.e. no party with overall control.

These figures will probably bemuse US readers, but I wonder how many UK readers are aware of this. You may find it amazing that the way our system works, a party only normally needs to obtain just over forty per cent of the votes, not fifty per cent, to form a government.

Matters were further complicated by Gordon Brown's proposal in February 2010 for a referendum on electoral reform, if re-elected in the general election. Until now we have had a first-past-the-post system (FPP), where the only votes that count are the first preferences. This is similar to the present system of electing the American president and its supporters argue that it has produced working majorities in most UK elections since 1945, the only exception having been in February 1974.

Brown proposed an alternative vote system (AV), where voters list candidates they wish to vote for in order of preference. These preferences determine which candidate is eliminated first and the process is continued until one candidate has more than 50% of the votes. It is important to realise that AV is not Proportional Representation (PR) and can produce even less proportionate results than FPP. Even if a proportionate result is achieved this can lead to weak governments, based on weak coalitions.

> There are ghastly examples, such as the Weimar Republic in the Germany of the twenties, the Italian and French constitutions of the post-war period, or the present constitution of Israel … this is a fraudulent 'deathbed conversion' which is supposed to trick the Lib Dems [a centrist party] into supporting Labour in tactical voting.
>
> Rees-Mogg, 2010

David Cameron, as part of the coalition deal with the Liberal Democrats, has had to give ground on the possibility of electoral reform in the new Conservative/Liberal Democrat coalition. The Liberal Democrats' aim is Proportional Representation, but it appears that Cameron has only agreed to a referendum on the Alternative Voting system, with the right to campaign against it.

UK readers will probably be just as bemused by the US system. America's electoral process is rooted in the principle of 'one person, one vote', but there is evidence to suggest that the principle is drowning in a flood of unlimited political campaign contributions that are, through their ability to secure privileged access to lawmakers, undermining the integrity of both elections and the legislative process.

As candidates and parties battle to win elections, they are forced to raise ever-greater sums of money. The current campaign finance system has taken on the dynamic of the Cold War arms race, with both sides unwilling to relinquish real or perceived political advantages that come from spending more and more money, particularly on negative campaign advertising. The course that both parties so zealously pursue poses a serious threat to the integrity of our democratic process.

That threat is the transformation of a representative democracy into a corporate democracy, in which the 'one person, one vote' principle is supplanted by a system that allocates influence over the political process in proportion to the amount of money an individual or group puts into that process.

The concept of democracy will be examined in greater depth in a later chapter. But for the moment, ask yourself whether you think that the pluralist conception of power and state produces a particular conception of democracy.

If so, what are these competing theories that seriously question the pluralist democratic view?

The competing theories are basically of two types.

First, there is what is called social class analysis, which emphasises the political power of capitalist elites based on the Marxist premise of the economic exploitation of one class by the other.

Remember, you do not necessarily have to be a Marxist to see the merits of the argument. We have just considered the central ideas of liberal democracy – the most widespread and significant political form in the world today – including its claims to offer formal equality, freedom and security to its citizens, on the basis of a particular conception of the state and its relation to civil society.

Marxism is important because it offers the most devastating critique of liberal democracy, based upon a contrasting account of human nature, the nature of power, the relation between the economy and politics, and the validity of liberal democratic claims to provide citizens with a meaningful degree of freedom, equality and justice.

It is a wholly distinct attempt to think through the meaning of these concepts, first under capitalism, and then under a socialist and communist organisation of society.

Until quite recently, almost half the world's population lived under governments that claimed allegiance to some form of Marxist doctrine. Even now, the debate between some form of liberal democracy and some form of socialism remains central to politics.

Throughout this book we have been looking at political ideas which have often been exemplified, if only imperfectly, in actual historical states. It can be hard to separate out theoretical arguments, and criticisms of them, from our knowledge of what became of particular states in practice.

There is a temptation here to say that if a particular state is short-lived, the principles on which it was based must be faulty somewhere. That is what Plato, for example, said about Athenian democracy. This needs great care. The demise of the Soviet form of socialism, reflecting a thousand contingent historical circumstances, is not a refutation of Marx's analysis of capitalism, even if the history of the USSR is an instructive counterpoint to Marx's account of how states might evolve towards the final goal of communism.

Marx had his own vision of what equality, freedom, citizenship and the fulfilment of human potential could mean, and of the political and economic structures that alone could bring them about.

There are a number of strands to these Marxist interpretations.

The structuralist approach, e.g. Nicos Poulantzas (1978), emphasises how the very way a capitalist society operates only allows and encourages the state to do things in some ways and not others – in other words, the state is not neutral.

The idea of the state as simply an instrument of the capitalist class was, however, simplistic. Poulantzas focuses on the structural constraints of the capitalist system that set limits to the state's autonomy and force it to work within the framework of an order that yields results invariably favourable to the dominant capitalist class.

Poulantzas argued therefore that the state allowed other interests to have powers, but only within certain parameters. By accommodating other interests to a degree, an inherently divisive system was able to reproduce itself while maintaining social stability.

Another structuralist is Althusser (1970) who identifies mechanisms for insuring that people within a state behave according to the rules:

- repressive state apparatuses (RSA), e.g. police, armed forces, prisons (criminal justice and prison systems)
- ideological state apparatuses (ISA), e.g. schools, religions, family, legal systems, politics, cultural activities such as arts and sports, systems of mass communication, all of which are institutions which generate ideologies (systems of ideas and values) which we as individuals and groups then internalise.

More recently, Agonists are sceptical about the capacity of politics to eliminate, overcome or circumvent deep divisions within our society, e.g. class, culture, gender and ideology. The traditional theories, which have been the backbone of political theory for the past thirty years, are essentially optimistic about the possibility of finding a harmonious and peaceful pattern of political and social cooperation.

Agonists, then, both claim that this optimism is unjustified and, hence, reorientate political theory to another question: how should we deal with irreducible difference?

In the view of agonists, proponents of the aforementioned traditions, in keeping their eyes fixed on forms of utopian cooperation, have failed to respond usefully to the messiness of contemporary political practice.

Agonism is also opposed to an important strand in the Marxist conception of politics known as 'materialism'. Marx would have agreed with the agonists that society had always been full of conflict, when he wrote: 'The history of all hitherto existing society is the history of class struggles.'

He also thought that the causes of conflict were inescapable features of present – i.e. capitalist society. But, in his view, history would develop in such a way as to eventually destroy capitalism, and replace it with a harmonious society, which was his conception of communism. Especially during the 1960s and 1970s many people, academics included, subscribed to a roughly Marxist analysis. Since then, many of those people have come to the view that the 'materialist conception of history' does not give sufficient reason for hope about a harmonious society to come.

Chantal Mouffe (2005) and Ernesto Laclau are among those who have come to agonism from a background in Marxism and the social movements of the middle part of the last century.

Thus, agonism can be seen as a response to the perceived failures of strands of idealism and materialism to accord with reality, and to provide useful responses to contemporary problems. It can also, in some sense, be seen as a development of theories that emphasised, even celebrated conflict, in a potentially less sensitive and responsible manner than agonism. For example, see Carl Schmitt's 1932 essay, 'The Concept of the Political'. In any case, it is clear that any conception of the political, which involves a celebration of conflict, may entail an endorsement of the domination of some portion of society over others. Agonism, in opposition to any such trend, is avowedly pluralist in its political outlook. It sees political tensions as having an essential place in society, but believes that they should be approached discursively, not in an attempt to eliminate 'the other'.

The second type of theory to attack pluralism is elite theory, which starts from the premise that elitism is inevitable in society. It is probably best to explain this historically.

The aristocratic view is based on the idea that a natural process sets the elite apart from the masses, the former having the required intelligence, skill and leadership and the latter being apathetic, incompetent and unable to govern themselves.

Pareto (1848–1923) argued that democracy was an illusion and that a ruling class always emerged and enriched itself. For him therefore, the key question was how actively the rulers ruled.

Mosca (1858–1941) stressed the universal necessity and inevitability of elite rule and described the ways by which the elite could control and perpetuate the prevailing ideas and institutions of the time.

More recently, in 1956, C Wright Mills wrote:

> The power elite is composed of men whose positions enable them to transcend the ordinary environments of ordinary men and women; they are in positions to make decisions having major consequences … they are in command of the major hierarchies and organisations of modern society. They rule the big corporations. They run the machinery of the state and claim its prerogatives. They direct the military establishment. They occupy the strategic command posts of the social structure, in which are now centred the effective means of the power and the wealth and the celebrity which they enjoy.

These ideas were further developed by William Domhoff, (1996), who in his 'governing class' model argues basically that those who have the money have the power.

He argues that the rich form a social upper class led by 'a power elite', which for historical reasons is particular powerful in America in that economic and political networks were more able to subdue ideological and military networks as compared to Europe.

The power elite has:

- developed institutions by which its children are socialised into an upper-class world view
- control of many corporations
- control of many non-profit organisations by which the upper class shape policy debates, e.g. think tanks and foundations
- influence in the processes of special interest, policy-making and candidate selection at the highest government levels.

Finally, elite managerial theory explains what the state does by looking at constraints from organisational structures, semi-autonomous state managers and interests that arise from the state as a unique power concentrating organisation.

Theda Skocpol in *Diminished Democracy* (2003) examines what will happen to US democracy if participatory groups and social movements wither, while civic involvement becomes one more occupation rather than every citizen's right and duty. She observes that thousands of non-profit groups have been launched in recent times, but that most are run by professionals who lobby Congress, or deliver social services to clients.

However, she argues that this decline in public involvement has not always been the case in this country – and that, by understanding the causes of this change, we might reverse it.

During the nineteenth and early twentieth centuries, farmers' groups, women's associations, unions, veterans' groups, fraternal orders, and crusades for social change and moral reform spread across the United States. Democratic government and voluntary associations have worked hand in hand through much of the nation's past. Then, after the 1960s, civic life suddenly changed. Many new advocacy groups appeared to speak on behalf of people formerly at the margins of social life and politics. But professionally managed agencies displaced membership groups, leaving regular Americans with fewer opportunities to unite across class lines and get involved in community and public affairs.

Her solution is that we must learn from the past to halt the diminishing democracy.

I hope this brief look at competing ideas regarding the state and power has been useful in helping you to see that the prevailing view today goes very much against the idea of a neutral state operating an effective democracy in so-called Western liberal democracies.

And do not forget that there are many more governments across the world that do not even bother to try to argue for the neutrality of the state. We will revisit elite theory later in the chapter on globalism, when we will examine the idea of a global power elite.

As you can see initially we were considering human nature,

the individual and society and social change. The introduction of social theory broadens things and adds questions regarding the nature of power in terms of the state, social groups and democracy.

At the time of writing, five key areas stand out for further investigation to assist you to broaden your political philosophy:

- religion and fundamentalism
- global capitalism and environmentalism
- isolationism, protectionism and populism
- libertarianism and egalitarianism
- endism and the 'myth of end'.

Summary

Social theory is more of a product of the modern industrial era, sometimes called modernity. It aims to provide a general interpretation of the social forces at work in the making and development of modern industrial society.

Social theory properly begins only with the recognition that society is a reality in itself. Societies have inner logics of development and that the social is always more than the sum of its parts.

Marx theory is both political and social. Marx established a tradition in social theory around the explanation of the rise and transformation of capitalist society.

Out of this intertwining of social and political theory emerged political sociology that looks at power and power relationships in society. One understanding of power is that it is 'the capacity of some persons to produce intended and foreseen effects on others'. However it is very much a 'contested concept'.

Political sociology has three main competing explanatory frameworks: pluralism, social class analysis and elite theory.

- -

Reader's Notes:

7

Religion and Fundamentalism

You are what you do.

Jean-Paul Sartre

A system of thought aiming at fundamental changes in the structure of society, and particularly at the replacement of the authoritarian state by some form of non-governmental cooperation between free individuals.

William Godwin

When I used to teach the contents of this book as a university course, I could always guarantee that at this point one of my students would ask me where religious or atheistic views fit into all of this.

Today I am sure I would be asked about religion and atheism and, in addition, fundamentalism and terrorism.

Most courses and books tend to keep the philosophy of politics and the philosophy of religion apart, but to a large number of students this is an important issue and an illogical separation, and therefore, in my view, one that must be addressed.

I am sure that readers can readily appreciate that within the student group there was always a mix of believers and non-believers with a wide range of differing perceptions in this area. This will be just the same for readers of this book.

So here goes, remembering that my aim is to take you from your own personal starting point, whether religious or not, and help you to develop your own political philosophy towards national and international developments.

Trust me, the last thing I want to do is upset your religious or non-religious beliefs, but I hope that you will concede that developing a sound political philosophy that gels with your religious or otherwise views will require some rethinking and accommodation. I will endeavour to be neutral regarding religion and concentrate on the relationship between religious and political philosophy.

First let us see if we can agree some philosophical positions for religious and non-religious views without taking sides in the debate.

Grayling (2007) has suggested that there are two fundamentally different ways of understanding the nature and sources of value that have competed and sometimes overlapped during the course of history:

> A broadly transcendental [asserting a fundamental irrationality or supernatural element in experience] and heteronomous [subject to external or foreign laws or domination; not autonomous] one that locates the source of moral value outside the human realm … that tells man what his goals are and how he should live … that places on the human realm a demand to realise aims and attain ends likewise located beyond the boundaries of this world … standardly, in a life after death.

And:

> A broadly secular attitude rooted in views about human nature and the human condition … where autonomy is premised as the basis of a good life … where the source of our values and resulting ethics come from within man himself, who is able to reason and choose for himself what his goals are and how he should live.

You can no doubt try to place yourselves on the spectrum just given, and that is your decision. To help you do this I would suggest that what you have here is a dimensional -ism from theism at the one end to atheism at the other.

As you move gradually from theism to atheism, the central importance of the transcendental and heteronomous elements of religion decline.

We can start perhaps with religious fundamentalists who literally accept the world view of the writings they regard as sacred, insisting on the morality and way of life prescribed by them. The Taliban and Orthodox Judaism are examples as are the creationists and 'intelligent designers' of the Christian Right in America.

A good example of a conservative philosopher is Anthony O'Hear, who in *After Progress* (1999) argues against the false promise of progress as embodied in science and the humanist values of reason, atheism, democracy and human rights.

> The meaning of life is just the little matter on which our official ideology of scientific enlightenment and liberal politics studiously refuses to pronounce; in place of anything like that, what we are offered are material prosperity, formal equality and political participation, and when these are not enough, drugs or therapy or yet more unrealisable political promises ... individuals, meanwhile, who for one reason or another cannot compete in society but who are fed on a half-understood diet of equality and human rights, become increasingly resentful and violent when they realise that they are never going to make the grade socially or economically.

Then there are those who accept that Kierkegaard is correct in arguing that faith, to be genuine, must have no aid from reason; the true believer must be prepared to make a non-rational 'leap of faith'.

There are those who call themselves religious who reject the transcendental but nevertheless feel that a religion's message gives them the good life that they aspire to lead. There is a fine line between the latter and those who call themselves humanist. Todorov (2002) perhaps describes it best when he argues

> That on the one hand they separate themselves from it; they want the individual to be able to choose freely whether to believe or not; they want societies to be governed by the will of the people and not divine right. They also think that Man and not only God is worthy of being an end in himself ... humanism which is not in itself a form of religion, is nonetheless not a form of atheism. It separates the management of human affairs from any theological basis of justification; but it does not demand an elimination of the religious dimension of experience.

Finally, on the continuum there are those who totally reject the idea that any purpose for mankind can be imposed from outside; such meaning as there is to human existence is found or imposed by humans themselves. Therefore a god or gods (or other supernatural beings) are man-made constructs, myths and legends.

I have tried to describe the dimensional -ism in a non-judgmental way that helps you to establish your place on it.

Just to give you an idea as to how complex and litigious this can all become, let me refer you to the 1957 tax case of Washington Ethical Society 'V' District of Columbia (101 US App. DC 371). The Society functions much like a church, but regards itself as a non-theistic religious institution, honouring the importance of ethical living without mandating a belief in a supernatural origin for ethics. The case involved denial of the Society's application for tax exemption as a religious organisation. The US Court of Appeals reversed the Tax Court's ruling, defined the Society as a religious organisation, and granted it tax exemption.

The implications of this judgment are that:

- this case affirmed that a religion need not be theistic to qualify as a religion under the law
- this case did not affirm that it established generic secular humanism as a religion.

Hopefully by now you are beginning to see the nature of the relationship between religious and political philosophy. Some of my students would always say something to the effect that they had never seen any connection between the two revealing, in my opinion, a narrow perception of politics and political philosophy, especially given the intertwining of social and political theory developed in the previous chapter. My reply is that political and religious philosophy has surely existed ever since two thinking human beings have existed.

Grayling does in fact define political philosophy as 'how to create a good society with the express intention of providing the best opportunities for its citizens to live the good life'. Many of you might accept this as a broad definition of religious philosophy.

Remember:

- an -ism is a collection or mix of ideas and values that exist at a certain moment in time and represent something that people feel is significant and important
- an -ism becomes an -ism of political philosophy when the ideas and values are concerned with achieving power over people by coercion or persuasion.

When person A tries to persuade person B to agree with their ideas, they are trying to get power over person B so that they will agree with person A's decisions. Person A might also use coercion as well as persuasion. Once either one or both happen, politics, albeit at an elementary level, is born, as is political philosophy that will analyse the power relationship.

I would suggest to you that there is clear evidence of persuasion and coercion being used throughout history under the name of most religions, from ancient history to the Crusades to 9/11.

Second, let us introduce ideology into the argument. To do this, let us go back to the pair of spectacles where it was argued that the lenses reflected the mix of ideas that were important to you. Let us say this time we will start with socialism and Welsh nationalism. But what if we next examine lenses that include the mix just given and then add, say, Presbyterianism?

I am sure it is not too difficult to envisage a Welsh miner with that mix of ideas to help him try to lead a good life, vote with thought and argue with reason.

The three key sets of ideas (socialism, nationalism and Presbyterianism) are a body of knowledge and values that have not necessarily taken on any ideological status at this stage.

What happens when an -ism becomes an ideological one?

This is not necessarily a problem if you have clearly thought it through and it gives you a clear sense of purpose and understanding in life. It can give you an important sense of conviction. However, you must never forget the aspects of an ideology outlined earlier and in particular their 'dynamism', 'cultural specificity', 'value assumptions' and possible 'inner contradictions'.

When an -ism takes on ideological status, however, it clearly becomes much more complicated. There are in fact two levels of increasing complexity.

Let us first imagine a situation where a devout Catholic wishes to give primacy to their religion in the way they perceive the world and behave in it.

I would suggest you try to imagine a pair of double-glazed lenses, the innermost lens representing the Catholicism and the outer lens the other -isms in their life. In other words the other -isms are themselves perceived through the Catholicism. Presumably in this instance if there were to be any contradictions, the Catholic view would prevail or an accommodation with the Catholic view would be met. A good example of this is the fact that many Catholics use contraception or support the war in Iraq.

This brings us to the next big question of whether or not assigning ideological status to a political -ism, say conservatism, is the same as assigning it to a religious -ism, say Protestantism.

Clearly there are two opposing views here. Some non-believers will see no difference, e.g. Marxism and Protestantism can both be seen as becoming ideologies. In contrast I have no doubt that many believers will perceive a major difference, and not agree to their faith being classified as an ideology. Whereas philosophy pursues the truth through reason, religion claims to know the truth through revelation and faith.

Wikipedia, however, suggests that religion is a set of beliefs and practices that are determined by one's view of reality (in other words, an -ism) and the supernatural.

However, for the purposes of this book, does this admittedly major difference matter when it comes to helping you realise your political philosophy? I suggest it does not.

All that happens is that the more transcendental (ideological) you are in your religious beliefs, the more the inner lens will dominate.

Thirdly and finally, we have to consider fundamentalism. This is a very difficult area in which to write impartially, but I will do my best by drawing attention to a number of differing viewpoints.

We will start with a couple of clarificatory points.

A distinction must be drawn between religious (that we will concentrate on) and non-religious uses of the term fundamentalism. For example, with regard to the latter, Richard Dawkins has been accused of 'atheistic fundamentalism'.

In *The Dawkins Delusion?* McGrath and McGrath (2007) compare Dawkins' 'total dogmatic conviction of correctness' to 'a religious fundamentalism which refuses to allow its ideas to be examined or challenged'.

This of course neatly brings us to the second point that is the distinction between the uses of religious fundamentalism in a neutral or pejorative way. For example, the phrase 'Muslim fundamentalists' can be used in a pejorative sense to characterise religious advocates as clinging to a stubborn, entrenched position that defies reasoned argument or contradictory evidence.

A more neutral approach, which will be used in this book, is to suggest that, for example, both Christian and Islamic fundamentalism suggest a movement or attitude within a movement stressing strict and literal adherence to a set of basic principles. Most of the world's major religions have, in fact, fundamentalist movements. Some fundamentalist movements claim to be founded upon the same religious principles as the larger group, but the fundamentalists more self-consciously attempt to build an entire approach to the modern world based on strict fidelity to those principles, to preserve a distinctiveness both of doctrine and of life.

With regard to differences of view, I suggest there are four main groups of religious fundamentalists who need to be distinguished to begin to understand the current antagonism between Islam and the so-called Western liberal democracies.

Firstly, there are Western and Eastern fundamentalists who can accommodate one another's religious views. Smith (2005) writes that

> Barring some extremists like Al-Qaeda, most Muslims do not interpret Qura'nic verses as promoting warfare; and that the phenomenon of radical interpretation of scripture by extremist groups is not unique to Islam.

> *Encyclopedia of Christianity* (2005)

According to Sells (2002),

> [Most Muslims] no more expect to apply [the verses at issue] to
> their contemporary non-Muslim friends and neighbours than
> most Christians and Jews consider themselves commanded by
> God, like the Biblical Joshua, to exterminate the infidels.

'Understanding, Not Indoctrination', *The Washington Post*, 2002

Similarly, Daniel Chirot (2002) said that

> Not many people in the world, either in Islamic countries, or
> Christian ones, or Hindu, or Buddhist, or anything else, really
> want to live a life of extreme puritanism, endless hate and suicidal
> wars. Extremist leaders can take power, and for a time, be backed
> by much of their population hoping to redress past grievances
> and trying to find a new utopia. But as with the most extreme
> Christian warriors during the European wars of religion ... it
> eventually turned out that few of their people were willing to go
> all the way in their struggles if that meant permanent violence,
> suffering and death. So it will be with Islamic extremism.

Many other similar quotations could have been found to
summarise this view.

Secondly there are Western fundamentalists who believe they
are at war with Islam. Here we need to consider the Christian
Right and the neoconservatives in the USA.

The origin of creationism is attributed to Chrysippus, a Stoic
philosopher. When asked if God even made bedbugs, his reply
was, 'In the bedbug God has given us a natural alarm clock.'

The issue is very much alive today in America with individual
states requiring creationism and intelligent design to be in the
school curriculum.

Evangelism is a force that cannot be ignored in America,
accounting for some forty per cent of the population.

If you want a more detailed look at the Christian Right in
America, I suggest you look at the writings of James Dobson on
the Internet. He has been referred to as 'the nation's most
influential evangelical leader' by *Time* magazine.

On 23 October 2008, Dobson published a 'Letter from 2012

in Obama's America' that proposed that an Obama presidency would lead to mandated homosexual teachings across all schools, the banning of firearms in entire states, the end of the Boy Scouts, home schooling, Christian school groups, Christian adoption agencies, talk radio, pornography on prime-time and daytime television, mandatory bonuses for gay soldiers, terrorist attacks across America, the nuclear bombing of Tel Aviv, the conquering of most of eastern Europe by Russia, the end of health care for Americans over eighty, out-of-control gasoline prices, and complete economic disaster in the United States, among other catastrophes. In the days after the 2008 presidential election, Dobson stated on his radio programme that he was mourning the Obama election, claiming that Obama supported infanticide, would be responsible for the deaths of millions of unborn children, and was 'going to appoint the most liberal justices to the Supreme Court, perhaps, that we've ever had'.

In complete contrast, Chris Hedges (2008) an ex-foreign correspondent for the *New York Times*, has written a controversial but interesting book entitled *American Fascists: the Christian Right and the War on America*.

It is important to remember that his book was published before the election of Obama. The following is a paraphrasing of the key ideas of his book.

He argues that the engine that drives the radical Christian Right in the United States, in his view the most dangerous mass movement in American history, is not religiosity but despair.

It is a movement built on the growing personal and economic despair of tens of millions of Americans, who watched helplessly as their communities were plunged into poverty by the flight of manufacturing jobs, and their families and neighbourhoods torn apart by neglect and indifference. They eventually lost hope that America was a place where they had a future. The end of the world is no longer an abstraction to many Americans.

Those in despair search desperately for a solution, the warm embrace of a community to replace the one they lost, a sense of purpose and meaning in life, the assurance that they are protected, loved and worthwhile.

Those in despair are the most easily manipulated and likely to be attracted to a promised fantastic utopia. The battle against abortion is one of the Christian Right's most effective recruiting tools. It plays on the guilt and shame of women who have had abortions, accusing them of committing murder, and promising redemption and atonement in the 'Christian' struggle to make abortion illegal – a fight for life against 'the culture of death'.

Hedges argues that, until now, we have turned our backs on the working class and stand passively and watch an equally pernicious assault on the middle class. There has been a creation of an American oligarchy. The top one per cent of households in the US has more wealth than the bottom ninety per cent combined.

As Plutarch reminded us: 'An imbalance between rich and poor is the oldest and most fatal ailment of all republics.'

Those in despair will willingly walk out on this world for the mythical world offered by radical preachers: a world of magic, a world where God had a divine plan for them and intervened on a daily basis to protect them and perform miracles in their lives.

The rage many express towards those who challenge this belief system, to those of us who do not accept that everything in the world came into being during a single week 6,000 years ago because it says so in the Bible, was a rage born of fear, the fear of being plunged back into a reality-based world where these magical props would no longer exist, and where they would once again be adrift.

The danger of this theology of despair is that it says that nothing in the world is worth saving. It rejoices in cataclysmic destruction. The obsession with apocalyptic violence is an obsession with revenge.

Those who lead the movement give their followers moral licence to direct this rage and yearning for violence against all who refuse to submit to the movement, from liberals and 'secular humanists', to 'nominal Christians', intellectuals, gays and lesbians, to Muslims.

The leaders of the Christian Right, from James Dobson to Pat Robertson, call for a theocratic state that will, if it comes to pass, bear within it many of the traits of classical fascism. They have created tens of millions of angry, disenfranchised Americans longing for revenge and yearning for a mythical utopia, Americans who embraced a theology of despair because they were offered nothing else.

All radical movements need a crisis or a prolonged period of instability to achieve power. We are in a period of crisis now – the opening these radicals seek – but this has to be balanced against the election of Obama as President.

Those of you who saw his inauguration and the crowds surely have to concede that they were excited because they see in Obama someone who can remove their fear and despair. How far this will moderate their evangelical militancy remains to be seen.

Secondly, in the US there was been the ascendancy of neoconservatism under the Bush administration.

Fukuyama (2006) suggests there are

Four common principles:

- a concern for democracy, human rights and more generally the internal politics of other states
- a belief that American power can be used for moral purposes
- a scepticism about the ability of international law and institutions to solve serious security problems
- a view that ambitious social engineering often leads to unexpected social consequences and thereby undermines its own ends.

Its key distinction is in international affairs, where it espouses an interventionist approach that seeks to defend what neoconservatives deem as national interests.

In America the Kagans (2009), along with the Kristols (2003, 2006) and the Podhoretzes (2004, 2007), are good examples of conservative dynasties that tried to assert neoconservative principles on the foreign policy of the Bush administration.

The Bush doctrine was laid out in his State of the Union speech in January 2002, following the 11 September 2001 attacks. The speech, written by neoconservative David Frum, named Iraq, Iran and North Korea as states that 'constitute an axis of evil' and 'pose a grave and growing danger'.

Bush suggested the possibility of pre-emptive war:

> I will not wait on events, while dangers gather. I will not stand by, as peril draws closer and closer. The United States of America will not permit the world's most dangerous regimes to threaten us with the world's most destructive weapons.

The Obama administration appears to be the death knell of neoconservatism. Following the election, Jonathan Clarke, a senior fellow at the Carnegie Council for Ethics in Foreign Affairs, expressed the following view.

> In many ways, the 2008 election represented a direct repudiation of the neocon style of foreign policy based on military-centred, unilateralist overreaching. At first sight, the incoming Obama administration appears to be the polar opposite of neoconservatism. Its instincts are multilateral, being committed, for example, to adhering to the Kyoto Protocol and to international agreements like the Geneva Convention. It places a high priority on diplomacy, with President-elect Obama being open to direct talks with long-ignored countries like Iran and Cuba. Defense Secretary Gates, who is remaining in office, has made it clear that he regards military intervention as the genuinely last option. Furthermore, the financial meltdown and the drains of the Iraq and Afghan wars have chipped away at the pre-eminence of US power. It is difficult to argue today that the US enjoys a unipolar advantage. The safest bet, therefore, is that we can bid adieu to the neocons and leave their role to be adjudicated by history. They themselves argue that they form part of the mainstream of American history. It seems more likely that they will come to be seen as an aberration.

This view is supported by Lawrence Freedman (2009), who stresses the need for America to rediscover the art of 'normal diplomacy' in the Middle East. He argues that dealing with the Middle East is 'an art, not a science', the problems can only be managed or endured.

> Part of the problem is America itself ... Just as the Americans have to learn to live with the unpredictability of the Middle East, so the Middle East has to live with the unpredictability of the

United States … Washington politics is intolerant of nuance and ambiguity … It tends to describe events in absolutes of good and evil.

Freedman, *A Choice of Enemies: America Confronts the Middle East*, 2009, p.475

Clearly Obama realises this in attempting to establish dialogues.

Thirdly, there are Eastern fundamentalists who see Western politics and society as actively anti-Islamic and promote the use of defensive force. They identify what they see as a historical struggle between Christianity and Islam, dating back as far as the Crusades.

Defensive jihad differs from offensive jihad in being *fard al-ayn*, or a personal obligation of all Muslims, rather than *fard al-kifaya*, a communal obligation, which if some Muslims perform it is not required from others. Hence, framing a fight as defensive has the advantage both of appearing to be a victim rather than aggressor, and of giving your struggle the very highest religious priority for all good Muslims.

It is worth noting that there are American writers who support the view that Islamic militancy towards America should be seen as a strategic reaction to American power, an idea associated with Johnson's (2000) 'blowback' thesis.

In this view, the presence of empires – both at the end of the last century and today – and the analogous unipolar (a distribution of power in which there is one state with most of the military influence) military position of the United States today provoke resistance in the form of terrorism. Johnson notes that

> The Russian, Ottoman and Habsburg Empires – which controlled multiple ethnic, religious and national peoples – led to a backlash, or blowback, by Serb, Macedonian and Bosnian terrorist organisations (the Black Hand, Young Bosnia, Narodnaya Volya). By analogy the powerful global position of the United States, particularly in its role of propping up repressive undemocratic regimes, constitutes something of a similar condition with Arab-Islamic terrorism as a result. The causal mechanism here is that the projection of military power plants

seeds of later terrorist reactions, as retaliation for previous American imperial actions.

Johnson, 2000

Fourthly, there are Eastern fundamentalists who see Western politics and society as actively anti-Islamic and promote the use of offensive force.

George Bush accepted 'Islamic-Fascism' as the ideological label for this group. While Islamic-Fascism immediately conjures up images of an evil to be resisted and is therefore useful as a public relations term, intellectually it does little for the serious study of Islam.

So what is this ideology he labelled Islamic-Fascism?

The answer can be found in a collection of Islamic thought called Qutbism, which refers to the writings of Sayyid Qutb and other Islamic theoreticians, e.g. Abul Ala Maududi and Hassan al Banna that provide the intellectual rationale.

Qutbism is not a structured body of thought from any single person, source, time or sect; rather it is a fusion of Islamic ideas that include elements from both the Sunni and Shia sects of Islam that have been combined with broader Islamic goals and methodologies. Qutbism integrates the Islamic teachings of Maududi and al Banna with the arguments of Sayyid Qutb to justify armed jihad in the advance of Islam. Qutbism advocates violence and justifies terrorism against non-Muslims and apostates in an effort to bring about the reign of God. Others, e.g. Ayman Al-Zawahiri, Abdullah Azzam and Osama bin Laden, built terrorist organisations based on the principles of Qutbism and turned the ideology of Islamic-Fascism into a global action plan.

Qutbism is structured on a common foundation of puritan Islamic orientations such as Wahabbi, Salafi and Deobandi. These orientations share several traits and beliefs, including beliefs that:

- Muslims have deviated from true Islam and must return to 'pure Islam' as originally practised during the time of the Prophet

- the path to 'pure Islam' is only through a literal and strict interpretation of the Quran and Hadith, along with implementation of the Prophet's commands

- Muslims should individually interpret the original sources without being slavishly bound to the interpretations of Islamic scholars

- any interpretation of the Quran from a historical, contextual perspective is a corruption, and that the majority of Islamic history and the classical jurisprudential tradition is mere sophistry.

While puritan Islamic orientations set the foundation, it was Islamic theoreticians who built Qutbism's intellectual framework.

One of the founding fathers of modern Islamic thought is Abul Ala Maududi (1903–1979). Maududi believed the Muslim community's decline resulted from practising a corrupted form of Islam contaminated by non-Islamic ideas and culture.

Maududi reminded Muslims that Islam is more than a religion; it is a complete social system that guides and controls every aspect of life, including government. He believed tolerance of non-Muslim rule and non-Islamic concepts and systems was an insult to God.

Therefore, the only way Muslims might practise pure Islam and assume their rightful place in the world is through the establishment of Islamic states, where Islam rules independent of non-Islamic influences. These Islamic states would eventually spread Islam across the globe and establish God's reign. Maududi argued the only practical way to accomplish Islamic rule is through jihad.

Maududi's *Jihad in Islam* articulated the goals of an evolving Islamic ideology by reiterating the strategic objective of global Islamic rule and designating jihad as the way to achieve it. Thinkers like Hassan al Banna, in *Jihad*, Muhammad Adb al Salam Faraj in *The Neglected Duty*, and Sayyid Qutb, *In the Shade of the Quran* and *Milestones* espoused similar ideas and attempted to put them into practice.

Hassan al Banna (1905–1949) believed, like Maududi, that a revival of 'pure Islam' was the antidote to Western domination and a cure for the malady infecting the Muslim world. A charismatic leader and organiser, al Banna implemented the Islamist vision by organising the Muslim Brotherhood in 1928 with the objective of establishing government rule on the basis of Islamic values.

His approach was a gradual one rather than a revolutionary one. By providing basic services to the community including schools, mosques and factories, he sought popular support for Islamic goals through persuasion.

However, despite this, al Banna never articulated a practical method for taking power. His lasting legacy was reminding Muslims that the Quran says jihad against unbelievers is an obligation of all Muslims. He also argued that jihad was not just the defence of Muslim lands but a means 'to safeguard the mission of spreading Islam'.

His contemporary Sayyid Qutb then expanded the idea of jihad to spread Islam and to establish the Islamic state.

Sayyid Qutb (1906–1966) is regarded as the founding father and leading theoretician of the contemporary extremist movement. Qutb became one of the leading spokesmen and thinkers of the Muslim Brotherhood, persuasively advocating the use of violence to establish Islamic rule and like Maududi inspired thousands to take up the cause of 'establishing God's rule on earth'.

Unlike al Banna, who tried to build an Islamic society from the bottom up, Qutb changed the strategy by developing a top-down approach that focused on removing non-Islamic rulers and governments.

Qutb argued that the entire world, including the Muslim, was in a state of *jahiliyah*, or ignorance, where man's way had replaced God's way.

According to Qutb, since *jahiliyah* and Islam cannot co-exist, offensive jihad was necessary to destroy *jahiliyah* society and bring the entire world to Islam. Until *jahiliyah* is defeated, all true Muslims have a personal obligation to wage offensive jihad. When Qutb added offensive jihad to the widely accepted concept of defensive jihad, Qutb broke with mainstream Islam:

> Those who say that Islamic jihad was merely for the defense of the 'home land of Islam' diminish the greatness of the Islamic way of life and consider it less important [than] their 'homeland … However, [Islamic community] defense is not the ultimate

objective of the Islamic movement of jihad but it is a means of establishing the Divine authority within it so that it becomes the headquarters for the movement of Islam, which is then to be carried throughout the earth to the whole of mankind...'

Sayyid Qutb, *Milestones*, 1964

In addition to offensive jihad, Sayyid Qutb used the Islamic concept of *takfir* or excommunication of apostates. Declaring someone *takfir* provided a legal loophole around the prohibition of killing another Muslim and in fact made it a religious obligation to execute the apostate. The obvious use of this concept was to declare secular rulers, officials or organisations, or any Muslims that opposed the Islamic agenda, a *takfir*, thereby justifying assassinations and attacks against them. Sheikh Omar Abdel Rahman, who was later convicted in the 1993 World Trade Centre attack, invoked Qutb's *takfir* writings during his trial for the assassination of President Anwar Sadat. The *takfir* concept along with 'offensive jihad' became the blank cheque for any Islamic extremist to justify attacks against anyone.

Qutb's theory of unrestricted jihad, '...Against every obstacle that comes into the way of worshipping God and the implementation of the divine authority on earth...' is the intellectual basis behind the exhortations of Abdullah Azzam and Ayman al-Zawahiri, and ultimately the establishment of Osama bin Laden's al-Qaeda.

Qutb's disciples, Abdullah Azzam and Ayman al-Zawahiri, introduced Osama bin Laden to Qutb's ideology. Azzam first met bin Laden when he lectured at King Adbul Aziz University in Jeddah, Saudi Arabia, where bin Laden was studying under Mohammad Qutb, Sayyid's brother.

In response to the Soviet invasion of Afghanistan, Azzam left Saudi Arabia and established the Maktab al-Khadamat or 'Services Offices' in Pakistan to organise, train and support international mujahideen fighting in Afghanistan. bin Laden joined Azzam in 1984 and supported the mujahideen effort through his Baitul-Ansar or 'House of Helpers'. Azzam's mentorship provided the young bin Laden with the practical experience to develop the logistical and organisational skills necessary for recruiting, training and funding a jihadi network with global reach. After the Soviet withdrawal from Afghanistan, Azzam attempted to shift the jihadi effort to Palestine. Azzam was killed in Peshawar by assassins in November 1989 and bin Laden assumed full control of the Maktab.

Ayman al-Zawahiri, a prolific writer on Qutb's ideas, met Osama bin Laden during the Afghan war. Their close relationship resulted in the 1989 merger of the Maktab and Egyptian Jihad that formed al-Qaeda. Al-Zawahiri served as the organisation's ideologist while bin Laden was the organiser and leader.

Al-Zawahiri authored al-Qaeda's manifesto *Knights Under the Prophet's Banner*, which clearly links the Islamist's goal with Qutb's strategy of unrestricted jihad. Significantly, it explains al-Qaeda's rationale for attacking the 'far enemy' (the US, Israel, and other non-Muslim powers) first. The 'far enemy first' strategy was revolutionary as it overthrew the accepted 'near enemy strategy' of al Banna, Qutb, Azzam, and Faraj. This shift was the result of careful strategic decision making by al-Zawahiri and bin Laden. It is only natural to assume that the two compared the failures of the Muslim Brotherhood, al-Jamaa al-Islamiya, Egyptian Jihad, and other organisations to prevail over the 'near enemy,' to the successes of the Afghan mujahideen in their victory over the Soviets. They reasonably concluded that the 'far enemy' strategy was the wiser course of action.

For these reasons al-Qaeda in the 1990s focused its efforts on the 'far enemy' and the United States in particular. Zawahiri and bin Laden pushed a shift from small isolated extremists attacking local apostate regimes to clear-cut and unified jihad against infidels. The intent was not so much as to destroy the West, but rather to unify Muslim masses behind al-Qaeda's goals.

The intent of progressively spectacular attacks against US and Western interests was to drive the United States from the Middle East, thus weakening apostate Muslim regimes and increasing al-Qaeda's prestige. They intended the attacks of 9/11 to provoke an inevitable infidel retaliation that would rally ordinary Muslims to global jihad in defence of Islam. Al-Zawahiri and bin Laden thought that by changing the target of the Qutbist strategy, they could turn the struggle into a war between Islam and the West.

Naturally, pro-Western secular regimes in Muslim lands would be the first casualties of this war. As these regimes fell, they would be replaced by Islamic rule, thus setting the initial stage for further Islamic conquests.

Osama bin Laden's chief contribution to Qutbism may be his management and organisational skills. The Muslim Brotherhood's collapse after al Banna's death demonstrated the fragility of hierarchical organisations dependent on a single leader. It can be assumed that bin Laden, as a business management student and protégé of Azzam, learned from al Banna's mistakes and designed al-Qaeda as a networked organisation of franchises rather than a conventional hierarchical organisation. His organisational design facilitated the rapid globalisation of Qutbism and distribution of resources, while building durability and protective firewalls between cells.

In summary therefore, Qutbism and al-Qaeda act according to the following principles.

- the Muslim community (or the Muslim community outside of a vanguard fighting to re-establish it) has been extinct for a few centuries having reverted to godless ignorance or *jahiliyah*, and must be reconquered for Islam.

- adherence to Sharia as sacred law accessible to humans, without which Islam cannot exist.

- adherence to Sharia as a complete way of life that will bring not only justice, but complete freedom from servitude, peace, personal serenity, scientific discovery and other benefits.

- avoidance of Western and non-Islamic 'evil and corruption', including socialism and nationalism.

- vigilance against Western and Jewish conspiracies against Islam.

- a two-pronged attack of preaching to convert and jihad to forcibly eliminate the 'structures' of *jahiliyah*.

- the importance of offensive Jihad to eliminate *jahiliyah* not only from the Islamic homeland but also from the face of the earth.

Charles Moore (2008) has written about his concern that the organisation Hizb ut Tahrir argues that their God-given law, Sharia law, is the only law, which should be obeyed, and that Muslims owe no allegiance to the UK.

Similarly, he writes of what he calls 'an ideologue named Mawdudi' who stated in the UK that 'Islam wishes to do away with all states and governments which are opposed to the ideology and programme of Islam [if necessary] by the power of the sword'.

For non-Islamic readers it may come as a surprise to know that Sharia law has been operating in the UK, in parallel to the English legal system, since 1982, when the Islamic Sharia Council was established. Today it oversees up to eighty-five Sharia courts that are permitted to rule only in civil cases. There are those who want the law extended to all criminal cases.

> In some ways I learned that this is happening already. The Somali Muslims in Britain have long relied on the Sharia principle of mediation and arbitration in criminal cases ... Sharia law was used to resolve the case of knife attacks ... The families of one victim and attacker were bought together under Somali elders ... [and it was decided] that the victim would be compensated by the attacker, who in turn was forgiven for the crime ... The literal meaning of Sharia is 'source of water in the desert', meaning the source of all spiritual life for Muslims. It is therefore a way of life rather than just a code of law ... Sharia law in Britain is here to stay ... it's a perilous tightrope we tread – the line between multicultural tolerance and the rights of the individual.
>
> Fernandes, 2009

For the purposes of this book, I suggest that one becomes a fundamentalist when the inner lens takes over almost entirely, and coercion may be considered along with persuasion.

Those under attack will conceive of the use of fear and coercion to spread an ideological view as terrorism.

But again I repeat the question as to how much does the diversity of view matter here in the context of your political philosophy. If you have a fundamentalist view about religion in terms of perceiving reality, you still have to come to a decision as to the extent to which you will reach an accommodation with the other -isms in your outer lens. Again, that is totally your decision.

Summary

Religious -isms are a collection or mix of ideas and values that exist at a certain moment in time and represent something that people feel is significant and important.

A religious -ism can be seen as an -ism of political philosophy when the ideas and values are concerned with achieving power over people by coercion or persuasion.

Fundamentalism occurs when there is a very strict adherence to one perception of reality.

Those under attack will conceive of the use of fear and coercion to spread an ideological view as terrorism.

- -
Reader's Notes:

8

Global Capitalism and Environmentalism

> Every man is virtuous when his particular will is in all things conformable to the general will, and we voluntarily will what is willed by those whom we love.
>
> Jean-Jacques Rousseau

> Is it the case that the world must suffer a major crisis ... before the United States sheds its laissez-faire philosophy and uses its unmatched powers to help establish working conditions of global governance?
>
> John Gray

> [I find the] collapse of the global marketplace ... easier to imagine than the continuation of the present regime.
>
> George Soros

The purpose of this chapter is:

- to explain global capitalism
- to examine the political arguments for and against it
- to consider environmentalism as a political issue.

Think back to the chapter on dimensional -isms and the capitalism and socialism dimension. At that early stage I was trying to examine the way your position on the dimension would influence the way you vote.

Now I would like to concentrate on the capitalist end and ask you to think internationally and globally. If you remember, Adam

Smith suggested three main concepts form liberalism or the foundation of free market economics, which are:

- division of labour
- pursuit of self-interest
- freedom of trade.

If you add to this the spread of new distance-abolishing technologies throughout the world, then you have the capacity for global capitalism and the rise of neoliberalism.

The alleged merits and demerits of a global free market are numerous and complex, but you must consider them to give needed breadth to your political philosophy.

The major recent advocate of the global market was the recent Bush administration in the USA that was heavily influenced by the philosophy of neoliberalism.

If Adam Smith returned and saw the more extreme aspects of neoliberalism, he would probably find them bizarre. Nevertheless, they derive from the ideas of early liberalism.

However, the belief in the market, in market forces, has separated from the factual production of goods and services. It has become an end in itself, and this is one reason to speak of neoliberalism and not of liberalism.

Paul Treanor (2009) has an excellent and provocative website covering liberalism, market and ethics. He suggests that a general characteristic of neoliberalism is

> The desire to intensify and expand the market, by increasing the number, frequency, repeatability and formalisation of transactions. The ultimate (unreachable) goal of neoliberalism is a universe where every action of every being is a market transaction, conducted in competition with every other being and influencing every other transaction, with transactions occurring in an infinitely short time, and repeated at an infinitely fast rate.

Treanor describes, in great detail, the new aspects of neoliberalism that have emerged. This is an abridged list.

How many of them do you recognise?

A new expansion in time and space of the market.

Neoliberals find new areas of marketisation. Adam Smith would not have believed that a free market was less of a free market because the shops are closed in the middle of the night. Expansion of trading hours is a typical neoliberal policy. For neoliberals a twenty-three-hour economy is already unjustifiable; nothing less than a twenty-four-hour economy will satisfy them. They constantly expand the market at its margins.

The emphasis on property, in classic and market liberalism, has been replaced by an emphasis on contract. In the time of Adam Smith, property in itself conferred status; he would find it strange that entrepreneurs sometimes own no fixed assets, and lease the means of production. Contracts are maximalised – e.g. the privatisation of the British railway network, formerly run by one state-owned company, led to 30,000 new contracts, and contract periods are reduced so that a service contract, for instance, for office cleaning, might be reduced from a one-year to a three-month contract, then to a one-month contract. Contracts of employment are shorter and shorter, in effect forcing the employee to reapply for the job more frequently. This flexibility means a qualitatively different working life. Many more job applications are required, spread throughout the working life.

Market forces are also reinforced by intensifying assessment, a development especially visible on the labour market. Even within a contract period, an employee will be subject to continuous assessment. The use of specialised software in some call centres has provided some extreme examples: the time employees spend at the toilet is measured in seconds: this information is used to pressure the employee to spend less time away from the terminal. Firms with contracts are also increasingly subject to continuous assessment procedures, made possible by information technology. For instance, courier services use tracking software and GPS technology, to allow customers to locate their packages in transit.

New transaction-intensive markets are created on the model of the stock exchanges, electricity exchanges and telephone exchanges. Typically for neoliberalism, there is no relationship between the growth in the number of transactions and the underlying production. New forms of auction are another method of creating transaction-intensive markets. Radio frequency auctions are an example. They replaced previous methods of allocation, especially licensing – a traditional method of allocating access to scarce goods with no clear private owner. Artificial transactions are created to increase the number and intensity of transactions. Large-scale derivative trading is a typically neoliberal phenomenon, although financial derivatives have existed for centuries. It is possible to trade options on shares, but it is also possible to create options on these options. This accumulation of transaction on transaction is characteristic of neoliberalism. New derivatives are created to be traded on the new exchanges, such as 'electricity futures'. There is no limit to this expansion, except computer power, which grows rapidly anyway.

The speed of trading is increased. Online market data is expensive, yet it is now available free with a fifteen-minute delay. The markets move so fast that the data is worthless after fifteen minutes: the companies can then give it away, as a form of advertising. Day-traders buy and sell shares in minutes. Automated trading programmes, where the computer is linked direct to the stock exchange system, do it in seconds, or less. It is this increased speed which has led to the huge nominal trading volumes on the international currency markets, many times the Gross World Product on a yearly basis.

Certain functions arise which only exist inside a neoliberal free market e.g. 'derivative professions'. A good example is the profession of a psychological-test coach. The intensity of assessment has increased, and firms now regularly use psychological tests to select candidates, even for intermediate-level jobs. So ambitious candidates pay for training in how to pass these psychological tests. Competition in the neoliberal labour market itself creates the market for this service.

There is also creation of sub-markets, typically within an enterprise. Sub-contracting is itself an old market practice, but was usually outside the firm. It is now standard practice for large companies to create competition among their constituent units. This practice is also capable of quasi-infinite extension, and its promotion is characteristic of neoliberalism. A few companies even require each individual employee to register as a business, and to compete with each other at the place of work. A large company can form millions of holdings, alliances and joint ventures, using such one-person firms as building blocks.

Supplier maximalisation extends the range of enterprises that compete for each contract. The ideal would be that every enterprise competes for every contract offered, maximising competition and market forces. In the case of the labour market, the neoliberal ideal is the absolutely flexible and employable employee, who can (and does) apply for every vacancy. In reality, an individual cannot perform every kind of work – but there is a real development towards non-specialised enterprises, especially in the producer services sector. In neoliberalism, instead of the traditional 'steel tycoon' or 'newspaper baron' there are enterprises which 'globally link people and knowledge, and cultures' or 'advise and implement solutions to management issues'. (In fact these are quotes from the accountants Price Waterhouse, but you cannot guess this from the descriptions.)

Neoliberalism is not simply an economic structure, it is a philosophy. This is most visible in attitudes to society, the individual and employment. Neoliberals tend to see the world in term of market metaphors. Referring to nations as 'companies' is typically neoliberal, rather than liberal. In such a view Deutschland GmbH competes with Great Britain Ltd, BV Nederland and USA Inc.

However, when this is a view of nation states, it is as much a form of neo-nationalism as neoliberalism. It also looks back to the pre-liberal economic theory – mercantilism – that saw the countries of Europe as competing units. The mercantilists treated those kingdoms as large-scale versions of a private household, rather than as firms. Nevertheless, their view of world trade as a competition between nation-sized units would be acceptable to modern neoliberals.

The market metaphor is not only applied among nations, but among cities and regions as well. In neoliberal regional policy, cities are selling themselves in a national and global marketplace of cities. They are considered equivalent to an entrepreneur selling a product, but the product is the city (or region) as a location for entrepreneurs. The successful 'sale' of the product is the decision of an entrepreneur to locate there, not simply the sale of land or factories. This view of cities as sub-firms within the fictive 'national firm' parallels the creation of sub-markets within real firms. The difference is that those sub-markets really exist; neoliberal city governments, on the other hand, act primarily on a belief in a metaphor.

Again, there is no hard evidence that the global marketplace of cities exists; again, neoliberalism is a philosophy, an attitude – rather than an economic reality. It has influenced European politics – the fear of this neoliberalism dominated the French campaign against the European Constitution.

There is certainly a neoliberal lobby within the EU, represented by the Lisbon Council, although it sees the world in terms of competing trade blocks rather than competing cities or regions. However, it is not clear how a continent could be run as a business firm. A good example of the underlying attitudes is the basic policy document of the city of Düsseldorf – the Leitbild, equivalent to a mission statement in English. It was adopted in 1997 and stresses continuously how the city is committed to the principle of competition. It goes on to emphasise that the success of a city is decided by both internal and external competition; only the good can survive.

The neoliberal urban vision was adopted, without debate, by many city governments in the 1990s. At some point, a belief in competition by population structure was incorporated – the idea that a successful city is inhabited only by successful people. This belief, nonsensical or not, has had an effect in a negative sense: some cities now pursue active policies aimed at relocating low-income households outside the city. In the Netherlands, a new law allows large cities to legally ban poor people from certain areas, or from the entire city.

As you would expect from a complete philosophy, neoliberalism has answers to stereotypical philosophical questions such as 'Why are we here?' and 'What should I do?' We are here for the market, and you should compete. Neoliberals tend to believe that humans exist for the market, and not the other way around: certainly in the sense that it is good to participate in the market, and that those who do not participate have failed in some way.

In personal ethics, the general neoliberal vision is that every human being is an entrepreneur managing their own life, and should act as such. Moral philosophers call this is a 'virtue ethic', where human beings compare their actions to the way an ideal type would act – in this case, the ideal entrepreneur. Individuals who choose their friends, hobbies, sports and partners to maximise their status with future employers are ethically speaking neoliberal. This attitude, not unusual any more among ambitious students, is unknown in any pre-existing moral philosophy, and is absent from early liberalism.

Such social actions are not necessarily monetarised, but they represent an extension of the market principle into non-economic areas of life.

The idea of employability is characteristically neoliberal. It means that neoliberals see it as a moral duty of human beings to arrange their lives to maximise their advantage on the labour market.

Paying for plastic surgery to improve employability is a typical neoliberal phenomenon. In practice many 'workfare neoliberals' also believe that there is a separate category of people who cannot participate fully in the market. Workfare ideologies condemn this underclass to a service function for those who are fully market-compatible.

The general ethical precept of neoliberalism can, therefore, be summarised approximately as:

- act in conformity with market forces
- within this limit, act also to maximise the opportunity for others to conform to the market forces generated by your action
- hold no other goals.

Hopefully, as you have been reading this précis of Treanor's ideas, you have recognised many of the features of neoliberalism that have been described. Perhaps you had not realised how they were all linked before.

I am sure many of you who work will be well aware of the

changes, as they will have had a major impact on your conditions of employment. When leaving university in my day – i.e. the sixties – one thought about which job, singular, one would like to go into, but today a young person in the same position will be lucky to be in that confident position.

If you tie this with neoconservatism, (the main ideas of which were developed in the last chapter), the other ideology that influenced the Bush administration, you will be able more readily to understand the policies pursued and to consider how they might have contributed to the economic recession of 2008 onwards.

We now need to consider the arguments against neoliberalism before considering alternatives. As you might imagine, there is a plethora of criticisms of the ideology of neoliberalism and the numbers are multiplying with the election of Obama.

There are going to be both Marxist and non-Marxist critiques. The dividing line between the two will be whether the desired outcome is a modified capitalist society or a non-capitalist society. As we have dealt quite fully with the Marxist view in the early part of the book, it is more appropriate now to consider non-Marxist views.

My main choice is the writings of Robert Kuttner who writes for the *American Prospect*, readily accessible on the Internet. He has written two excellent books (2007, 2009) that cover his key views. Essentially Kuttner writes from a middle-ground position on the Political Compass chart that we described earlier.

He argues that the claim that the free market with minimal regulation produces the best economic outcome was the centre-piece of the conservative political resurgence that has just ended with the defeat of Bush. He believes that there are three funda-mental things wrong with the utopian claims about markets.

First, they misunderstand the dynamics of human motivation. The school of experimental economics, pioneered by psychologists Daniel Kahneman and Amos Tversky (2000), has demonstrated that people do not behave the way the model specifies. People will typically charge more to sell you something they own, even though they could buy the identical article for less; economic theory would predict a single 'market-clearing' price. People help strangers, return wallets, leave generous tips in restaurants they will never visit again, give donations to public radio in the US, when theory would predict they would rationally 'free-ride', and engage in other acts that suggest they value general norms of fairness. To conceive of altruism as a special form of selfishness misses the point utterly.

Second, they ignore the fact that civil society needs realms of political rights where some things are not for sale. Although the market model imagines a rational individual, maximising utility in an institutional vacuum, real people also have civic and social selves. The act of voting can be shown to be irrational by the lights of economic theory, because the 'benefit' derived from the likelihood of one's vote affecting the outcome is not worth the 'cost'. But people vote as an act of faith in the civic process, as well as to influence outcomes. In a market, everything is potentially for sale. In a political community, some things are beyond price. One's person, one's vote, one's basic democratic rights do not belong on the auction block. We no longer allow human beings to be bought and sold via slavery (though influential Chicago economists have argued that it would be efficient to treat adoptions as auction markets). While the market keeps trying to invade the polity, we do not permit the literal sale of public office.

Third, even in the economic realm, markets price many things wrong, which means that pure markets do not yield optimal economic outcomes, with the need therefore for some regulation. History demonstrates that in much of economic life, pure reliance on markets produces sub-optimal outcomes. Market forces, left to their own devices, lead to avoidable financial panics and depressions, which in turn lead to political chaos. Historically, government has had to intervene, not only to redress the gross inequality of market-determined income and wealth, but to rescue the market from itself when it periodically goes haywire, as for example at the end of 2008.

So the fact remains, argues Kuttner, that the mixed economy – a strong private sector tempered and leavened by a democratic polity – is the essential instrument of both a decent society and an efficient economy.

Kuttner believes that the second coming of laissez-faire had multiple causes.

In part, it reflects the faltering of economic growth in the 1970s.

It also reflects a relative weakening of the political forces that support a mixed economy, namely:

- the declining influence of the labour movement
- the erosion of working-class voting turnout
- the suburbanisation of the Democratic party in America
- the restoration of the political sway of organised business
- the reversion of formal economics to pre-Keynesian verities.

With regard to the latter, Kuttner gives the examples of public choice theory and the law and economics movement, where Chicago-style economists have colonised other academic disciplines.

Public choice theory (Buchanan, 1962), a very influential current in political science, essentially applies the market model to politics. Supposedly, self-seeking characterises both economic man and political man. Public choice claims that office holders have as their paramount goal re-election, and that groups of voters are essentially 'rent seekers' looking for a free ride at public expense, rather than legitimate members of a political collectivity expressing a democratic voice. Organised interest groups crowd out ordinary citizens, so the 'people' never get what they want.

Thus, since the democratic process is largely a sham, as well as a drag on economic efficiency, it is best to entrust as little to the public realm as possible. Lately, Kuttner points out, nearly half the articles in major political science journals have reflected a broad public choice sensibility.

The law and economics movement (Cooter, 2007), likewise, has made deep inroads into the law schools and courts, subsidised by tens of millions of dollars from right-wing foundations.

The basic idea of law and economics is that the law, as a system of rules and rights, tends to undermine the efficiency of markets. It is the duty of judges, therefore, to make the law the servant of market efficiency, rather than a realm of civic rights. Borrowing from public choice theory, law and economics scholars contend that since democratic deliberation and hence legislative intent are largely illusory, it is legitimate for courts to ignore legislative mandates, to protect the rights of minorities and instead to protect the efficiency of markets. Regulation is generally held to be a deadweight cost, since it cannot improve upon the outcomes that free individuals would rationally negotiate.

These intellectual currents are strategically connected to the political arena. Take the journal titled *Regulation*, published for many years by the American Enterprise Institute, and currently published by the Cato Institute. Though it offers lively policy debates over particulars, virtually every article in *Regulation* is anti-regulation. Whether the subject is worker safety, telecommunications, the environment, electric power, health care or whatever, the invariable subtext is that government causes problems and markets are self-purifying. It is hardly surprising that the organised Right publishes such a journal. What is more depressing, and revealing, is that there is no comparable journal with a predisposition in favour of a mixed economy.

This intellectual apparatus has become the scaffolding for the proposition that governments should leave markets alone. This, of course, is particularly ironic given that the lack of regulation is generally thought to be one of the main reasons for the economic collapse starting in late 2008.

Kuttner's views have been supported more recently by Shiller (2006, 2009). As early as 2005, in his book *Irrational Exuberance*, Shiller warned of the dangers of two uncontrolled speculative 'bubbles' not grounded in sensible economic fundamentals.

The first was the enormous stock market boom that started around 1982 and picked up incredible speed after 1995, and the second the real-estate boom.

Shiller warned,

> Significant further rises in these markets could lead, eventually, to even more significant declines. The bad outcome could be that eventual declines would result in a substantial increase in the rate

of personal bankruptcies, which could lead to a secondary string of bankruptcies of financial institutions as well. Another long-run consequence could be a decline in consumer and business confidence, and another, possibly worldwide, recession.

Schiller, 2005

His most recent book *Animal Spirits*, written jointly with Akerlof, argues that the global financial crisis has made it painfully clear that powerful psychological forces are imperilling the wealth of nations today.

He challenges the economic wisdom of neoliberalism that got us into the mess and, together with Akerlof, reasserts the necessity of an active government role in economic policy-making by recovering the idea of animal spirits. This was a term John Maynard Keynes used to describe the gloom and despondence that led to the Great Depression and the changing psychology that accompanied recovery. Like Keynes, they know that managing these animal spirits requires the steady hand of government; simply allowing markets to work won't do it. In rebuilding the case for a more robust, behaviourally informed Keynesianism, they detail the most pervasive effects of animal spirits in contemporary economic life, such as confidence, fear, bad faith, corruption and a concern for fairness. They argue that economic theory must incorporate the powerful forces of human psychology that are afoot in the world economy today.

Alongside Shiller, Dean Baker's new book, *Plunder and Blunder: The Rise and Fall of the Bubble Economy* (2009), has also explored the stock and housing bubbles at the heart of the current economic crisis.

The economic downturn, on track to be the worst since the Depression, is due, as he argues, to the collapse of the housing and stock-market bubbles that wiped out $6 trillion and counting of housing wealth and $8 trillion of stock-market wealth.

The most infuriating aspect of this disaster is that it was completely preventable. The basics of the housing bubble were straightforward. House prices began soaring in the mid-1990s, hugely outpacing the overall rate of inflation. This followed a 100-year-long trend in which nationwide house prices had just kept even with the rate of inflation.

125

There was no fundamentals-based explanation for the explosion of house prices on either the demand or supply side. Furthermore, there was no remotely comparable increase in rental prices. If the fundamentals of the housing market were to have explained the run-up in house prices, then there should have been a comparable rise in rents. Instead, rents only slightly outpaced inflation in the 1990s, and inflation-adjusted rents actually fell slightly in the 2000s.

The huge overvaluation in house prices guaranteed trouble when prices adjusted. Homeowners consumed based on the wealth in their home. When housing prices plunged, so too did consumption. The effect of this plunge in demand has been amplified by the collapse of the huge pyramid of creative financing that grew up in the shadow of the bubble and in turn fed its growth. Ever-greater levels of leverage on ever-riskier loans were the path to big profits in the boom years. This was also the path to bankruptcy following the bubble's collapse.

Not only did Federal Reserve Board Chairman Alan Greenspan and the other leading lights of the economic profession fail to see the $8 trillion housing bubble, they somehow failed to recognise the explosion of risky mortgages and the highly leveraged chain of finances built on top of these mortgages.

Certain experts are given the megaphone, and for a reason. Many of the experts providing the advice were the same ones making the money. As Dean Baker lays bare, the stockbrokers exhorting us to invest were making a killing from the fees. The housing experts who received the most press worked for realtors, homebuilders and financiers. Perhaps most important, the newspapers needed the real estate classifieds to make their business model work. To keep their jobs, all of these people needed us to keep believing in a better, richer tomorrow. And so they kept the music playing and taking our money long after the party should have ended. As Citigroup's chief executive, Charles O Prince knew all too well, 'As long as the music is playing, you've got to get up and dance.'

Back to Kuttner, who argues that the moral claim of the free market is based on a number of fallacies.

A – Markets Maximise Liberty

In a market economy, individuals are free to choose, as Milton Friedman famously wrote. They are free to decide what to buy, where to shop, what businesses or professions to pursue, where to live, subject 'only' to the constraints of their individual income and wealth. The extremes of wealth and poverty seemingly mock the claim that markets epitomise human freedom – a poor man has only the paltry freedoms of a meagre income. What choice do you have in terms of your children's education if you live in a poor area and cannot afford to transport your child outside of the local area to a more successful school?

B – The Purchasing Power Awarded by Markets is Economically Fair

If Bill Gates has several billion dollars to spend, that is only because he has added several billions of dollars of value to the economy, as validated by the free choices of millions of consumers. An unskilled high-school dropout, in contrast, has little freedom to consume, because his labour offers little of value to an employer. There may be extenuating prior circumstances of birth or fortune, but each of us is ultimately responsible for our own economic destiny.

C – Markets are Roughly Efficient

The prices set by supply and demand reflect how the economy values goods and services. So the resulting allocation of investment is efficient, in the sense that an alternative allocation mandated by extra-market forces would reduce total output. This is why professional economists who have liberal social values as citizens generally argue that if we do not like the social consequences of market income distribution, we should redistribute after the fact rather than tamper with the market's pricing mechanism.

Next, Kuttner explains how the prevalence of 'externalities' can reduce the efficiency of a market.

These are costs or benefits not captured by the price set by the immediate transaction. The best-known negative externality is pollution. The polluter 'externalises' the true costs of his waste products onto society by dumping them, at no personal cost, into a nearby river or into the air. If the full social cost were internalised, the price would be higher.

Positive externalities include research and education. Individuals and business firms underinvest in education and research because the benefits are diffuse. The firm that trains a worker may not capture the full return on that investment, since the worker may then take a job elsewhere. The fruits of technical invention, likewise, are partly appropriated by competitors. As economists put it, the private return does not equal the social return, so we cannot rely on profit-maximising individuals for the optimal level of investment. By the same token, if we made the education of children dependent on the private resources of parents, society as a whole would underinvest in the schooling of the next generation. There is a social return on having a well-educated workforce and citizenry.

A tour of the actual economy reveals that some sectors lend themselves to markets that look roughly like the market of the textbook model, while others do not.

Either way, Kuttner argues that markets can actually be enhanced by extra-market interventions.

Let us take your local supermarket as a case study, as they are argued to be a reasonable approximation to a perfect market.

On the one hand the pricing and supply of retail food is mostly unregulated, and fiercely competitive. Somehow, the average consumer's lack of infinite time to go shopping, and less-than-perfect information about the relative prices of a thousand products in several local stores, exactly allows the supermarket to earn a normal profit.

Supermarkets connect the retail market to the agricultural one. The supermarket also provides part of the local market for labour and capital. Though cashiers and meat cutters are not the most glamorous of jobs, the supermarket manages to pay just enough to attract people who are just competent enough to perform the jobs acceptably. If a supermarket's profits are below par over time, the price of its shares will fall. That also operates as a powerful signal as to where investors should put their capital, and on how executives must supervise their managers and managers their employees.

Though there may be occasional missteps, and though some supermarkets go bankrupt, the interplay of supply and demand in all of these sub-markets contributes to a dynamic equilibrium. It results in prices that are 'right' most of the time.

The supermarket stocks, displays and prices thousands of different highly perishable products, in response to shifting consumer tastes, with almost no price regulation.

However, supermarkets are not perfectly efficient.

Firstly, although retail grocers operate on thin profit margins, the wholesale part of the food distribution chain is famous for enormous mark-ups. A farmer is likely to get only ten cents out of a box of cornflakes that retails for $3.99.

Secondly, even supermarkets themselves are far from perfectly free markets.

Their hygiene is regulated by government inspectors, as is most of the food they sell. Government regulations mandate the format and content of nutritional labelling. They require clear, consistent unit pricing, to rule out a variety of temptations of deceptive marketing. Moreover, many occupations in the food industry, such as meat cutter and cashier, are substantially unionised, so the labour market is not a pure free market either. Much of the food produced in the United States is grown by farmers who benefit from a variety of interferences with a laissez-faire market, contrived by government to prevent ruinous fluctuations in prices. The government also subsidises education and technical innovation in agriculture.

Therefore, even in this nearly perfect market, a modicum of regulation is entirely compatible with the basic discipline of supply and demand. It can be argued that this enhances efficiency by making for better-informed consumers and less opportunistic sellers. Because of the imperfect information of consumers, it is improbable that repealing these regulations would enhance efficiency.

Now, however, consider a very different sector: health care.

Medical care in the US is anything but a textbook 'free market', yet market forces and profit motives in the health industry are rife.

On the supply side, the health industry violates several conditions of a free market. Unlike the supermarket business, there is not 'free entry'. You cannot simply open a hospital, or easily set up as a doctor. This gives health providers a degree of market power that compromises the competitive model and raises prices.

On the demand side, consumers lack the special knowledge to shop for a doctor the way they buy a car, and lack perfectly free choice of health insurer. And since society has decided that nobody shall perish for lack of medical care, demand is not constrained by private purchasing power, which is inflationary.

Health care also offers substantial 'positive externalities'. The value to society of mass vaccinations far exceeds the profits that can be captured by the doctor or drug company. If vaccinations and other public health measures were left to private supply and demand, society would seriously underinvest. Society invests in other public health measures that markets under-provide.

The health care system also depends heavily on extra-market norms: the fact that physicians and nurses are guided by ethical constraints and professional values that limit the opportunism that their specialised knowledge and power might otherwise invite.

The fact that health care is a far cry from a perfect market sets up a chain of perverse incentives. A generation ago, fee-for-service medicine combined with insurance reimbursement to stimulate excessive treatment and drive up costs. Today many managed care companies reverse the process and create incentives to deny necessary care to those in need. In either case, this is no free market. Indeed, as long as society stipulates that nobody shall die for lack of private purchasing power, it will never be a free market. That is why it requires regulation as well as subsidy.

Here is the nub of the issue. Are most markets like supermarkets – or like health markets?

The conundrum of the market for health care is a good example of an oft-neglected insight known as the General Theory of the Second Best. Lipsey and Lancaster showed in a 1956 paper that if one optimality condition in an economic model is not satisfied, it is possible that the next-best solution involved changing other variables away from the ones that are usually assumed to be optimal.

This means that in an economy with some unavoidable market failure in one sector, there can actually be a decrease in efficiency due to a move toward greater market perfection in another sector. In theory, at least, it may be better to let two market imperfections cancel each other out, rather than making an effort to fix either one.

Thus, it may be optimal for the government to intervene in a way that is contrary to laissez-faire policy. This suggests that economists need to study the details of the situation before jumping to the theory-based conclusion that an improvement in market perfection in one area implies a global improvement in efficiency.

A Second Best market (such as health care) is not fully accountable to the market discipline of supply and demand, so typically it has acquired second-best forms of accountability, e.g. professional norms, government supervision, regulation and subsidy, to which market forces have adapted. If the health care system is already a far cry from a free market on both the demand side and the supply side, removing one regulation and thereby making the health system more superficially market-like may well simply increase opportunism and inefficiency. In many economic realms, the second-best outcome of some price distortion, offset by regulation and extra-market norms, may be the best outcome practically available.

Another good Second Best illustration is the banking industry.

Until the early 1970s, banking in the United States was very highly regulated. Regulation limited both the price and the quantity of banking services. Bank charters were limited. So were interest rates. Banks were subject to a variety of other regulatory constraints. Of course, banks still competed fiercely for market share and profitability, based on how well they served customers and how astutely they analysed credit risks.

Partially deregulating the banking and savings and loan industries in the 1980s violated the General Theory of the Second Best. It pursued greater efficiency, but led to speculative excess. Whatever gains there were to the efficiency of allocation were swamped by the ensuing costs of the bailout.

We have seen since late 2008 the phenomenal sums the US

and UK governments have used to bail out their banks. The saga of banking regulation raises the question of contending conceptions of efficiency.

The efficiency prized by market enthusiasts is 'allocative'. That means the free play of supply and demand via price signals will steer resources to the uses that provide the greatest satisfaction and the highest return. Regulation interferes with this discipline, and presumably worsens outcomes. But in markets like health care and banking, the market is far from free to begin with.

'Allocative' efficiency leaves out the issues of 'Keynesian efficiency' – i.e. whether the economy as a whole has lower rates of growth and higher unemployment than it might achieve. Nor does allocative efficiency deal with the question of 'Schumpeterian (1994) efficiency' or technical progress, which is the source of improved economic performance over time.

Schumpeter argues that innovation in oligopolistic markets is more robust than in price competitive markets which can be ruinous. In other words, because firms fear that competitors will gain from their advances in technology, markets will underinvent in innovation.

Standard market theory lacks a common metric to assess these three contending conceptions of efficiency. Countermanding the allocative mechanism of the price system may depress efficiency in Adam Smith's sense. But if the result is to increase Keynesian efficiency of high growth and full employment, or the Schumpeterian efficiency of technical advance, there may well be a net economic gain.

Increasing allocative efficiency when unemployment is high does not help. It may even hurt, to the extent that intensified competition in a depressed economy may throw more people out of work, reduce overall purchasing power and deepen the shortfall of aggregate demand.

By the same token, if private market forces underinvest in technical innovation, then public investment and regulation can improve on market outcomes. Patents, trademarks and copyrights are among the oldest regulatory interventions acknowledging market failure, and creating artificial property rights in innovation. As technology evolves, so necessarily does the regime of intellectual property regulation.

Only a minority of the diverse sectors of the economy operate efficiently with no regulatory interference. Some sectors, such as banking and stock markets, entail both fiduciary responsibilities and systemic risks.

In the absence of financial regulation, conflicts of interest and the tendency of money markets to speculative excess could bring down the entire economy, as financial panics periodically did in the era before regulation and, more recently, after the deregulation of the Bush administration.

In summary, capitalism requires ground rules. It is wrong to insist that the best remedy is no regulation at all. The choice is between good regulation and bad regulation.

The basic competitive discipline of a capitalist economy can coexist nicely with diverse extra-market forces; they can even render the market more efficient.

Richard Vietor of the Harvard Business School observes in his 1994 book, *Contrived Competition*, that imperfect, partly regulated markets are still highly responsive to competitive discipline. The market turns out to be rather more resilient and adaptive than its champions admit. In markets as varied as banking, public utilities, and health care, entrepreneurs do not sicken and expire when faced with regulated competition; they simply revise their competitive strategy and go right on competing. Norms that commit society to resist short-term opportunism can make both the market and the society a healthier place. Pure markets, in contrast, commend and invite opportunism, and depress trust.

A review of the virtues and limits of markets necessarily takes us back to politics. Even a fervently capitalist society, it turns out, requires prior rules. As new products and business strategies appear and markets evolve, so necessarily does the regime of rules.

Contrary to the theory of perfect markets, much of economic life is not the mechanical satisfaction of preferences or the pursuit of a single best equilibrium.

On the contrary, many paths are possible – many blends of different values, many mixes of market and social, many possible distributions of income and wealth – all compatible with tolerably efficient getting and spending. The grail of a perfect market, purged of illegitimate and inefficient distortions, is a fantasy.

The real world displays a very broad spectrum of actual markets with diverse structural characteristics, and different degrees of separation from the textbook ideal. Some need little regulation, some a great deal, either to make the market mechanism work efficiently or to solve problems that the market cannot fix. In short, rules require rule setters. In a democracy, that enterprise entails democratic politics.

The issue of how precisely to govern markets arises in libertarian, democratic nations like the United States, and deferential, authoritarian ones like Singapore. It arises whether the welfare state is large or small, and whether the polity is expansive or restrained in its aspirations. Rule setting and the correction of market excess are necessarily public issues in social-democratic Sweden, in Christian democratic Germany, in feudal-capitalist Japan, and in Labour Britain.

The political process, of course, can produce good sets of rules for the market, or bad ones. Thus, the quality of political life is itself a public good – perhaps the most fundamental public good. A public good is something that markets are not capable of valuing correctly. Trust, civility, long-term commitment and the art of consensual deliberation are the antitheses of pure markets, and the essence of effective politics.

As the economic historian Douglass North, the 1993 Nobel Laureate in economics, has observed, competent public administration and governance are a source of competitive advantage for nation states. Third-world nations and post-communist regimes are notably disadvantaged, not just by the absence of functioning markets, but also by the weakness of legitimate states. A vacuum of legitimate state authority does not yield efficient laissez-faire; it yields mafias and militias, with whose arbitrary power would-be entrepreneurs must reckon. The marketisers advising post-Soviet Russia imagined that their challenge was to dismantle a state in order to create a market. In fact, the more difficult challenge was to constitute a state to create a market.

Norms that encourage informed civic engagement increase the likelihood of competent, responsive politics and public administration, which in turn yield a more efficient mixed economy. North writes:

The evolution of government from its medieval, Mafia-like character to that embodying modern legal institutions and instruments is a major part of the history of freedom. It is a part that tends to be obscured or ignored because of the myopic vision of many economists, who persist in modelling government as nothing more than a gigantic form of theft and income redistribution.

North, 2009

The more that complex mixed markets require a blend of evolving rules, the more competent and responsive a public administration the enterprise requires. Strong civic institutions help constitute the state, and also serve as counterweights against excesses of both state and market.

Lately, the real menace to a sustainable society has been the market's invasion of the polity, not vice versa. Big money has crowded out authentic participation. Commercial values have encroached on civic values. Unless we are to leave society to the tender mercies of laissez-faire, we need a mixed economy.

Capitalism entails public policies, which in turn are creatures of democratic politics. The grail of a market economy untainted by politics is the most dangerous illusion of our age.

A major critic of globalisation is Naomi Klein (2008), who in her book *The Shock Doctrine* reveals the huge profits made by companies from catastrophes, both natural and man-made. She describes it as 'the sprawling disaster capitalism complex'.

She is outraged by the rapacity of corporations that see market opportunities rather than human suffering in wars and disasters, with the privileged becoming wealthier and the disadvantaged increasingly marginalised. Disasters discriminate because the rich are equipped with the shock absorbers that the poor cannot afford.

In the developed world, globalisation has unravelled any notions of a social compact between the rich and the poor. Corporations move their wealth abroad to avoid tax and at the same time establish labour-intensive production in countries where unionisation is non-existent and wages low.

Alongside this is the growth of 'security apartheid' with gated communities growing rapidly in cities around the world. This is Klein's description of Baghdad's Green Zone in 2004:

135

It feels oddly like a giant fortified Carnival Cruise ship parked in a sea of violence and despair. If you can get on board you can have poolside drinks, bad Hollywood movies and Nautilus machines. If you are not among the chosen you can get yourself shot just by standing too close to the wall.

Klein, 2008

In New Orleans in the wake of Hurricane Katrina, Klein found 'poor refugees living in desperate, out of the way trailer camps where private security companies treated survivors like criminals'. In stark contrast were

> ...the gated communities built in the wealthier parts of the city. Within weeks of the storm, residents there had water and powerful emergency generators. Their sick were treated in private hospitals, and their children went to new charter schools. As usual, they had no need of public transport.

She uses the Iraq war to illustrate her theory clearly that the unrestrained Chicago School ideology argued that pure capitalism is best built from scratch.

> The plan was not to build a model democracy in Iraq but a system violently incompatible with democracy, a model market free society with minimum taxes and regulation, a quiescent labour force and all productive assets in private hands.

Klein quotes Polanyi (1991), who argues that physical coercion is required to establish a market society. Capitalism can only be created if centrally organised violence is employed without moral scruples, because ordinary people will not willingly adapt to social dislocation and the obsolescence of their skills.

It is not surprising to find, therefore, that the company Halliburton made huge profits from the Iraq war. The former CEO of the company and still a shareholder is Dick Cheney, until recently the Vice-President of the USA.

Finally in terms of criticisms of globalism come the warnings by David Rothkopf (2009) of the 'global power elite'.

He describes an elite of 6,000 out of 6 billion whose power

transcends national boundaries and who operate covertly. Their purpose is not to further national interest but to shape global forces purely for the purposes of wealth creation from which they will be the main benefactors. This new elite is totally unaccountable so that they are bypassing democracy and destroying political representation.

The success of the global elite could be responsible for the relative shift of wealth from the middle classes to the wealthy. The phenomenon is called median wage stagnation (Summers, 2007).

For example, between 2000 and 2006, the US economy expanded by 18%, whereas real income for the median working household dropped by 1.1% in real terms as against an increase of 32% for the top 10% and 203% for the top 1%.

Wage earners no longer getting the benefits of improved productivity is something that has not been experienced before in modern America. There are strong parallels between the distribution of income just before the 1929 crash and the crash in 2008.

What are the alternatives?

I will give you three for now to consider vis-à-vis the lenses in your spectacles. It is, however, an issue that we will return to later on.

The first is the idea of creative capitalism being advocated by Bill Gates (Kingsley 2010). The heart of the argument is that profit and social responsibility are not necessarily mutually exclusive. If I can take you back to our initial look at capitalism and Marxism you may remember the essentially capitalist idea of profit as the spur for growth and the Marxist idea of profit as exploitation.

A useful distinction can be drawn between 'acceptable' and 'unacceptable' capitalism. The latter is where only economic costs are considered. A good example of this would be a decision to drill for oil in the centre of the Lake District, with no consideration given to the damage to the environment and the tourist industry. If such social costs are excluded, the profit would be much higher but is this 'acceptable'?

Creative capitalism would take the broadest view possible of social costs and responsibility so that self-interest serves the larger interest. Companies, with government and non-governmental help, can make a profit, enhance their reputations and help to improve the lives of those who have not traditionally been aided by capitalist markets.

Bill Gates admits that he has been influenced by C K Pralahad's (2004) book *The Fortune at the Bottom of the Pyramid*, which shows that there are markets all over the world that have been missed with the poorest two-thirds of the world's population having five trillion dollars in purchasing power. So you might want to refine the concept of capitalism in the lenses of your spectacles.

Secondly, there is the idea of a 'global commonwealth' as suggested by Jeffrey Sachs (2008) in his book *Commonwealth Economics for a Crowded Planet*. Sachs argues that in this coming century many of our basic assumptions about economic life are going to be overturned as we witness the end of Western dominance of global economics and politics, and the continuing growth of China and India on the world stage.

Four earth-changing trends are stressed.

- The world on average is getting richer in terms of income per capita while the gap in income per capita between the West and Asia is narrowing, with the latter soon becoming the centre of gravity of the world economy.

- The world's population continues to rise, as does average output, so the scale of world economic production is increasing.

- This is creating multiple man-made economic crises, including climate change.

- Many of the poorest are stuck at the bottom, with nearly ten million children dying each year.

The defining challenge therefore of the twenty-first century is to face the reality that humanity shares a common fate on a crowded planet. Whether we continue to fight each other or come together in a 'commonwealth' is in our hands.

This clearly shows the acceptance of the notion of individual responsibility that is considered to exist for all mankind.

Finally, there is cosmopolitanism, which can be traced back to the founding father of the Cynic movement, Diogenes of Sinope (412 BC) who argued that he was a citizen of the world.

Cosmopolitans are moral universalists, believing that the same moral standards apply to all human beings. The boundaries between states, cultures and so on are morally irrelevant.

After World War Two and as a reaction to the Holocaust, the concept of crimes against humanity became a generally accepted category in international law.

Ulrich Beck (2006) argues that cosmopolitanism sees a meta-power game with global capital, states and civil society as the key players. Clearly the concept of the United Nations is passé here and will eventually be replaced by global institutions.

Again there is plenty to think about in terms of your perception of the way forward for global capitalism.

Beyond the traditional ethical disputes concerning the good life for human beings and what political situation would best suit our development, others take up an alternative conception of humanity and its relationship with the living world.

Broadly termed environmentalism, this political philosophy does not concern itself with the rights of people or of society, but of the rights of the planet and other species than humans. Environmentalism starts on a different premise: human beings are not at the centre of our politics, nature is. Environmentalism, therefore, considers our place on earth to be of secondary importance to that of the natural world.

In its moderate version, environmentalism claims that human beings are custodians of nature, to whom we must show respect and perhaps even certain ethical and political obligations (obligations akin to those some theological positions hold of people to their god) to the natural world. This implies that people are accorded an equal ethical status as that of other living species.

Generally, environmentalists distinguish themselves from conservationists who, from various positions along the spectrum of political theory, argue that landscapes or animals ought to be protected from extinction only if they are beneficial or pleasing to humanity in some form or other.

Environmentalists usually reject such human-centred utilitarianism in favour of a broad ethical intrinsicism – the theory that all species possess an innate value, independent of any other entity's relationship to them.

Criticisms levelled against this argument begin with asking what the moral relationship between a predator and its victim is or ought to be. The central issue for environmentalists is to explain the moral relationship between human and beast, and the resulting asymmetrical justifications and judgments levelled against humanity. According to the environmentalists' general ethical position, it is morally appropriate, so to speak, for the lion to hunt the gazelle or the ant to milk the caterpillar, but not for people to hunt the fox or milk the cow – and likewise, it can be asked whether it is morally appropriate for the wildcat or bear to attack people but not for people to defend themselves from these animals.

The political philosophy of environmentalism then turns on creating the proper structures for human social life in this context. The most useful arguments are that man stops pillaging the earth's resources by either prohibiting further exploitation or at least slowing the rate at which he is presently doing so. Sustainable resource management is at the centre of such environmentalism.

Summary

The belief in the market, in market forces, has separated from the factual production of goods and services. It has become an end in itself, and this is one reason to speak of neoliberalism and not of liberalism. A general characteristic of neoliberalism is the desire to intensify and expand the market, by increasing the number, frequency, repeatability and formalisation of transactions.

Neoliberals tend to believe that humans exist for the market, and not the other way around: certainly in the sense that it is good to participate in the market, and that those who do not participate have failed in some way. In personal ethics, the general neoliberal vision is that every human being is an entrepreneur managing their own life, and should act as such. Moral philosophers call this a virtue ethic, where human beings compare their actions to the way an ideal type would act – in this case the ideal entrepreneur.

There are three fundamental things wrong with the utopian claims about markets.

- They misunderstand the dynamics of human motivation.
- They ignore the fact that civil society needs realms of political rights where some things are not for sale.
- Even in the economic realm, markets price many things wrong, which means that pure markets do not yield optimal economic outcomes.

Disasters discriminate because the rich are equipped with the shock absorbers that the poor cannot afford. Pure capitalism is best built from scratch. The plan was not to build a model democracy in Iraq but a system violently incompatible with democracy, a model market-free society with minimum taxes and regulation, a quiescent labour force and all productive assets in private hands.

A global power elite have emerged that take decisions that have no root in any single country. Instinctive patriotism and the concept of national interest are being continually diluted.

Global capitalism can positively lead to creative capitalism, a global commonwealth and cosmopolitanism, and negatively to an increasing number of exploited and disadvantaged peoples, areas, countries and environmental disasters.

Environmental problems are man-made. They result from global capitalism's search for exploitable resources and profit.

- -
Reader's Notes:

9

Isolationalism, Protectionism and Populism

> What generates war is the economic philosophy of nationalism:
> embargoes, trade and foreign exchange controls, monetary
> devaluation, etc. The philosophy of protectionism is a philosophy
> of war.
>
> Ludwig von Mises

> Economic isolationalism can lead to a negative cycle of events
> such as those we saw in the 1930s, which made a bad situation
> much, much worse.
>
> Robert Zoellick

> Populism is an ideology which pits a virtuous and homogeneous
> people against a set of elites and dangerous 'others' who are together
> depicted as depriving (or attempting to deprive) the sovereign
> people of their rights, values, prosperity, identity and voice.
>
> Albertazzi, 2008

This chapter has four sections:

- an introduction which will cover definition and topicality
- a historical look at isolationism and economic recession in the UK and USA
- the arguments for and against protectionism
- the rise of populism and its implications.

The purpose of this chapter is to explain the concepts of isolationism, protectionism and populism and their current significance to political debate.

Using the Internet and Answers.com we obtain a definition of isolationism as 'a national policy of abstaining from political or economic relations with other countries' and protectionism as 'the advocacy, system or theory of protecting domestic producers by impeding or limiting, as by tariffs or quotas, the importation of foreign goods and services'.

Populism is defined by Krastev (2009, p.15) as 'a world view that considers society ultimately separated into two antagonistic groups, the "pure people" and the "corrupt elite" '.

If this book had been written at a time of economic growth and prosperity, it is unlikely that these ideas would have merited a separate chapter. They become of considerable importance, however, in a period of global economic crisis.

Looking at the world situation at the time of writing (2010), world trade has increased every year since 1982, but fell in 2009 by nine per cent, the steepest annual fall since World War Two.

Tom Barkley (2009) writes in a *Wall Street Journal* blog about information obtained from a World Bank Report that despite a pledge by the group of twenty leaders in November 2008 to avoid protectionist measures, seventeen of the countries have since erected new trade restrictions.

This is despite the fact that, with the global economy teetering on the abyss of severe recession, political pressures demanding protection from import competition to protect employment are surfacing with increasing intensity around the world.

Overall, the report found that forty-seven trade-restricting measures had been implemented. Developed countries have relied exclusively on subsidies, imposing twelve such measures, while nearly half of the thirty-five measures adopted by developing countries were tariffs.

Subsidies to prop up the auto sector amount to $48 billion, with high-income countries accounting for $43 billion of that, including $17.4 billion in the US alone.

The bank gave some specific examples:

- Russia has raised tariffs on used cars
- Argentina has imposed new licensing arrangements for imports

- China has banned Irish pork
- India has banned Chinese toys
- thirteen countries have granted subsidies to their automobile industries.

In addition MacShane (2009) has drawn attention to the fact that

> Racism and xenophobia are now part and parcel of European elections. Sarkozy and Merkel made their views against the accession of Turkey, a majority Muslim nation, the archstone of their campaign. The manifesto of the centre-right EEP Federation explicitly referred to Europe as a Judeo-Christian concept. No room for Muslims then…
>
> The Federation of Poles of Great Britain recently published a dossier of eighty headlines from the *Daily Mail* which in their judgment amounted to anti-Polish xenophobia. This helps create the swamp the BNP grows in. The more Poles, Slovaks and other foreigners are presented by the Right as a problem, the more the BNP and UKIP vote grows.

So it would appear that an economic recession increases protectionism and racism.

Chris Dillow (2009), an economics writer at the *Investors Chronicle* in the UK, argues and explains how in ethical terms, the effects of recession are pernicious.

Firstly, recessions are a minority activity; the pain is not evenly spread. It falls upon the small proportion of those who lose their jobs or businesses, or who find it harder to get into work. A study (1993) of the last serious downturn by Paul Geroski and Paul Gregg, of Bristol University, estimated that the worst hit ten per cent of companies accounted for eighty-five per cent of job losses between 1989 and 1991.

Secondly, for most of us the main effect of recession is insecurity. And when people are insecure and anxious, they care less for others. As Adam Smith said, 'Before we can feel much for others, we must in some measure be at ease ourselves' (1976b, p.84).

Recessions mean that we are not at ease, and, as Smith recognised, are more selfish as a result.

Smith was anticipating Abraham Maslow's (1943) theory of the hierarchy of needs.

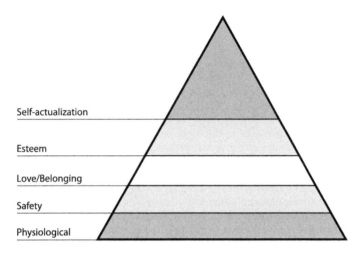

This says it is only after we have satisfied our basic needs for financial security that we care about others. When our security is in doubt, concern for others takes a back seat.

Thirdly, times of economic insecurity are associated with increasing crime, intolerance, racism and hostility to immigration, together with the rise of isolationalism, protectionism and populism, while better times led to more liberal attitudes (Friedman, 2005).

One reason for people committing crime is that if you are out of work, if you cannot make money honestly, making it dishonestly becomes relatively more attractive. And a big cost of getting caught ? the threat of losing your job ? disappears. This does not, of course, mean all the unemployed become criminals. We are talking about what happens at the margin. But this margin can be quite extensive.

The best research here comes from the US, where economists can look at variations in unemployment by state and so control nationwide factors such as demography (younger people commit more crime than older ones) or culture. One paper (1998) by

Rudolf-Winter Ebmer, of the University of Linz, and Steven Raphael, of the University of California, San Diego estimates that a 1% point rise in unemployment is associated with a 4.5% rise in the number of burglaries and 6.5% rise in car theft. A huge chunk of the fall in US crime in the 1990s, they concluded, was due merely to falling unemployment.

Recessions can also increase racism. The last one hit black workers harder than whites. Between 1990 and 1992, the unemployment rate among white workers rose by 2.6%, from 6.8% to 9.4%. But the jobless rate among black people rose by 9.4%, from 12.5% to 21.9% (Dillow, 2009).

In large part this is because black men are, on average, less qualified than their white counterparts, and employers prefer to shed less-skilled workers.

But it can also be that recessions give bosses freedom to indulge racist attitudes. When the labour market is slack, they can pick and choose more freely who to hire and fire. Kenneth Couch (2005) of the University of Connecticut has shown that the US racial unemployment gap varies over the business cycle in a manner consistent with the fact that discrimination is easier in recession.

Alongside the increase in racism is increased hostility to immigrants and isolationism. Two examples will suffice:

In Northern Ireland more than a hundred Romanians had to be placed in a secret location in Belfast after attacks on their homes in the south of the city. There have been other attacks on foreigners' homes in loyalist east Belfast in recent months. A police investigation is centred on youths with far-Right links suspected of being behind an attack last April on Poles in the Lisburn Road.

The Romanian ambassador, Ion Jinga, stated, 'I was shocked because I didn't expect such negative extremism could happen here, it was the first time when Romanians have been targeted in Britain.' (*Guardian*, 2009)

In the USA (Espenshade and Belanger 1998), there is clear evidence that one of the most important factors regarding public opinion about immigration is the level of unemployment; anti-immigrant sentiment is highest where unemployment is highest and vice versa.

A May 2006 *New York Times*/CBS News poll showed that fifty-three per cent of Americans feel that 'illegal immigrants mostly take the jobs Americans don't want'. In an opinion poll by Zogby International, voters were also asked, 'Do you support or oppose the Bush administration's proposal to give millions of illegal aliens guest worker status and the opportunity to become citizens?' Only thirty-five per cent gave their support, and fifty-six per cent said no (Miller, 2007).

In the recent economic collapse there has been a sharp increase in the influx of illegal immigrants willing to work for cheap labour. This makes it harder for unskilled or less-educated American workers to compete in industries where illegal immigrants are concentrated, such as hotels and restaurants, construction, manufacturing and farming.

Finally, with regard to populism, the 2008 US presidential elections were fought against a backdrop of economic collapse:

- Governor Mike Huckerbee had an economic populist message supporting 'Main Street America' and supporting the 'fairtax'

- Senator John McCain and his running mate Governor Sarah Palin also ran pledging to clean up corruption and Wall Street, small portions of a populist platform

- Senator Hillary Clinton gave a promise of universal health care running with a populist message

- President Barack Obama also ran with a populist message promising tax cuts to ninety-five per cent of American families.

In Europe, in the 2009 elections to the European Parliament, there was a strongly Euro-sceptic result. The three anti-Lisbon parties (Conservatives, UKIP, Greens) increased their share of the vote. The two pro-Lisbon parties (Labour, Lib Dems) lost ground. When you factor all the little anti-Brussels parties – English Democrats, No2EU, BNP, DUP, Christians, United Kingdom First – the differential is still more pronounced. Seven out of every ten ballots went to sovereignist or euro-sceptic parties.

For both the UK and the US, isolationism refers to a long-standing reluctance to become involved in other countries' alliances and wars, together with the belief that freedom and democracy could be better advanced by means other than war.

The UK has been habitually isolationist even during the centuries when it was acquiring a quarter of the world. The British have always regarded the English Channel as a 'cordon sanitaire' to protect them from what they regarded as the continental disease of war. We hesitated over joining the EU and now hesitate over the Euro. There is clear evidence that many are still strongly opposed to both. In the 2008–09 recession there has been increased support for the United Kingdom Independence Party (UKIP), whose main aim is to take the UK out of the EEU.

Most Europeans, and especially the Germans, see the European constitution as that of a bureaucratic state justified in terms of the philosopher Hegel, who believed the group – that is the state – was more important than the individual. The British, on the other hand, see Europe as a liberal democratic alliance, which can be described in terms of John Locke and America's Declaration of Independence. The global recession has exposed the deep fractures in Europe between the 'haves' – the relatively strong economies of France, Germany, Benelux and Scandinavia – and the 'have nots' – Greece, Portugal, Spain, Italy and Ireland. As Warren Buffett allegedly put it, 'It is only when the tide goes out that you discover who has been swimming naked.' This has reinforced the isolationist view in the UK that it would have been disastrous for us to have entered the euro.

For the past two years, it is argued, like the Greeks, we would have had no latitude to conduct economic policy. We would not have been allowed to reduce interest rates or devalue sterling. As a consequence unemployment would have been much higher and our national debt even higher. The majority isolationist view is that we are better as a self-governing country than a European protectorate.

In the US, the isolationist perspective dates to colonial days. Many people who had fled from Europe, where there was religious persecution, economic privation and war, populated the colonies. Their new homeland was looked upon as a place to make things better than the old ways.

The great rule of conduct for us, in regard to foreign nations, is in extending our commercial relations, to have with them as little political connection as possible. Europe has a set of primary interests, which to us have none, or a very remote relation. Hence she must be engaged in frequent controversies, the causes of which are essentially foreign to our concerns. Hence, therefore, it must be unwise in us to implicate ourselves, by artificial ties, in the ordinary vicissitudes of her politics, or the ordinary combinations and collisions of her friendships or enmities.

George Washington, September 1796

More recently Fromkin (1994, p.29) has stated 'Ever since 1898 [the beginning of the Spanish/American War], the fundamental question about American foreign relations had been whether the United States would choose to play a continuing role in world affairs.'

The United States remained politically isolated throughout the nineteenth century and the beginning of the twentieth, an unusual feat in Western history.

Germany's submarine attacks against American ships during World War One provoked the US into abandoning the neutrality it had upheld for so many years. The country's resultant participation in World War One against the Central Powers marked its first major departure from isolationist policy. When the war ended, however, the United States was quick to leave behind its European commitment.

Indeed, isolationism would persist for a few more decades. During the 1920s, American foreign affairs took a back seat. In addition, America tended to insulate itself in terms of trade. Tariffs were imposed on foreign goods to shield US manufacturers.

America turned its back on Europe by restricting the number of immigrants permitted into the country. Until World War One, millions of people, mostly from Europe, had come to America to seek their fortune and perhaps flee poverty and persecution. Britons, Germans and Jews constituted the biggest groups. In 1921, the relatively liberal policy ended and quotas were introduced. By 1929, only 150,000 immigrants per year were allowed in.

During the 1920s and 1930s, the preponderance of Americans remained opposed to enmeshment in Europe's alliances and wars. Isolationism was solid in hinterland and small-town America in the Midwest and Great Plains states, and among Republicans.

The year 1940 signalled a final turning point for isolationism. German military successes in Europe prompted nationwide American rethinking about its posture toward the war. If Germany and Italy established hegemony in Europe and Africa, and Japan swept East Asia, many believed that the western hemisphere might be next. Even if America managed to repel invasions, its way of life might wither if it were forced to become a garrison state. By the autumn of 1940, many Americans believed it was necessary to help defeat the Axis, even if it meant open hostilities.

Everything abruptly changed when Japan naval forces sneak-attacked Pearl Harbour on 7 December 1941. Germany and Italy declared war on the United States four days later. America galvanised itself for full-blown war against the Axis powers.

After the war the isolationist point of view did not figure as prominently in American policies and affairs. Countervailing tendencies were at work. The Roosevelt administration and other leaders inspired Americans to favour the establishment of the United Nations (1945), and the threat embodied by the Soviet Union under Joseph Stalin dampened any comeback of isolation-ism.

The post-war world environment, in which the United States played a leading role, changed with the triumph of urban industry and finance, expanded education and information systems, and advanced military technology and leadership by internationalists. Nevertheless, internally isolationism remained, to be rekindled at times of economic distress or terrorist attack. Historically, both the UK and the US become more isolationist in these periods.

The third section will consider the economic arguments as to why and how protectionism hurts an economy.

The fact that trade protection hurts the economy of the country that imposes it is one of the oldest but still most startling insights economics has to offer. The idea dates back to the origin of economic science itself and Adam Smith's arguments for free trade.

By specialising in production instead of producing everything, each nation would profit from free trade.

In international economics, it is the direct counterpart to the proposition that people within a national economy will all be better off if they specialise at what they do best instead of trying to be self-sufficient.

To begin to understand this, we should keep our eye on two essential points which are:

- protectionism means using force in restraint of trade
- the key is what happens to the consumer.

Invariably, we will find that the protectionists are out to exploit and impose severe losses not only on foreign consumers but also especially on the home country. And since each and every one of us is a consumer, this means that protectionism is out to disadvantage us for the benefit of a specially privileged, subsidised and inefficient few who cannot make it in a free and unhampered market.

We should recognise that all government action means coercion, so that calling upon the government to intervene means urging it to use force and violence to restrain peaceful trade.

Take, for example, the alleged Japanese menace. Is the 'flood' of Japanese products really a menace, to be combated by the government? Or is the new Japan a godsend to consumers?

All trade is mutually beneficial to both parties – in this case Japanese producers and home consumers – otherwise they would not engage in the exchange. In trying to stop this trade, protectionists are trying to stop home consumers from enjoying high living standards by buying cheap and high-quality Japanese products. Instead, are we to be forced by protectionist interests to return to the inefficient, higher-priced products we have already rejected? In short, inefficient producers are trying to deprive us of products we desire so that we will have to turn to inefficient firms.

Rothbard (1986) counters the main fallacious arguments put forward by protectionists.

'FAIR' TRADE

Take, for example, the standard complaint that while the protectionist 'welcomes competition', this competition must be 'fair'. Whenever someone starts talking about 'fair competition' or indeed, about 'fairness' in general, beware. For the genuinely 'fair' is simply the voluntary terms of exchange, mutually agreed upon by buyer and seller. As most of the medieval scholastics were able to work out, there is no 'just' (or 'fair') price outside of the market price.

So what could be 'unfair' about the free-market price? One common protectionist charge is that it is 'unfair' for, say, an American firm to compete with, say, a Taiwanese firm which needs to pay only half the wages of the American competitor. The US government is called upon to step in and 'equalise' the wage rates by imposing an equivalent tariff upon the Taiwanese. But does this mean that consumers can never patronise low-cost firms because it is 'unfair' for them to have lower costs than inefficient competitors?

What the protectionists do not bother to explain is why US wage rates are so much higher than Taiwan. Wage rates are high in the US because American employers have put these rates up. Like all other prices on the market, wage rates are determined by supply and demand, and the increased demand by US employers has put wages up. What determines this demand? The 'marginal productivity' of labour.

The demand for any factor of production, including labour, is constituted by the productivity of that factor – the amount of revenue that the worker, or the pound of cement or acre of land, is expected to bring in. The more productive the factory, the greater the demand by employers, and the higher its price or wage rate. American labour is more costly than Taiwanese because it is far more productive.

What makes it productive? To some extent, the comparative qualities of labour, skill and education. But most of the difference is not due to the personal qualities of the labourers themselves, but to the fact that the American labourer, on the whole, is equipped with more and better capital equipment than his Taiwanese counterparts. The more and better the capital investment per worker, the greater the worker's productivity, and therefore the higher the wage rate.

In short, if the American wage rate is twice that of the Taiwanese, it is because the American labourer is more heavily capitalised, is equipped with more and better tools, and is therefore, on average, twice as productive. In a sense it is not 'fair' for the American worker to make more than the Taiwanese, not because of his personal qualities, but because savers and investors have supplied him with more tools. But a wage rate is determined not just by personal quality but also by relative scarcity, and in the United States the worker is far scarcer compared to capital than he is in Taiwan.

Putting it another way, the fact that American wage rates are on average twice that of the Taiwanese does not make the cost of labour in the US twice that of Taiwan. Since US labour is twice as productive, this means that the double wage rate in the US is offset by the double productivity, so that the cost of labour per unit product in the US and Taiwan tends, on average, to be the same. One of the major protectionist fallacies is to confuse the price of labour (wage rates) with its cost, which also depends on its relative productivity.

Thus, the problem faced by American employers is not really with the 'cheap labour' in Taiwan, because 'expensive labour' in the US is precisely the result of the bidding for scarce labour by US employers. The problem faced by less efficient US textile or auto firms is not so much cheap labour in Taiwan or Japan, but the fact that other US industries are efficient enough to afford it, because they set wages that high in the first place.

So, by imposing protective tariffs and quotas to save, bail out and keep in place less efficient US textile or auto or microchip firms, the protectionists are not only injuring the American consumer. They are also harming efficient US firms and industries, which are prevented from employing resources now locked into incompetent firms, and who could otherwise expand and sell their efficient products at home and abroad.

'DUMPING'

Another contradictory line of protectionist assault on the free market asserts that the problem is not so much the low costs enjoyed by foreign firms, as the 'unfairness' of selling their products 'below costs' to American consumers, and thereby engaging in the pernicious practice of 'dumping'. By such dumping, they are able to exert unfair advantage over American firms who presumably never engage in such practices and make sure that their prices are always high enough to cover costs.

But if selling below costs is such a powerful weapon, why do business firms within a country never pursue it?

The first response to this charge is, once again, to keep our eye on consumers in general and, in this example, on American consumers in particular. Why should it be a matter of complaint when consumers so clearly benefit? Suppose, for example, that Sony is willing to injure American competitors by selling TV sets to Americans for a dollar each. Surely as far as consumers are concerned, the more 'dumping' that takes place, the better.

But what of the American TV firms, whose sales will suffer so long as Sony is willing to virtually give their sets away? Well, surely, the sensible policy for RCA, Zenith and so on would be to hold back production and sales until Sony drives itself into bankruptcy. But suppose that the worst happens, and RCA, Zenith and so on are themselves driven into bankruptcy by the Sony price war? Well, in that case, we the consumers will still be better off, since the plants of the bankrupt firms, which would still be in existence, would be picked up cheaply at auction, and the American buyers at auction would be able to enter the TV business and outcompete Sony because they now enjoy far lower capital costs.

For decades, indeed, opponents of the free market have claimed that many businesses gained their powerful status on the market by what is called 'predatory price-cutting' – that is, by driving their smaller competitors into bankruptcy by selling their goods below cost, and then reaping the reward of their unfair methods by raising their prices and thereby charging 'monopoly prices' to the consumers.

The claim is that while consumers may gain in the short run by price wars, 'dumping', and selling below costs, they lose in the long run from the alleged monopoly. But, as we have seen, economic theory shows that this would be a fool's game, losing money for the 'dumping' firms, and never really achieving a monopoly price. Historical investigation has not turned up a single case where predatory pricing, when tried, was successful – and there are actually very few cases where it has even been tried.

Another charge claims that Japanese or other foreign firms can afford to engage in dumping because their governments are willing to subsidise their losses. But again, we should still welcome such an absurd policy. If the Japanese government is really willing to waste scarce resources subsidising American purchases of Sony, so much the better. Their policy would be just as self-defeating as if the losses were private.

There is yet another problem with the charge of 'dumping'. There is no way whatever that outside observers, be they economists, businessmen or other experts, can decide what some other firms' 'costs' may be. 'Costs' are not objective entities that can be gauged or measured. Costs are subjective to the business-man himself, and they vary continually, depending on the businessman's time horizon or the stage of production or selling process he happens to be dealing with at any given time.

Suppose, for example, a fruit dealer has purchased a case of pears for $20, amounting to $1 a pound. He hopes and expects to sell those pears for $1.50 a pound. But something has happened to the pear market, and he finds it impossible to sell most of the pears at anything near that price. In fact, he finds that he must sell the pears at whatever price he can get before they become overripe. Suppose he finds that he can only sell his stock of pears at 70¢ a pound. The outside observer might say that the fruit dealer has, perhaps 'unfairly' sold his pears 'below costs', bearing in mind that the dealer's costs were $1 a pound.

'INFANT' INDUSTRIES

Another protectionist fallacy held that the government should provide a temporary protective tariff to aid, or to bring into being, an 'infant industry'. Then, when the industry was well established, the government would and should remove the tariff, and toss the now 'mature' industry into the competitive swim.

The theory is fallacious, and the policy has proved disastrous in practice. For there is no more need for government to protect a new, young industry from foreign competition than there is to protect it from domestic competition.

In the last few decades, the 'infant' plastics, television and computer industries in the US made out very well without such protection. Any government subsidising a new industry will funnel too many resources into that industry as compared to older firms, and will also inaugurate distortions that may persist and render the firm or industry permanently inefficient and vulnerable to competition. As a result, 'infant-industry' tariffs have tended to become permanent, regardless of the 'maturity' of the industry. The proponents were carried away by a misleading biological analogy to 'infants' who need adult care. But a business firm is not a person, young or old.

OLDER INDUSTRIES

Indeed, in recent years, older industries that are notoriously inefficient have been using what might be called a 'senile-industry' argument for protectionism. Steel, auto and other out-competed industries have been complaining that they 'need a breathing space' to retool and become competitive with foreign rivals, and that this breather could be provided by several years of tariffs or import quotas.

This argument is just as full of holes as the infant-industry approach, except that it will be even more difficult to work out when the 'senile' industry will have become magically rejuvenated. In fact, the steel industry has been inefficient ever since its inception, and its chronological age seems to make no difference.

Are there, in fact, any theoretical possibilities in which protection could improve a nation's economic well-being?

First, as Adam Smith himself noted, a country might be able to use the threat of protection to get other countries to reduce their protection against its exports. Thus, threatened protection could be a tool to pry open foreign markets, like oysters, with 'a strong clasp knife', as Lord Randolph Churchill put it in the late nineteenth century. If the protectionist threat worked, then the country using it would gain doubly: from its own free trade and from its trading partners' free trade. However, both Smith and later economists realised that success only occurs if the threats work.

US trade policy today is premised on a different assessment: that US markets can, and should, be closed as a means of opening new markets abroad. This premise underlies sections 301–310 of the 1988 Omnibus Trade and Competitiveness Act, which permit, and sometimes even require, the US government to force other countries to accept new trade obligations by threatening tariff retaliation if they do not. But those trade obligations do not always entail freer trade. They can, for instance, take the form of voluntary quotas on exports of certain goods to the US.

Thus, they may simply force weak nations to redirect their trade in ways that strong nations desire, cutting away at the principle that trade should be guided by market prices.

The second exception in which protection could improve a nation's economic well-being is when a country has monopoly power over a good.

Since the time of Robert Torrens and John Stuart Mill – that is, since the mid-1800s – economists have argued that a country that produces a large percentage of the world's output of a good can use an 'optimum' tariff to take advantage of its latent monopoly power, and thus gain more from trade.

This is, of course, the same as saying that a monopolist will maximise his profits by raising his price and reducing his output. Two objections to this second argument immediately come to mind.

First, with rare exceptions such as OPEC, few countries seem to have significant monopoly power in enough goods to make this an important, practical exception to the rule of free trade.

Second, other countries might retaliate against the optimum tariff.

One may well think that any market failure could be a reason for protection. Indeed, economists fell into this trap for nearly two centuries, until the 1950s. Economists now argue, instead, that protection is an inappropriate and inefficient way to correct domestic market failures.

For example, if wages do not adjust quickly enough when demand for an industry's product falls, as was the case with US auto workers losing out to foreign competition, the appropriate policy is for the government to intervene in the labour market, directly aiming remedial policy at the source of the problem.

This is the principal insight from the post-World War Two theory of commercial policy: it significantly narrows the rationale for protectionism and has revolutionised the conventional understanding of the relative merits of free trade and protectionism.

Many economists also believe that even if protection were appropriate in theory, it would in practice be 'captured' by groups who would misuse it to pursue their own narrow interests instead of the national interest. One clear cost of protection is that the country imposing it forces its consumers to forgo cheap imports. But another important cost of protection may well be the lobbying costs incurred by those seeking protection. These lobbying activities, now extensively studied by economists, are variously described as 'rent seeking' or directly unproductive profit-seeking activities. They are unproductive because they produce profit or income for those who lobby, without creating valuable output for the rest of society.

It is also important to consider the ways in which protectionists can create new ways to protect against foreign competitors.

Protectionists always seem to be one step ahead of free traders in creating new and ingenious ways to protect against foreign competitors. One way is by replacing restrictions on imports with what are euphemistically called 'voluntary' export restrictions (VERs) or 'orderly' market arrangements (OMAs). Instead of the importing country restricting imports with quotas or tariffs, the exporting country restricts exports. The protectionist effect is still the same.

The real difference, which makes exporting nations prefer restrictions on exports to restrictions on imports, is that the VERs enable the exporters to charge higher prices and thus collect for them the higher prices caused by protection. That has been the case with Japan's voluntary quotas on exports of cars to the United States. The United States could have kept Japanese car imports in check by placing a tariff on them. That would have raised the price, so consumers would have bought fewer. Instead, the Japanese government limited the number of cars shipped to the United States. Since supply was lower than it would have been in the absence of the quotas, Japanese car-makers were able to charge higher prices and still sell all their exports to the United States. The accrual of the resulting extra profits from the voluntary export restraint may also, ironically, have helped the Japanese auto producers find the funds to make investments that made them even more competitive.

The growth of VERs in the 1980s was a disturbing development for a second reason as well. They selectively target suppliers instead of letting the market decide who will lose when trade must be restricted. As an alternative, the United States could provide just as much protection for domestic auto makers by putting a quota or tariff on all foreign cars, letting consumers decide whether they wanted to buy fewer Japanese cars or fewer European ones. With VERs, in other words, politics replaces economic efficiency as the criterion determining who trades what.

Protectionism has recently come in another form more insidious than VERs. Economists call the new form 'administered protection'. Nearly all rich countries today have 'fair trade' laws. The stated purpose of these laws is twofold:

- to ensure that foreign nations do not subsidise exports (which would distort market incentives and hence destroy efficient allocation of activity among the world's nations)
- to guarantee that foreign firms do not dump their exports in a predatory fashion.

National governments thus provide for procedures under which a countervailing duty (CVD) against foreign subsidy or an anti-dumping (AD) duty can be levied when subsidisation or dumping is found to occur. These two 'fair trade' mechanisms are meant to complement free trade.

In practice, however, when protectionist pressures rise, fair trade is misused to work against free trade. Thus, CVD and AD actions are often started against successful foreign firms simply to harass them and coerce them into accepting VERs. Practices that are thoroughly normal at home are proscribed as predatory when foreign firms engage in them. As one trade analyst put it, 'If the same anti-dumping laws applied to US companies, every after-Christmas sale in the country would be banned.'

Much economic analysis shows that, in the 1980s, fair trade mechanisms turned increasingly into protectionist instruments used unfairly against foreign competition. US rice producers got a countervailing duty imposed on rice from Thailand, for example, by establishing that the Thai government was subsidising rice exports by less than one per cent – and ignoring the fact that Thailand also imposed a five per cent tax on exports. We usually think that a foreign firm is dumping when it sells at a lower price in our market than in its own. But the US government took an anti-dumping action against Poland's exports of golf carts, even though no golf carts were sold in Poland.

Economists have been thinking about how these fair trade mechanisms can be redesigned so as to insulate them from being 'captured' and misused by special interests.

So, finally, if isolationism and protectionism are so bad for us, why does everyone reach for them in bad times? There are two main reasons:

First, while the benefits are widely spread and difficult to measure, the costs are concentrated and often easy to see. The gains manifest themselves in things like lower prices at super-markets, but consumers are many and varied, and not politically organised. By contrast, the losers such as car workers made redundant or put on short time are vocal and politically organised. In such situations it is not easy to get across the message that it is imports and not exports that are the whole point of trade; we trade precisely so we can enjoy those goods in whose production others have a comparative advantage.

Second, trade is a global phenomenon, while politics is national. When unemployment lines lengthen, politicians tend to prioritise the immediate concerns of their constituents. In the short term, import quotas can save jobs, and such factors become of even greater importance in election years or in a depression.

Those of you reading this book that have lost jobs in the recent economic collapse may very well wish to include protectionism in their spectacles!

The protectionist arguments, many seeming plausible at first glance, do not stand up to close examination, betraying ignorance of current economic theory.

Taking an overall long-term view, the impetus for protectionism comes from the quest for coerced special privilege and restraint of trade at the expense of efficient competitors and consumers.

However, in the short term, there is no denying that it can protect employment, and in a democracy it is often politically motivated policies designed to win elections that prevail.

In the final section of this chapter we will consider populism, which has been a common political phenomenon throughout history. For example, Spartacus could be considered a famous populist leader of ancient times through his slave rebellion against the rulers of Rome.

There is, however, a tendency for populism to increase during times of perceived bad government and/or economic recession. Wikipedia provides an excellent background.

The word populism is derived from the Latin word *populus*, which means people in English (in the sense of 'nation'). Therefore, populism espouses government by the people as a whole (that is to say, the masses). This is in contrast to elitism, aristocracy and plutocracy, each of which is an ideology that espouses government by a small, privileged group above the masses.

Populism therefore is a discourse that claims to support 'the people' versus 'the elites'. Generally, populism invokes an idea of democracy as being, above all, the expression of the people's will.

In recent years, due to the heightened attention on populism, advances have been made in defining the term in ways that can help to distinguish between movements which are populist and those that simply borrow from populism. One of the latest of these is the definition by Albertazzi and McDonnell who, in their volume *Twenty-First Century Populism*, define populism as 'an ideology which pits a virtuous and homogeneous people against a set of elites and dangerous "others" who are together depicted as depriving (or attempting to deprive) the sovereign people of their rights, values, prosperity, identity and voice' (2008, p.15).

In fact, given its central tenet that democracy should reflect the pure and undiluted will of the people, populism can sit easily with ideologies of both Right and Left, or claim to be neither 'left wing', nor 'centrist' nor 'right wing'.

At the core of this ideology there are four intertwined principles.

1   The people are one and are inherently 'good'. They are a homogeneous and virtuous community. Divisions within them are false, created and nurtured by the intellectual and political elites, and can be overcome as they are of less consequence than the people's common 'nature' and identity.

2   The people are sovereign. Those who govern are morally obliged to do so in the interests of the people who must once more become 'masters in their own homes', in the widest sense of the term. As Gerry Stoker puts it, populism 'posits that the people are one, and their voice, if properly understood, has a unified and unifying message' (Stoker, 2006, p.139).

3   The people's culture and way of life are of paramount value. This is (alleged to be) rooted in history and tradition, and is thus solid, 'right' and conducive to the public good — hence the need to 'love', 'save', 'protect', 'treasure' and 'rediscover' our culture.

4   The leader and party/movement are one with the people. Populism celebrates 'the ordinariness of its constituents and the extraordinariness of their leaders' (Taggart, 2000, p.102). As Max Weber says, whether or not charismatic leaders really possess the qualities claimed is not so relevant; the important point is that their followers are convinced that they are their man (or, occasionally, woman) 'of destiny' (Weber, 1978).

The rise of populism in Western Europe is, in large part, a reaction to:

*   the failure of traditional parties to respond adequately in the eyes of the electorate to a series of phenomena such as economic and cultural globalisation

- the speed and direction of European integration and immigration
- the decline of ideologies and class politics
- the exposure of elite corruption
- 'political malaise', manifested in steadily falling turnouts across Western Europe, and declining party memberships
- ever-greater numbers of citizens in surveys citing a lack of interest and distrust in politics and politicians
- an anti-political climate in which people perceive politics to be more convoluted, distant and irrelevant to people's lives and politicians to be more incapable, impotent, self-serving and similar to one another than in the past.

Like all ideologies, populism proposes an analysis designed to respond to a number of essential questions: 'What went wrong; who is to blame; and what is to be done to reverse the situation?' (Betz and Johnson, 2004, p.323).

Put simply, the answers are:

- the government and democracy, which should reflect the will of the people, have been occupied, distorted and exploited by corrupt elites
- the elites and 'others' (i.e. not of 'the people') are to blame for the current undesirable situation in which the people find themselves
- the people must be given back their voice and power through the populist leader and party. This view is based on a fundamental conception of the people as both homogeneous and virtuous.

With regard specifically to bad government, Ivan Krastev (2006) argues that a major reason for the growing tide of European populism is disgust with corruption. Today's European populists like democracy. What they oppose 'is the representative nature of modern democracies, the protection of the rights of minorities, and the constraints to the sovereignty of the people'.

He believes that corrupt elites have become 'increasingly suspicious of democracy'; 'angry publics' have become 'increasingly anti-liberal'. Furthermore, he argues that Liberal governments have misread the anti-corruption sentiments of the population they governed in four distinct ways.

First, liberals perceived corruption as an institutional issue requiring a response focusing on more transparency and institutional reforms. But in the eyes of the public, corruption was a moral issue ('God does not take bribes'), requiring honest politicians in power.

Second, liberals regarded anti-corruption discourse as being about fairness, whereas for the public it was a discourse about growing social inequality.

Third, liberals believed that corruption was caused by the state being too powerful and large, and advocated rapid privatisation and a small state. But a majority of people thought the power of the market was to blame, and came to expect a revision of the most scandalous privatisation deals.

Fourth, liberals saw anti-corruption discourse as a chance to legitimise capitalism. But the conspiracy-minded majority saw it as an opportunity to delegitimise it without the risk of being accused of communism or other infectious diseases.

The last decade has seen liberals caught in a trap that they themselves constructed. The war on corruption made populism respectable; thus to attack populism today can be made to seem like defending corruption.

Much of the above seems to be an accurate description of what has happened in the UK.

The New Labour project was ultimately a statement of lack of trust in the people (Lerman, 2009). The only way they could be brought round to vote the 'right' way was by appealing to their narrow self-interest and to be told that there was no alternative. What was sold as the politics of choice was precisely the opposite.

The global financial and economic collapse revealed the bankruptcy of this fundamentally anti-democratic approach, and yet the Labour elite drank so deeply at this well that they have lost the ability to see that the instincts of the electorate can be a force for good.

The Tories, meanwhile, are pulling in two directions. They

too, very belatedly, decided that the will of their party had to be overcome for the sake of getting elected. So, Cameron has 'decontaminated the brand' and fully embraced the bland. But as the party that has not been in government for years and does not have the responsibilities of power to weigh it down, it can respond more quickly to the popular mood and is flirting with populism more riskily than the other main parties.

Whatever may have initially prompted William Hague and David Cameron to decide to pull out of the European People's Party in the European Parliament and into a new caucus of Euro-sceptics, the European Conservatives, getting into bed with the Polish Law and Justice Party and the Czech Civic Democrats lines the Tories up with people espousing distinctly populist policies and holding deeply troubling views. And they may well have to link up with other populist parties to qualify for official caucus status in the new parliament.

The British mood increasingly resembles the populism taking hold across Europe. The party leaders here think they can surf the wave, but most populist politics are, in Krastev's (2006) words, 'dangerous mutations'. Flirting with them may well backfire. His research on populism and the politics of anti-corruption led him to conclude that 'the more governments make fighting corruption a priority, the more people are inclined to view these very governments as corrupt'.

The UK is not central Europe, but, as well as corruption, the problems fuelling populism – Euro-scepticism, xenophobia, fear of loss of national identity, immigration, weakened national sovereignty, Islamophobia, the impact of recession – are Europe-wide. It would be dangerously complacent to think that we can continue to be the European exception.

While political turmoil persists in the UK, we should take notice of the fact that populism is on the rise all over Europe and a populist agenda is prevailing at the centre of many countries' national politics.

Summary

Isolationism is 'a national policy of abstaining from political or economic relations with other countries', and protectionism is 'the advocacy, system, or theory of protecting domestic producers by impeding or limiting, as by tariffs or quotas, the importation of foreign goods and services'.

The fact that trade protection hurts the economy of the country that imposes it is one of the oldest but still most startling insights economics has to offer. People within a national economy will all be better off if they specialise in what they do best instead of trying to be self-sufficient.

Protectionism arises in ingenious ways. Protectionists always seem to be one step ahead of free traders in creating new ways to protect against foreign competitors. Much economic analysis shows that, in the 1980s, fair trade mechanisms turned increasingly into protectionist instruments used unfairly against foreign competition.

So if isolationism and protectionism are so bad for us, why does everyone reach for them in bad times? There are two main reasons. First, while the benefits are widely spread and difficult to measure, the costs are concentrated and often easy to see. Second, trade is a global phenomenon, while politics is national. Short-term policies often prevail in democracies.

Populism is an ideology which pits a virtuous and homogeneous people against a set of elites and dangerous 'others' who are together depicted as depriving (or attempting to deprive) the sovereign people of their rights, values, prosperity, identity and voice.

- -

Reader's Notes:

10

Libertarianism and Egalitarianism

> The historical development of capitalism ... has left remaining no other nexus between man and man than naked self-interest and callous cash payment.
>
> Karl Marx

> We are going to hell in a hand-cart, as free markets rip up established communities. The idea of a world of liberal, democratic and prosperous states on the American model is ... a fantasy.
>
> Andrew Marr

This chapter will make you think about the relationships between freedom, equality, fairness, justice, democracy and civil disobedience. First some definitions from the net:

> Libertarianism is a term used by a broad spectrum of political philosophies which prioritise individual liberty and seek to minimise or even abolish the state.
>
> Wikipedia

> Political philosophy that takes individual liberty to be the primary political value ... seeks to define and justify the legitimate powers of government in terms of certain natural or God-given individual rights. These rights include the rights to life, liberty, private property, freedom of speech and association, freedom of worship, government by consent, equality under the law, and moral autonomy (the pursuit of one's own conception of happiness, or the 'good life') ... government power should be limited to that which is necessary to accomplish this task.
>
> Britannica Online

Egalitarianism (derived from the French word *égal*, meaning equal) is a political doctrine that holds that all people should be treated as equals and have the same political, economic, social and civic rights.

Wikipedia

Egalitarianism – 1: a belief in human equality especially with respect to social, political, and economic rights and privileges. 2: a social philosophy advocating the removal of inequalities among people.

Merriam-Webster Online

Well that all seems to be quite clear – or does it?

Presumably you would agree that having to pay tax reduces your freedom to the degree that you are no longer free to spend the income that has been taken away from you.

But on the other hand, how do you remove inequalities without redistributing income? So to increase equality you have to reduce liberty? Therefore, it is surely a matter of getting the right balance between the two.

But wait a minute – are we sure that we know what we mean by liberty and equality?

Berlin's 1958 essay, 'Two Concepts of Liberty', described a difference between negative liberty, which limits the power of the state to interfere, and positive liberty, in which a paternalistic state helps individuals achieve self-realisation and self-determination. He believed these were rival and incompatible interpretations of liberty and held that demands for positive liberty lead to authoritarianism.

Therefore to achieve a balance you must mean positive liberty.

Likewise, with equality, Milton Friedman argues that equality of opportunity in the sense of identical opportunity for all individuals is impossible.

One child is born blind, another with sight. One child has parents deeply concerned about his welfare who provide a background of culture and understanding, another has dissolute, improvident parents. Children at birth clearly do not have identical opportunities in relation to abilities or environment.

Milton and Rose Friedman,
Free to Choose, New York (1980) p.131–2

Furthermore, he argues that we must distinguish between 'equality of opportunity' and 'equality of outcome'. Equality of opportunity provides in a sense that all start the race of life at the same time. Equality of outcome attempts to ensure that everyone finishes at the same time.

Equality of opportunity is best expressed in the phrase 'career open to talents'. No arbitrary obstacles should prevent people from achieving those public positions which their talents fit and which their values lead them to seek. Neither birth, nationality, colour, religion, sex, nor any other equivalent characteristic should determine the public opportunities that are open to a person, only talent and achievement. Thus, equality of opportunity simply spells out the concept of equality before the law.

And it has meaning and importance precisely because people are different in their genetic and cultural characteristics, and hence both want to and can pursue different careers. It is important to note that such equality of opportunity does not present any conflict with freedom – quite the opposite.

Equality of opportunity and freedom are two facets of the same basic concept. Equality of outcome is a radically different concept. Equality of outcome attempts to ensure that everyone finishes at the same time. To slightly change what the Dodo said in *Alice in Wonderland*, 'Everybody must win and all must have prizes.'

That is, argues Friedman, the goal of radical socialism. Everyone must be a winner, everyone must be equal. Socialists do not really point towards absolute equality but they point to vague ideas of fairness and justness.

This concept differs radically from the idea of equality of opportunity. Equality of opportunity provides scope for freedom and is, in fact, complementary to freedom. On the other hand, government measures to achieve 'fair shares for all' reduce equality. Government attempts to promote equality by positive action and discrimination have many undesirable consequences.

Three questions may be noted.

- If rewards are based not on achievement and effort but on fairness, what incentive is there to work?

- Who is to decide on fairness?
- What are the criteria of fairness?

Therefore, to achieve balance, are you also going to ignore the arguments of Milton Friedman?

Let us look to the philosophers for guidance. No book on political philosophy can ignore the ideas of John Rawls, whose book *A Theory of Justice* was published in 1971. Rawls made later revisions to his ideas.

Rawls was concerned with justice and fairness and the relationship between freedom and equality.

To achieve a just and moral society two principles must be adhered to.

- Each individual is to have an equal right to the most extensive total system of equal basic liberties compatible with a similar system of liberty for all.

- Social and economic inequalities are to be arranged as to be to the greatest benefit of the least advantaged, and all associated offices and positions are to be open to all under conditions of fair equality of opportunity.

In these two principles there are in fact four points which are that:

- there should be as much freedom as possible
- people should be equally free
- inequalities should be to everyone's advantage (the difference principle)
- the better positions must be open to all (compare 'equality of opportunity').

It is as if he supposes that freedom is a good thing and inequality a bad thing.

How can inequality ever be advantageous to the person who gets the smaller share?

The answer is that inequalities may constitute incentives, which increase the size of the cake to be shared, so that the smaller piece may be larger absolutely than an equal share of the smaller cake that would have existed if no such incentive had been offered.

Clearly Rawls is on the egalitarian side of the argument, whereas in complete opposition to these ideas are those of Robert Nozick, whose book *Anarchy State and Utopia* was published in 1974.

His opening remark (p.ix) is: 'Individuals have rights … so strong and far-reaching that they raise the question of what, if anything, the state and its officials may do.'

At first sight the proposition that the state can do nothing appears to be 'anarchy' (meaning not chaos, but 'non-rule' – 'an' being in Greek a negative prefix). Anarchy might be a happy state of affairs in which people live together more or less cooperatively without government. Anarchy is what John Locke and other seventeenth century writers called the 'State of Nature'; they assumed that anarchy is natural and original, and civil society (society ruled by government) artificial.

However, Nozick is not an anarchist. He is, more accurately a 'libertarian,' a proponent of the minimal or 'night watchman' state.

> The nature of the state, its legitimate functions and justifications, if any, is the central concern of this book … Our main conclusions about the state are that a minimal state, limited to the narrow functions of protection against force, theft, fraud, enforcement of contracts, and so on, is justified; that any more extensive state will violate persons' rights … and is unjustified … the state may not use its coercive apparatus for the purpose of getting some citizens to aid others, i.e. no compulsory charity.
>
> Nozick, 1974, p.11

In this book he attacks the notion of egalitarian social justice. In essence he argued that the state could not be justified as the redistributor of wealth without violating the rights of the individual.

He attacked Rawl's concept of 'distributive justice'. Where Rawls argued that inequalities could be compatible with justice if they benefit the worst-off, Nozick argued that 'whatever arises from a just situation must itself be just'.

Nozick put forward his own notion of 'entitlement justice', which argues that everyone is entitled to all they have acquired, provided they gained their possessions justly, and even if large inequalities result in the process.

So which concept of justice do you favour?

And we still haven't looked at one of the biggest problems of all in terms of the form of government that will control the balance between liberty and equality. In others words, we need to consider our understanding of 'democracy'.

As a bridge, and to show the diversity of thinking in this area, we will concentrate first on the thoughts of Henry Thoreau, a highly original thinker, who lived in Concord, Massachusetts from 1817 to 1862. At this time in America, liberal and conservative thinkers alike endorsed the three broad concepts of nationalism, representative democracy and capitalism. In his book *Walden* and political philosophy essay on 'Civil Disobedience' (1848), Thoreau emphatically rejects all three.

First, let us look at nationalism and Thoreau's famous statement that 'government is best which governs not at all'. Although conceding that the state might sometimes be expedient, he thought it to be 'half-witted' and insisted that no intrinsic connection exists between politics and ethics. Not only does he deny that the state has any moral authority, but he also accuses it of thwarting both the liberty and moral development of individual human beings.

This of course runs completely against the prevailing consensus of the time, from Plato to Aristotle, Rousseau and Thoreau's contemporary Hegel. For Hegel, a person achieves freedom only within and through the state, while for Thoreau the state inevitably thwarts individual liberty.

Second, there is representative democracy where Thoreau first attacked voting and elections – 'All voting is a sort of gaming … even voting for the right is doing nothing for it' – and dismissed a system of majority rule as 'There is … little virtue in the action of masses of men'.

Finally he indicted the rule of law, arguing that when the injustice of the law and the state becomes intolerable, 'then, I say, break the law'.

Thoreau is affirming the right of individual conscience as

against the claim of any state, albeit monarchy or representative democracy.

He went briefly to jail for refusing to pay his poll tax. When Emerson famously asked Thoreau why he went to jail, Thoreau responded, 'Why did you not go to jail?'

Finally, Thoreau attacked capitalism for its exaltation of money: 'A man is rich in proportion to the number of things that he can let alone [and] money cannot purchase one necessary of the soul.'

Thoreau was a contemporary of Marx although it is not thought that he had read his work. What is fascinating then is that we have two attacks on capitalism written at the same time but with a fundamental difference between them.

Unlike Marx, Thoreau indicts capitalism on moral grounds. Marx thought in terms of class struggle and historical inevitability rather than individual conscience, moral virtue and voluntary poverty. Whereas Marx's mode of resistance is collective and aims at a collective communist society, Thoreau would reject any form of collectivism, affirming individualism and the sanctity of conscience.

And now let us take a more detailed look at democracy in terms of the form of government that will control the balance between liberty and equality.

Most of you reading this book will probably be favourably disposed towards the idea of democracy. Is that because most of you may have been brought up in a democracy and do not really know any different? How many of you have thought in any depth about what democracy actually is and what in reality it actually delivers?

In this chapter we will concentrate on democracy nationally but in the penultimate chapter we will consider it globally.

> The received wisdom in the UK and the US is that democracy, when adequately qualified and explicated, can be seen to lay down a programme of change in and through which pressing, substantive issues will receive a better opportunity for deliberation, debate and resolution than they would under alternative regimes ... it offers, in theory at least, a form of politics and life in which there are fair and just ways of deliberating over and negotiating value disputes.

> David Held, 2008, p.261

But what if I suggested to you that democracy in the West has a semi-sacred status accorded to it that it by no means deserves?

To provoke thought, here are some of the reasons of Paul Treanor (2009) as to the weaknesses of democracy. He suggests that there are many aspects of democracy that are morally and ethically questionable.

1 Democratic theory can legitimise a political community and then legitimise the selfish decisions of that community.

Let us start with a short story:

In a large ocean there are two neighbouring islands: faultless democracies with full civil and political rights. One island is extremely rich and prosperous, and has ten million inhabitants. The other is extremely poor: it has a hundred million inhabitants, who live by subsistence farming. After a bad harvest last year, there are no food stocks, and now the harvest has failed again: ninety million people are facing death by starvation. The democratically elected government of the poor island asks for help, and the democratically elected government of the rich island organises a referendum on the issue. There are three options: Option A is a sharp increase in taxes, to pay for large-scale permanent structural transfers to the poor island. Option B is some increase in taxes, to pay for immediate and sufficient humanitarian aid, so that famine will be averted. Option C is no extra taxes and no aid. When the votes are counted, all of the voters have chosen Option C. After all, who wants to pay more taxes?

So 90 million people starve. Yet all electoral procedures on both islands are free and fair, the media are free, political campaigning is free; there is no political repression of any kind.

According to democratic theory, any outcome of this democratic process must be respected. Two perfect democracies have functioned perfectly: if you believe the supporters of democracy, that is morally admirable. But it clearly is not: surely there is something fundamentally wrong with democracy if it allows this outcome.

The defect is not hard to find: The people most affected by

the decision are excluded from voting. The issue is the composition of the demos, the decision-making unit in a democracy. This theoretical possibility corresponds with the real-world Western democracies. Millions of people are dying of hunger and preventable disease, yet the electorate in rich democracies will not accept mass transfers of wealth to poorer countries. They will not accept mass immigration from those countries either.

2   The claim of democracy for legitimacy leads to the false claim that no value may override democracy.

What would happen if legitimacy disappeared completely? In principle, you could hold free and fair multi-party elections in an open society – and then overthrow the democratically elected government, after each election. That could happen every week, but it would not be considered 'democracy'. This emphasises the formalism and procedurals of democracy: once followed, the democratic procedures are claimed to produce legitimacy. The government, which is elected by the democratic procedures, becomes the absolutely legitimate government. If legitimacy is strong, then it becomes culturally taboo to overthrow it.

To be a democrat means that you think this should happen: you believe that the democratically elected government is legitimate and must be accepted as legitimate (unless it is itself anti-democratic). The procedures are not an ornament, they are the essence.

This legitimacy claim is a major ethical defect of democracy – because procedure is no substitute for morality. Most democrats go much further, and would claim explicitly that a democratically elected government, which has acted on a decision made in accordance with democratic procedures and the rule of law, should not be overthrown, even if the action is morally wrong.

At the heart of democracy is something that is morally unacceptable. What democrats are saying is that no value may override democracy. In terms of regime preference, they are saying, for instance, that a democracy that tortures is preferable to a dictatorship which does not. The word 'democratic' is widely used as a synonym for 'legitimate', in both the political and moral sense.

In the democratic ethic, the only remedy for any defect of democracy is democracy itself. In a democracy, there is certainly no political authority external to the democratic process: there is no 'appeal to a higher tribunal'. No other method or process is accepted as a legitimate response to the democratic process, and certainly not the use of force. The word 'undemocratic' is used as a synonym for 'criminal' or 'hostile'. It is used to suggest an attack on society, a form of terrorism.

These claims for democratic legitimacy indicate the primary function of democratic theory in Western democracies. It serves to legitimise the existing order, however wrong that order may be.

Democracy in fact, blocks the transition to a post-democratic world. Self-preservation probably characterises most social structures. In liberal-democratic states, there are usually specific legal prohibitions against overturning democracy. All such prohibitions are unethical, for it is unethical to block change. If necessary, innovation should take precedence over democracy. However, as we have seen, democrats claim that democracy itself has priority over other values.

More than any other regime of government, democracy is concerned with its own maximisation.

Not only is democracy for ever, it is forever becoming more democratic. It is normal for democrats to demand more democracy. It is not simply a monopoly in time and space. It goes beyond monopoly: even if the entire world is democratic, for ever, many democrats will still insist on more democracy. Since the world is not yet one hundred per cent democratic, 'democratisation' refers to spatial expansion. There are organisations in Western states (government-funded and private) that exist for the specific purpose of converting other states into democracies.

Proposals for a Union of Democracies existed before World War Two, and there were older proposals for unions of 'civilised states'. At the time both of these meant the US, Britain and its 'white colonies', and a few west-European and Scandinavian states. After the end of the Cold War the idea enjoyed a revival – indicative of the mood of democratic expansionism. Democratic expansionists believe that they are entitled to impose democracy, without limit in time or space.

Inherent in democracy is a claim to a democratic world order – and by definition, any global claim is a monopoly claim. Like universal religions such as Christianity, Islam and 'Marxism', democracy can ultimately tolerate no competitors, no 'other gods'. Democracy intensifies itself, and maximises its spatial extent.

Five different versions of the history of democratic expansion are compiled at Steve Muhlberger's site entitled Chronology of Modern Democracy: Five Different Views (Francis Fukuyama, Samuel P Huntingdon, Tatu Vanhanen, the Freedom House's End of Century Survey, and Matthew White). The last includes online maps of regime types at ten-year intervals. Multi-party democracies are coloured blue (the traditional colour of conservatism), and in the map series a wave of blue is slowly covering the planet. The democratic theorists are not just describing what is happening, they say clearly that they want it to happen.

So democracy is not only a system of government, it is a war against anti-democracy.

3   The treatment of minorities is perhaps the most recognised defect of democracies.

Between the mid-1930s and the mid-1970s, the Swedish government forcibly sterilised thousands of women, because of 'mental defects', or simply because they were of 'mixed race'. Yet Sweden has been a model democracy for the entire period. The problem is that democracy offers no protection to marginalised and despised minorities. The usual answer of democrats is that constitutionally enforced individual rights can prevent excesses. There are two problems with that.

First, no constitutional rights are absolute: President Bush showed how easy it is to overturn fundamental constitutional protections. Simply by redefining some American citizens as 'illegal enemy combatants', he was able to intern them. Some groups are in any case openly excluded from the usual democratic rights, most notably illegal immigrants.

The Australian government detains asylum seekers in internment camps in the desert: its hard line accurately reflects the attitudes of a racist electorate. The detainees cannot vote, cannot engage in political activities and have no free press, but Australia is still considered a democracy.

The second problem is that basic rights allow wide limits. Treatment of minorities may be harsh and humiliating, without infringing their rights. A recent example in the Netherlands is a proposal to impose compulsory genital inspections for ethnic minorities. The aim is to combat female genital mutilation, but every ethnic Somali parent, regardless of their own circumstances, would be obliged to present their daughters for annual genital inspection. Eritreans, Egyptians and Sudanese might be included under the legal obligation, even if they were naturalised Dutch citizens. The proposal has majority support in Parliament. It is not law yet, but since Somalis are a marginalised and often despised minority in the Netherlands, there is nothing they can do to prevent its implementation.

So long as they avoid certain types of policy, and outright violence, democracy allows a democratic majority to impose its will on a minority. They can impose their language and a culture, and both impositions are normal practice in nation states. They can also impose their values, which may be unacceptable to the minority: the best example is democratic prohibitions of alcohol or drugs.

Alcohol prohibition in the United States, enforced through a constitutional amendment, was a direct result of democracy. Since there was (and is) no 'right to drink', the Christian anti-alcohol majority could simply use the democratic process to make their values the national values. Prohibition was repealed in 1933, but the 'War on Drugs' of the last twenty years is at least as comprehensive in terms of policy and effects. Successful prohibition movements are a special case of the inherent anti-minority bias in democracies.

There is a more general effect: it is very difficult for an innovative minority to succeed in a democracy – and it is a minority that first proposes most innovations. Like many political systems, democracy has an inherent bias in favour of the existing, as against the possible. Innovations must go through the political process, which in that sense is an anti-innovative barrier, but the existing social order does not have to prove its existence rights. A large-scale example of failed innovation in democracies is the European high-speed rail network, first proposed in the 1970s. Since then, not even planned national networks have been completed. The pan-European project failed primarily due to lack of political enthusiasm.

But should it be abandoned, simply because there is insufficient 'will of the people'? If an innovation has no democratic mandate then a democracy will not implement it – but should democracy have this priority over innovation? The issues are scarcely considered in democratic theory: the priority is simply taken for granted.

4   The prohibition of secession is unacceptable.

Unlike the legitimacy claim, the democratic principles concerning secession are often discussed – for instance, in Canada, in connection with Quebec secessionism.

Unlimited secession would make democracy pointless. If free and fair multi-party elections are held in an open society, but anyone who disagrees with the result can set up a separate state, no democrat would accept that as a democracy. For democrats there must be a unit, beyond which secession is not permitted: this unit is the demos. Again, its modern expression is the democratic nation state. The indivisibility of the demos is as important as legitimacy, because legitimacy collapses in the face of secessionism. Secessionists see the existing government as 'foreign', and they no longer feel any obligation to its laws, institutions and policies. So a democratic government ultimately depends on military power to sustain itself in office, and to prevent the unlimited secession of minorities.

This aspect of the democratic ethic brought democrats into a long-term alliance with nationalism. No guns, no democracy. A good example here is the lack of a Kurdish state. Most of the Kurds live in the adjoining states of Iraq and Turkey, both democracies.

5   Democracy has failed to eliminate social inequality, and this
      seems a permanent and structural failure.

It is undeniable that all democratic societies have social inequalities – substantial differences in income, in wealth and in social
status. These differences have persisted: there is no indication that
inequality will ever disappear in democracies. In the stable
Western democracies, inequality is apparently increasing. The
pattern established in the United States is, that the lowest
incomes do not grow: all the benefits of economic growth go to
the higher-income groups.

Some form of social inequality is therefore inherent in
democracy. In a theoretical democracy of one hundred voters, a
party of fifty-one voters can confiscate the property of the other
forty-nine. They can divide it among themselves. However, if one
voter is sick on election day, they lose their majority. A party of
fifty-two has more chance to divide the property of the minority,
but now the minority is forty-eight and there is slightly less to
divide. A party of ninety-nine will have guaranteed success against
a minority of one, but the shares after division will be minimal.

In practice, a coalition of two thirds, or three quarters, can
successfully disadvantage a minority (one third, one quarter). For
instance, the majority might exclude the minority from the main
labour market, creating an excluded underclass. There is evidence
that in Northern Ireland, preferential treatment in the labour
market has always been given to Protestants, the majority
religious group.

The emergence of an underclass is usually seen as a structural
change within a society, but it might be simply a side effect of
democracy. Every democracy is a temptation (to the majority) to
disadvantage minorities. In practice, every existing liberal
democracy is a dual society, with some politically marginalised.

In the past, aristocratic conservatives feared that democracy
would allow the poor to confiscate the wealth of the rich. In
reality, the historical trend seems exactly the opposite. Guarantees
of fundamental rights do not prevent a low-status minority being
targeted, politically and socially. In several European countries,
political parties compete against each other, to show how tough

they are against an unpopular minority – for instance, asylum seekers. There is nothing the minority can do. Unfortunately, this development is probably still in the early stages: the worst is yet to come. In a democracy, those at the bottom of the social scale can expect steadily worsening conditions of life.

Let us give some examples from health statistics that are an excellent indicator of structural inequalities in democracies.

First, inequalities in mortality are a moral defect of democracies. Public health and epidemiology journals are full of examples of health inequalities. In Britain, the 1998 Acheson Report on health inequalities showed that they had worsened since the last major study, the Black Report in 1980. Those were the years of the Conservative governments in Britain, so perhaps the Conservative policies are responsible. But that is the point: those Conservative governments were democratically elected. If democracy were a system that prevented inequalities in death rates, then democracy would prevent a government that worsened those inequalities. If democracy were a system that prevented inequalities in death rates, then there would be no inequalities anyway. But there are, and democracy is apparently making them worse.

Second, things are even worse if we consider excess mortality and the distribution of wealth at a global level.

Although the democratic states are the most prosperous in history, democracy has failed to eliminate inequality at global level. Despite the great personal wealth evident in some democratic nations, millions of people in the poorest regions of Africa live under conditions comparable to mediaeval European averages. The general global distribution of wealth has not shifted substantially in the last 150 years. This also seems a permanent and structural failure of democracy. Democracy does not induce the rich to give their money to the poor: not locally, not globally, not as individuals, not as societies, not as states.

A causal relationship between democracy and famine exists primarily at a global level. In nation states, by definition, the national territory is reserved for members of the nation. The democratisation of a nation state reinforces their inherent qualities. The electorate generally does not want to give 'their money' to foreign countries, and they do not want to dilute their standard of living by mass immigration. A democratic and national world order does not cause droughts or crop failures. However, it destroys two standard historical responses to famine: redistribution of food and migration to non-famine areas. The national-democratic world order imprisons the poor in poverty and ill health.

There is already enough data on long-term patterns of economic growth to conclude that the rich-poor gap among states is increasing. Research by Angus Madison for the Organisation for Economic Cooperation and Development (OECD), indicated that the gap (in GDP/capita) between Western Europe and sub-Saharan Africa was about three to one in 1820. By 1990 it had increased to twenty to one. During this long period Western Europe was not continuously democratic, so this Europe-Africa gap is not equivalent to the gap between democracies and non-democracies.

However, that has changed: in the last generation, the terms 'democracy' and 'rich country' have become almost equivalent. According to the 2004 World Bank estimates, over 1.1 billion people live on less than one dollar a day, the same as a decade earlier. (These figures are already corrected for the differences in purchasing power.) In sub-Saharan Africa the proportion living under this official 'extreme poverty' limit rose to forty-six per cent.

The income ratio – of the poorest twenty countries to the richest twenty – has doubled in the last forty years. And for that time at least, most of these rich countries were democracies. There are a few rich non-democracies, such as the United Arab Emirates, and some poor democracies such as Cape Verde.

Certainly there is no 'political will' in the democracies to introduce the massive transfer taxes that would be necessary to close the gap. Democracies seem structurally unable to generate this political will.

6   There is a built-in conservative bias in democracy. Democratic culture structurally limits innovation.

The uniformity and conformity of liberal-democratic societies has been criticised, for almost as long as they have existed – from the nineteenth century on. At first, these criticisms amounted to nostalgia for aristocratic individualism, and it is still a favourite tactic of democrats to label all criticism of democracy as 'elitist'.

However, not all anti-conformist criticism can be dismissed as aristocratic nostalgia. The aristocratic culture of noble eccentricity gradually became culturally marginalised. Instead, new forms of individualist 'eccentricity' emerged within mass culture, especially from the 1960s onwards.

The resistance of democracy to innovation is clearly related to the reluctance to accept any criticism of it. Although pro-democratic theorists often say they are not claiming democracy is perfect, in practice it does have a semi-sacred status.

So in democratic societies, criticism of democracy, even without questioning its fundamental principles, is regarded with suspicion and hostility. Especially, democrats are reluctant to accept that a democratic system can be corrupted. They may try to associate this criticism with fascism: corruption and 'decadence' were indeed major themes of anti-democratic propaganda in the 1930s. Logically, that implies that there is an underlying belief that democracy is in some way 'pure' or 'perfect'. In turn this creates a tendency to social self-worship, shown at its most extreme in the United States. Widespread belief that the existing society is perfect or quasi-sacred creates a climate for complacency and social conformity, not for innovation.

A conservative and anti-utopian bias has specific effects inside a nation state. The 'democratic values' in a democratic nation state are the values of the dominant ethno-cultural group, which first constituted that nation state. Danish democratic values are Danish values; Norwegian democratic values are Norwegian values. Rejection of these values would require an individual moral choice, and the truly democratic citizen does not exercise individual moral judgment, but blindly accepts election results. That mentality is unlikely to produce innovation in the core values: most will be transmitted unchanged from one generation to the next. Paradoxically, the source of values in a democracy is often not the voters, but the voters' ancestors.

7   Democracy in Europe came from the barrel of a gun, or from the power of the dollar, but rarely from the people.

By the end of World War Two in 1945, citizens of Western Europe or the United States found it normal to enforce democracy by war. During the geopolitical stability of the Cold War, however, fear of a nuclear holocaust eroded that attitude. Now, democratic conquest is back, inside and outside Europe. Once again, democratic values are explicitly claimed to justify war.

Most democratic regimes in Europe were enforced from outside anyway – by invasion, occupation or as a condition of economic aid.

The present democracies in Europe do not match the democratic mythology. They are not the product of successive popular uprisings against absolutist monarchies or totalitarian regimes. A far more appropriate term is 'democratic conquest'. There is nothing inherently noble, admirable or moral in such a war of conquest.

The invasion of Iraq, for the declared purpose of 'regime change', is probably the best example of democratic conquest.

8   Model democracies exclude (and often politically persecute) anti-democrats who are often excluded from the use of human and political rights, and anti-democratic parties are sometimes forbidden.

The suppression of political parties is normal practice in established liberal democracies. Western media and governments usually support such 'democratic forces' in other countries: the implication is that they have a special claim to be elected. If democracy were politically neutral, candidates' support for democracy would be irrelevant. In reality, democrats are pro-democracy – as you would expect – as are democratic systems.

It is even possible to define democracy by these characteristics – as a political system where democratic forces hold absolute political power, at least in relation to non-democrats, and where they institutionally persecute anti-democrats. It is not a comprehensive definition, but it is descriptive of most democracies. If democracy were truly a superior system of government, then it would (presumably) not need this harassment of its opponents.

Democrats often claim that living in a democracy is equivalent to 'freedom' – usually meaning political freedom. Nevertheless people are also un-free in democracies – in ways that seem specific to liberal market democracy itself. In general, it is the market that limits social and economic freedom, rather than their political regime.

The operation of the labour market, and the conditions of employment, provide the best examples. Some US employers in the services and retail sectors require their employees to smile permanently, at least in the presence of customers. In a few cases, employers have required plastic surgery as a condition of employment. These are impositions, and restrict personal freedom. The point is that they are apparently culturally specific to the liberal market democracies. Unlike, for instance, poverty or inequality, they are not reported in any historical non-democratic society. Apparently, the market democracies have certain specific un-freedoms, which undermine their claim to be 'free'.

9   Democrats believe it is necessary to maintain the demos as a political unit: this has led to an association of democracy and conservative nationalism, together with a tendency to undermine the legitimacy of democratic decisions.

Modern democracy is inextricably linked to nations, to nationalism and to the nation state as a form of state. Liberal democracy and nationalism developed together in Europe. To a large extent, democracy and nationalism are parallel.

Democracy presupposes a demos, a community in which 'politics' takes place. The demos of modern democracies, and the nation of modern nation states, are the same thing. Western politicians speak interchangeably of 'the nation', 'our nation', 'the people', 'the community'. Democrats, almost by definition, believe it is necessary to maintain the demos as a political unit: this has led to an association of democracy and conservative nationalism.

Most democrats believe that a democracy is legitimate regardless of the criteria used to select the demos. Even a completely closed racial community, with zero immigration, can be a democracy. (According to democratic theory, it would be more legitimate than a dictatorship that allowed free immigration.) Although several Western democracies have a 'right to emigrate', no democracy has ever had a right to immigration. In practice the criteria of citizenship in democracies is biological descent: typically, more than ninety per cent of the citizens acquired that status from their parents.

Opponents of immigration in democratic states even use democracy as an argument – claiming that the cohesion of the political community will be undermined. In the EU, conservative nationalists use the explicit argument that no European-scale geopolitical entity can be legitimate, because there is no European demos.

Democracy therefore reinforces nationalism as a state formation ideology. That is wrong in itself, and it encourages nationalist violence in state formation. New nation states are comparatively rare (about one per year on average), and some were formed without bloodshed – such as Slovakia. But blood was certainly shed to found some others, or to save an existing state. That happened partly because nationalists (on both sides) believed their nation state was essential to democracy.

The equivalence of demos and nation also undermines the legitimacy of democratic decisions. Imagine a referendum on the prohibition of pork, which Muslims consider unclean. If the referendum is held in France or Germany the result will be: no prohibition. If held in Saudi Arabia, there will certainly be prohibition. If the referendum is only for women, worldwide, then there will probably be no prohibition. But if the referendum is only for veiled women, then pork will be forbidden. You can get any result in this referendum, by choosing the unit of decision.

That is a general characteristic of democracy – although to get some decisions, you would have to be very selective. Supporters of democracy claim that a democratic decision is legitimate, because it is the result of a free and fair decision-making process. But what if the opposite decision can be obtained in an equally free and fair democracy, with different voters? Why is one free and fair decision to be respected, and the other not? In practice the legitimation of the decision is historical. The unit of decision is the nation state, based on a historic group: only their decisions are recognised as legitimate.

10 In practice all democracies limit immigration, to preserve existing community.

If democracy was intended to give maximum power of decision to individual persons, then all democracies would allow voting from outside. In reality, the claim to democracy has been treated as equivalent to the sovereignty claim, with sometimes only a few colonial administrators being expelled, sometimes millions of people. People are not only forced into nation states, they are also forced out of them. An election cannot legitimise ethnic cleansing of the electorate before the election.

Historical expulsions are not the main cause of exclusion from voting. Most 'excluded potential voters' were not expelled from the democracy: they never lived there anyway. If the idea of a fixed territorial-political unit was abandoned, all these billions of potential voters could arrive to vote. The reality in democratic states is exactly the opposite: non-resident aliens are never allowed to vote. The fact that a nation is democratic is said to legitimise its immigration laws. But this is a circular reasoning: if the potential immigrants were allowed to vote, they would usually outvote the resident population (and grant themselves citizenship). Again, an election cannot in itself legitimise exclusion from that election, no matter how fair it is. An ethnically pure nation with totally closed borders might still be a perfect democracy, but that does not justify such states: instead it suggests something is wrong with democracy.

Have you had enough? Do you give in? Are you now an anti-democrat? Of course not, because what are the alternatives? However, perhaps I, or in truth Paul Treanor, have convinced you that it is more a case of being a democrat 'warts and all' and that everyone should have a fuller understanding of living in a democracy.

Finally, while trying to get you to think about what you understand by democracy, it would in my opinion be wrong not to introduce you to the ideas of David Held. His book *Models of Democracy* (2008) examines nine models of democracy before developing his own model of 'democratic autonomy' in response to both perceived inadequacies in the traditional models, and the challenge to democracy represented by contemporary developments.

Held's own model actually has two sides. First, a conception of 'democratic autonomy' within the nation state itself; second, an account of the complementary structure of 'cosmopolitan democracy' at the regional and global levels.

We will examine his first model of 'Democratic Autonomy' in this chapter and his second model of 'Cosmopolitan Democracy' in the following chapter, for reasons that will become apparent.

In his model of 'Democratic Autonomy', Held is seeking to think through, from first principles, what a genuinely democratic version of our present society and political system might look like, and then to outline a set of practices and institutions that would be necessary to bring it into being. He attempts to rescue what is most valuable from classic and contemporary models of democracy, while avoiding, as we have just examined, their characteristic weaknesses.

He goes beyond many previous accounts by extending their scope to inequalities associated with race, gender and family life. He makes the case for the return of a more active conception of citizenship, within a broader account of the political sphere. He takes on board the meaning of new technological advances for the possibilities of representation and democracy more generally. In short, he produces a blueprint for how contemporary democracy could be extended, deepened and made real.

What seems to be genuinely new and radical about the (Gieben) model is that it simultaneously confronts and attempts to deal with the following.

1   The economic problem, identified by Marxists and others, of the unequal distribution of property, wealth and power under liberal democracy, and the way individual legal and political rights are weakened by the lack of economic rights.

2   The related problem with the state under modern capitalism, in that its freedom of action, and hence the possibility of genuine democratic control over the policy agenda, is curtailed by corporate power.

3   The 'other' major problem with the state, identified by liberal critics of socialism and of collectivism more generally, of protecting the rights of the individual and 'policing the frontiers of freedom' against overwhelming and unaccountable concentrations of political power, and an expensive and self-interested bureaucracy.

4   The problem in civil society, neglected by most traditional schools of political thought, of the way that inequalities related to gender and race (usually but not always linked to economic inequalities) infringe the claims of citizenship.

5   The problem of legitimacy, and in particular, of apathy and non-participation by a large minority of citizens.

Summary

Libertarianism seeks to prioritise individual liberty and minimise or even abolish the state, whereas egalitarianism is a social philosophy advocating the removal of inequalities among people by state intervention.

Equality of opportunity argues that no arbitrary obstacles should prevent people from achieving those public positions which their talents fit and which their values lead them to seek. Thus, equality of opportunity simply spells out the concept of equality before the law. Equality of outcome is a radically different concept. Government attempts to promote equality of outcome by positive action and discrimination.

Rawls argued for a concept of 'distributive justice', suggesting that inequalities could be compatible with justice if they benefit the worst-off; Nozick argued instead that 'whatever arises from a just situation must itself be just'. He put forward his own notion of 'entitlement justice', which argues that everyone is entitled to all they have acquired, provided they gained their possessions justly, and even if large inequalities result in the process.

The received wisdom in the UK and the US is that democracy, when adequately qualified and explicated, can be seen to lay down a programme of change in and through which pressing, substantive issues will receive a better opportunity for deliberation, debate and resolution than they would under alternative regimes. It offers, in theory at least, a form of politics and life in which there are fair and just ways of deliberating over and negotiating value disputes.

At best, democracy is no more than a system of government, but in Western democracies it has acquired a sacred status, and it is taboo to question it. Yet there is no moral basis for this cult of democracy.

A democracy is different from other possible societies, cultures and regimes: by definition it substitutes itself for them. This substitution is not inherently good: democracies have specific defects, in their culture and society.

Reader's Notes:

11

Endism and the Myth of End

> We have always believed in the power of words to change history.
>
> Vaclav Havel

> Any attempt to impose one's own will or values upon others or to unify the world under a certain model of civilisation will definitely fail … No one economic system is good for all countries. Each must follow its own path as China has.
>
> Qiao Shi

The issues to be explored in this chapter are effectively introduced by Chantal Mouffe.

> As this turbulent century draws to a close, liberal democracy seems to be recognised as the only legitimate form of government. But does that indicate its final victory over its adversaries, as some would have it? There are serious reasons to be skeptical about such a claim. For once, it is not clear how strong is the present consensus and how long it will last. While very few dare to openly challenge the liberal democratic model, the signs of disaffection with present institutions are becoming widespread. An increasing number of people feel that traditional parties have ceased to take their interests into account and extreme right-wing parties are making important advances in many European countries. Moreover, even among those who are resisting the call of the demagogues, there is a marked cynicism about politics and politicians, and this has a very corrosive effect on popular adhesion to democratic values. There is clearly a negative force at work in most liberal democratic societies, which contradicts the triumphalism that we have witnessed since the collapse of Soviet communism.
>
> Mouffe, 2000, p.17

The philosopher Kant pointed out quite logically that the human race must be regressing, progressing or mired in stagnation. Is politics all about obtaining power over people to converge on a desirable and inevitable end? Or are there different and ongoing battles throughout time so that the, human race will always be 'regressing, progressing or mired' with no end in sight?

Does this mean that there will never be an end, and that we live in a world of tragic contingencies, or do you see history as the unfolding of an inevitable narrative?

I have kept the biggest issue until the last so that hopefully you can get your mind around it.

In other words, are your special lenses with their unique mix of value, theory and fact taking you to a perceived end, or are they merely guiding you along an uncertain and never-ending route?

Hopefully you understand by now that the essentially utopian nature of religious philosophies and Marxism makes their position clear. So clearly if you believe in a utopian philosophy you are an 'endist'. In which case please read this chapter in a critical way, trying to accommodate the criticisms of endism with your developing political/religious philosophy.

If you start this chapter as an undecided, then try to use the ideas to help you reach a conclusion as to whether or not there is an ideology that you believe to be the final form of human government.

If after deliberation you reject endism or if you have already rejected endist explanations, then try to clarify in your mind exactly what you put in their place. I am sure there are many readers who may by now be realising they are not endists and who are wondering where that leaves them.

Finally, a special paragraph for the non-utopian religious person i.e. someone who chooses to follow the morality of the religion, chooses not to accept its transcendentalism, but still perceives of themselves as religious. Just one example: how many of you are aware of the Jefferson Bible? Thomas Jefferson believed that the ethical system of Jesus was the finest the world has ever seen. In compiling what has come to be called 'The Jefferson Bible, 1820', he sought to separate those ethical teachings from the religious dogma and other supernatural elements that are intermixed in the account provided by the four Gospels. He presented these teachings, along with the essential events of the life of Jesus, in one continuous narrative. Surely it is a perfectly tenable position for someone to see themselves as religious while living their life by the ethical system of Jesus? If this is you, you might like to examine your position against the main arguments for humanism. 'Think Humanism' on the Internet would be a good start.

So are there any other ideologies that claim to be endist? The main one that we need to consider is that of democratic liberalism.

Therefore in the rest of this chapter we will concentrate first on the democratic liberalist arguments for an end to history and secondly, those philosophers who argue against this and what they see as the 'myth of the end'.

We have just seen Held's argument that democracy is 'the received wisdom in the UK and the US'.

The industrial and post-industrial revolutions were overall periods of progression with the eighties and nineties being increasingly seen as the victory of Western liberal democracy over Marxism.

Churchill once stated that 'It has been said that democracy is the worst form of government except all the others that have been tried.'

These days, however, we no longer see democracy as a sort of necessary evil in the way Churchill did. Instead, today's public in the UK and US are generally strong supporters of democracy. Not only is democracy now generally believed to be the most enlightened form of government, it is also believed to be the only form of government able to offer long-term economic prosperity.

Therefore, on material grounds alone, it is believed that the masses will eventually rebel against any other system, making democracy the only sustainable form of government.

Francis Fukuyama, in fact, declared that history was at an end (although he later qualified this) with the world converging on one final political and cultural resting place.

In 1989, he wrote an article called 'The End of History?' (in the journal *The National Interest*), in which he described what he saw as a growing 'consensus concerning the legitimacy of liberal democracy as a system of government', and the delegitimisation of all rival ideologies.

In the article he summed up his euphoric modern viewpoint.

> The notion that mankind has progressed through a series of primitive stages of consciousness on his path to the present, and that these stages corresponded to concrete forms of social organisation, such as tribal, slave-owning, theocratic and finally democratic-egalitarian societies, has become inseparable from the modern understanding of man ... [We may be in the process of witnessing] the end of history as such: that is, the end point of mankind's ideological evolution and the universalisation of Western liberal democracy as the final form of human government.

The article immediately became very controversial, and was often praised immoderately or identified as a symptom of post-Cold War triumphalism.

Later in his book *The End of History and the Last Man* (1992) he went into greater detail about his philosophical conclusions and concerns about the post-Cold War world.

His thesis had three main components:

- Conflicts between ideologies are the motor of history. History can be thought of as a sequence of stages of ideology with liberal democracy being the final conflict-free development. Fascism and communism have failed and contemporary challengers, religious movements such as Islam and nationalist one such as those found in Eastern Europe fail to provide coherent alternatives in the long term.

- The end of history does not mean the end of all conflict, but no new systems will emerge to supersede liberal democracy.

- The end of history will be a sad time; 'life will come to resemble that of a dog'. (1992, p.331)

His writings encapsulated the idea that after 1989 America appeared to have no serious competitor. This encouraged the view that democracy is for ever. This view was encouraged in the nineties by the Bush administration.

> We've reached another great turning point – and the resolve we show will shape the next stage of the world democratic movement … So it is the policy of the United States to seek and support the growth of democratic movements and institutions in every nation and culture, with the ultimate goal of ending tyranny in our world.
>
> Bush, Second Inaugural Address, January 2004

Now we go on to the myth of end alternatives to 'endism', and to do this of course will require looking at those arguments for 'endism' that are seen as unacceptable. It is very important that you understand here that I will be referring to philosophical objections to 'endism' in general.

COSMOPOLITAN DEMOCRACY

David Held (2008) argues that there are serious questions to be asked about Fukuyama's thesis.

- Liberalism is treated as a unity whereas in reality it is an ideologically contested terrain.
- There is no attempt to explore the balance between liberalism and democracy.
- The whole meaning of democracy and its variants is left unanalysed.
- The extent to which market relations are themselves power relations that can influence the democratic process is ignored.
- There is no examination of the extent to which the liberty to accumulate unlimited economic resources poses a threat to the extent to which political liberty can be enjoyed by all citizens.

- The potential for struggles between different ideological accounts of the nature of the economic system and of desirable alternative forms of economic organisation at national and international levels is seriously under-estimated.

- Liberalism will face increasing challenges as the search for a fair and safer economic order goes on.

- The dismissal of religious and nationalist movements is unconvincing. Fundamentalism is on the rise and not just in terms of Islam.

- The claims with regard to the end of history are implausi-ble. We cannot rule out the possibility of new ideologies with mass mobilising potential that are capable of legiti-mating new regimes, benevolent or authoritarian. History is not closed and the very form and shape of democracy will remain contested for generations to come.

We have already looked at David Held's model of democratic autonomy but Held realises that the model of democratic autonomy he sketches at the national level is not enough. If its aim is to give citizens a genuine degree of democratic control over the forces that shape their lives, then it needs to be linked to a model of cosmopolitan democracy on the world stage.

Held argues that globalisation and the increasing intercon-nectedness of nations and societies contradict some of the fundamental assumptions on which almost all democratic theory has been based, assumptions about:

- the nature of a constituency
- the meaning of representation
- the proper form and scope of political participation
- the relevance of the democratic nation state as the guarantor of the rights, duties and welfare of subjects.

And that in turn raises crucial questions about 'the coherence, viability and accountability of national decision-making entities'. Held concludes that there has certainly been:

- a further 'internationalisation' of domestic activities
- an intensification of decision making in international frameworks
- an alteration of the powers of the modern sovereign state by international and transnational relations.

This limits state autonomy and increasingly impinges on state sovereignty. It fundamentally challenges the idea of the democratic nation state within fixed boundaries, in which a legitimate government pursues policies that determine its own fate and has the consent of those they affect.

Held's analysis has in fact shown a number of ways in which 'the very process of governance seems to be "escaping the categories" of the nation state'. In the face of these momentous developments, 'the model of democratic autonomy … has to be rethought in relation to a series of overlapping local, regional and global structures and processes'. Doing so has led Held to the cosmopolitan model of democracy.

In his final model we are all citizens of a number of overlapping communities – nations, regions, global networks – affected by forces, problems and organisations that transcend national boundaries.

To bring about better democratic control of issues which escape the nation state, 'the territorial boundaries of systems of accountability [must] be restructured'.

For this, we need to rethink the role of the regional and global regulatory agencies, reforming some (like the UN) and installing new ones, to produce a layer of democratic government capable of overriding states 'in clearly defined spheres of activity', where these have 'demonstrable transnational and international consequences'.

If you find these arguments compelling you may feel a cosmopolitan democracy that does not claim endism is the most desirable outcome.

RECOLONIALISATION AND THE RETURN OF THE PROTECTORATE

Re-colonisation is apparently the present specific form of democratic expansion.

The minimal Western definition of democracy, in places such as Kosovo, Timor and now Iraq, is simply 'rule by democratic forces'. In order to rule, these democratic forces must kill (or at least defeat) the anti-democratic forces, usually with Western help. But the 'democratic forces' in such territories are generally a small elite anyway: pro-American, English-speaking and usually upper-middle class.

On this definition, the new democracy leads to the creation of a specific political structure in such territories. Bosnia, Kosovo and Timor have seen a remarkable development in geopolitics, the return of the protectorate.

A military governor governed occupied Iraq, at first, in true colonial style. At the time of writing (2010) the real power in Iraq still rests with the United States. In the new protectorates, the majority of the population are excluded from the political and administrative structure by language and cultural barriers. On Timor, there were riots when the UN administration made knowledge of English a condition for employment – excluding ninety per cent, perhaps even ninety-nine per cent, of the population. Here and in other countries, 'democratic transition' and 'democratisation' are processes administered in English. The protectorate imported administrators, and was externally financed, at least in the beginning. The powers of these administrators are very great – including in Kosovo controlling the choice of music played on local radio stations.

The accurate term for such political regimes is 'colonial'. They display the classic characteristic of a colonial regime, namely the imbalance in the exercise of power. Australian troops imposed a new Portuguese-financed civilian administration in East Timor, but the Timorese population was not given a piece of Australia, to administer by their standards. Nor are they allowed to vote in Australian or Portuguese elections. Kosovars were not given a piece of the United States, where they can tell the local radio stations what music to play.

Yet this one-sided process is described as 'democratisation'. Whatever the justification for the arrival of the troops, the democratisation becomes the justification for their stay. A new type of territorial unit has emerged – the democratising protectorate – but it is firmly within the general category of 'colonies'.

The next twenty years might see a spectacular growth in the number of protectorates. Much of Africa is affected by intermittent or endemic conflicts, including 'official' wars among states. All of these are potential justifications for intervention, and often there are pro-intervention lobbies in the West. The most serious are the Sudan civil war and the interconnected wars in the Democratic Republic of Congo, Rwanda and Burundi.

A few Latin American states with endemic internal conflicts, such as Colombia, might also become protectorates: they are already targets of military intervention in varying degrees. And there are always other justifications available, such as 'weapons of mass destruction', or simply the threat that they exist. A general recolonisation, unthinkable during the Cold War, is now a medium-term possibility.

Colonialism can be distinct from democratic expansionism. The wave of colonisation in Africa from 1870 to 1910, the 'scramble for Africa', was not driven by any ideals of democracy. It was driven by commercial pressure and great-power rivalry, and legitimised by doctrines of racial superiority and the 'civilising mission'. However, the crusade for democracy and human rights could become the 'civilising mission' of a global recolonisation – and democratising protectorates the standard form of colony. In a worst-case scenario, about 1 billion people could live in such protectorates in 2020 – ruled by administrators from Europe and North America, and a local English-speaking elite.

Influenced by a global pro-democracy elite, Western public opinion might genuinely believe that this is the final triumph of democracy. However, in the protectorates, 'democracy' is simply the militarily enforced rule of non-European ethnic groups by imported administrators.

That is no different from the political regime of nineteenth-century colonies, and it is difficult to claim it has any special moral legitimacy, especially when cultural and linguistic barriers separate the administration from the population. 'Liberated Iraq' will no doubt provide more examples of life under a democratising imperialism.

LIBERAL AUTHORITARIANISM

First, Bevin Chu (2007) warns us of the dangers of false assumptions and suggests an experiment. Sit down in front of your PC and Google the words: 'authoritarianism, liberalism, Western, Chinese'.

Type them into the search box in any order you choose, hit return, and you will get page after page on 'Western liberalism' and 'Chinese authoritarianism'.

These pages will very likely assume that the West is heir to a noble tradition of democracy and republicanism rooted in Periclean Greece and Republican Rome, and demand that a 'congenitally authoritarian' China emulate the Land of the Free, Home of the Brave by adopting 'American-style democracy'. Never mind that the Founding Fathers of these United States made quite clear that they detested democracy, and went to great pains to note that they founded a constitutional republic, not a democracy. These pages may well assume that China is heir to an ignoble tradition of 'Oriental despotism', and demand that China jettison its benighted 'Oriental despotism' in favour of enlightened 'Western progressivism'. Never mind that China's unfortunate 'dictatorship of the proletariat' is a Western European political invention, devised in Great Britain by two progressive Western European political philosophers named Karl Marx and Friedrich Engels. As the old joke goes, 'When you assume, you make an ass of you and me.'

This section is heavily indebted to an essay written by William Hooper (February 2008), entitled 'Not the End of History? Democracy vs Authoritarianism'. His arguments are very interesting and I quote from a recent email from him.

> I really believe we are living through very exciting times and the essence of them has not been appreciated. Essentially, I believe we are moving through a change in thinking as dramatic as the Enlightenment. The new realisation is that setting political policy according to moral assumptions not only leads to poor policy-making economically, but also in a sense ethically. Instead, policy should be computed using the scientific method in the most depersonalised manner and this will produce the most 'enlightened' policy. Plato already said as much, but it is hugely

radical. Today our policy-making is set by Christian morality. I am saying that just as the best carpentry is done by carpenters who study the effect of their efforts, the best political policy can be scientifically derived without reference to our preconceived moral concepts.

The rise of China is big news across the world – but everyone is coming at it from the point of view of failed democracy. That is fine but it goes much deeper. The authoritarianism I am really suggesting is much more than a benevolent committee of experts – it is something that is fundamentally different and not values-based.

William Hooper

Liberal democracy as the final form of human government implies of course that there is no room for liberal authoritarianism. However, the democratic arguments that no other system can thrive is now being increasingly challenged by the economic success of China, Malaysia, Singapore, Vietnam and Russia.

The triumphalist pronouncements that the most appropriate formula to attain development is a market economy combined with a liberal democratic polity, and that globalisation is creating conditions for the consolidation of a world of liberal democracies, seem barren and indeed rhetorical in these countries.

Empirically, the realities of the free market economies of (soft) authoritarian states, especially of China, Singapore, Malaysia, and Vietnam, are tangible manifestations that these pronouncements are false.

As in the respective cases of these Asian states, globalisation may in fact mean the end of liberal democracy – characterised by limited accountable government, relatively un-free and unfair competitive elections, partially curtailed substantial civil and political rights, and compromised associational autonomy.

Historically, if there is any cogent lesson that we could draw from the past decades, it is that capitalism can thrive and survive without democracy, and that socialism cannot survive without democracy.

Many orthodox thinkers still see the success of China as an anomaly that cannot last. They believe that corruption is endemic to the authoritarian system and this will eventually cause economic growth in China to stall. Indeed, economic historians point out that many regimes in the past, such as Russia under Stalin and Italy under Mussolini, showed initially high growth rates after adopting an authoritarian model and then fell into decline.

However, there are many who acknowledge that the authoritarian model may be more sustainable than previously believed. Perhaps the level of corruption endemic to the authoritarian system has been overestimated; perhaps also other economic factors benefit from authoritarianism that mitigates the corruption issue. For example, Robert Kagan (2008), foreign-policy analyst at the Carnegie Endowment for International Peace, has said:

> We lived under the illusion that economic success required political liberalisation. All the optimism of the 1990s rested on this assumption. Now it appears that the causality is less certain. Autocratic governments can sustain economic growth, and indeed their economic success helps them sustain their autocracy. This means, if nothing else, that we must be ready for a world in which powerful autocracies endure and perhaps even thrive … The old struggle, the one that long predated the Cold War, has returned.

> Kagan, 2008, p.192

Similarly there are a growing number of economists who are now arguing that the spectacular economic success of 'the China Model', which has been sustained for almost thirty years now, and which dwarfs the achievement of emerging democracies such as India, demonstrates that authoritarianism can, in fact, deliver higher levels of economic growth than democracy, even in the longer term. We must, it is argued, learn from China's example and recognise that our increasingly politicised democracies are failing us.

The United Kingdom is the oldest modern democracy and it typifies the decline. Long ago the disproportionate wealth of the elite allowed them to present the people with a limited selection of candidates supported by patronage, and the UK flourished as a democratic oligarchy. In the 1920s, trade unions upended this system by creating the Labour Party. Today, UK politics is firmly in the control of the masses and many feel the quality of policy making has fallen to an all-time low. Meanwhile, the economy appears to be in terminal decline.

If it becomes clear that a more authoritarian system offers significant economic advantages, it may eventually become popular. Suppose, for the purposes of argument, that an authoritarian system did offer higher rates of economic growth, lower rates of unemployment, better infrastructure, more efficient government spending, lower taxes and a higher standard of living. Would people accept these many advantages in return for reduced policy responsibility?

Given the current disillusionment with politicians, how many people put concern with taxation and economic growth far ahead of politics and appear almost equally happy with any modern civilised government? For example, low tax regimes such as Monaco and Singapore are popular even though they are not democracies.

Also, aside from Switzerland, few countries hold many referendums, yet people do not appear to miss this greater democratic power. If the world's oldest and richest democracies are led by unpopular and untalented leaders such as, until 2008, George Bush and Gordon Brown, is it any wonder that elected governments in Pakistan quickly lose popular support? The Chinese government is, by contrast, extremely popular with its people (although critics complain this is because dissenting opinion is crushed).

Many of you are perhaps thinking, 'If democracy is so bad, why is the USA so relatively rich?' The USA's economic success over the last couple of hundred years could be argued to be less about democracy than it is about policy gridlock, which has kept the government small and allowed the markets to flourish (indeed, the more democratic countries of Europe have fared worse). It can also be argued that in a severe recession, future challenges will require genuine and bold government policy responses that are very difficult to make in a democracy. It will be interesting to see how effectively the UK and USA democracies combat the 2009 economic crisis.

A gridlocked system is less democratic, since elected

representatives have less power, and if the USA does owe much of its success to gridlock, then the case for limiting democracy is obviously proved. The argument can only be about the degree to which democracy should be reined back.

Please remember that liberal authoritarian models attempt to tone down democracy; they certainly do not wish to create an entirely authoritarian country governed by a despotic emperor who rules by fear.

President Musharraf, for example, in Pakistan, described himself as a liberal authoritarian. He missed few opportunities to extol the virtues of a free press and did more than any leader in Pakistan's history to make that freedom available with his decision to open up the airwaves and allow a mushrooming of cable channels. He also believed in freedom of religion, fought against violent extremism and was never credibly accused of corruption, unlike his democratically elected predecessors. He worked closely with the International Monetary Fund (IMF) instituting many laudable reforms that boosted economic growth. Now that he has relinquished the helm, many feel the country is again headed toward disaster.

All this has parallels with the twentieth century rise of the 'political class' which refers to a shift in the balance of power away from the establishment and towards a new generation of professional politicians whose policy much more closely reflects the opinions of the voting public. For example, critics accused the UK Prime Minister Tony Blair elected in 1997 of introducing new levels of 'spin' to democratic government. Blair developed very close relations with the media and employed a tabloid newspaper editor as government spokesman.

Although the general public complain about spin, they clearly fail to work with political argument at much more than the superficial or emotional level, which is, of course, the cause of the problem. This is not to say that education levels today are worse than before – in the past the general public probably tended to set more store by the perceived personality of their king than they did his policy. The Roman Emperor Caligula was popular with his people because he projected an endearing public profile; neither his real personality nor his policy-making actually deserved merit.

For all the modern idealism, Churchill's idea of necessary evil keeps creeping back. Is democracy in fact a singularly unsuccessful model which is unapplied to any other field of endeavour, but which exists in government only to prevent greater evil? If so, is every other possible model really so at risk of greater evil?

What about the USA? Although socialism was popular with the masses, many in the elite feared it. Where the elite resisted the will of the masses popular revolt often ended in socialist tyranny. Government in the USA also resisted the popular tide, e.g. with the 1918 Sedition Act, but much more effectively. Indeed, the fight against socialism and communism became a cornerstone of American policy. Up until at least the 1990s the USA was arguably the least socialist country in the world. Even today it remains the only major industrialised nation without universal health care (although this is promised by Obama). Arguably the economic success of the USA today once hinged on the ability of its politicians to manipulate or override their public.

Alan Greenspan has described democracy as a safety release value in that a notionally democratic system manipulated by the elite allowed the air to escape safely from the socialist pressure cooker. Thus the entire Cold War, escalated by the US, did not necessarily reflect a genuine reflection of the Soviet threat, but could be argued to be rather a fight, by the American elite, to suppress a political system which the masses might have embraced. However, although this smoke-screen of fear and misinformation had the laudable goal of manipulating democracy, the loss of transparency became so great that even the elite began to lose clarity. Today these dangers stalk Putin, and some modern liberal authoritarians are more wary.

In the UK, by contrast, thanks to the creation of the Labour party that was funded by the trade unions, democratic government began embracing socialism in the 1920s. Ramsay MacDonald rose from humble origins to become the first Labour Prime Minister in 1924, although his first government lasted less than one year. Labour returned to power in 1929 but was soon overwhelmed by the crisis of the Great Depression. In 1931 MacDonald formed a 'National Government' in which a majority of MPs were from the Conservatives. As a result, he was expelled from the Labour Party who accused him of 'betrayal'. Nevertheless, socialism had taken root.

At the end of the World War Two, the pace of socialist change in the UK picked up considerably. Experts in financial markets began moving funds offshore; e.g. investment in the non-democratic UK colony of the Bahamas boomed. The Attlee government responded to this capital flight with foreign exchange controls that lasted for the next thirty years or so. By the 1970s, the UK was one of the most socialist countries in the advanced world with a marginal rate of income tax peaking at ninety-eight per cent. Some socialist policies, such as the creation of the National Health Service, were successful, but many others were not. Indeed, the economic health of the nation deteriorated to such an extent that in 1976 the UK was put on to an IMF programme.

Eventually, the UK electorate tired of socialism and in 1979 they elected as Prime Minister the pragmatic right-wing politician Margaret Thatcher. Thatcher's reforms, which were based on received economic wisdom rather than ground-breaking new ideas, eventually transformed the UK from being one of the poorest countries in Western Europe to one of the wealthiest.

France never sank as low as the UK in the 1970s; consequently the electorate have not fully tired of socialism, and therefore they still refuse to allow Thatcherite reforms in France. As a result they are poorer than the UK electorate today. Critics of democracy claim that this example typifies the erratic and snail-paced evolution of democratic economic policy.

On a more micro level the potential advantages of authoritarian infrastructure and planning permission decisions are even more apparent. It is interesting to compare Beijing's new airport with Heathrow's Terminal 5 in the UK. China's stunning new airport was designed by Norman Foster and is currently over twice as large as the next largest airport in the world (including Heathrow Terminals 1–5 added together). The total time from design, through construction, to opening of the airport was just four years. By contrast, the possibility of a new Heathrow terminal was first mooted in 1982. In 1989 an architect was selected to design it. In 1992 BAA announced it would be submitting a planning application. In 1993 the application was submitted. In 1995 a public enquiry began considering it. In 1999 they gave the go-ahead. In 2001 the government validated the result and gave the project planning permission. In 2008 construction was completed and the airport opened. The democratic process arguably turned a four-year project into a twenty-five-year project. Even after all this, no new runways were built at Heathrow, leaving the problem of chronic congestion unaddressed.

Many experts also argue that replacing Heathrow with a new airport in the Thames Estuary linked by a high-speed train to central London (China's Maglev airport train could make the journey in fifteen minutes) would be a much better option, not least because flight paths over land could be virtually abolished. However, UK politicians regard this option as hopelessly ambitious and therefore impractical in the democratic UK, regardless of its theoretical advantages.

Many people on all sides of the debate believe that the democratic model is struggling to respond to three huge issues: globalisation, climate change and the depletion of natural resources.

The democratic system cannot easily adapt to a radically changing world in which difficult and painful decisions have to be made. For example, heavily unionised US car manufacturers are left trailing by foreign competitors. In the African county of Mali, the average woman gives birth to 7.38 children, but in authoritarian China the 'one-child policy' has cut fertility rates from over 5 births per woman to 1.7 in 2009. Although global warming threatens the planet, the irrational masses in democratic Europe continue to fight over the merits of nuclear power; meanwhile the rational Chinese government prepares for cheap CO_2 free nuclear mass production.

Adam Posen (1998) argues that within developed countries today, enlightened policy making often appears inversely correlated to democratic power.

> The irony for those who have been congenitally suspicious of excessive power being concentrated in Brussels is that the more the central body has had authority over economic policy, the

greater the liberalising influence – whether it was the US breaking down barriers to interstate commerce or the Commission implementing the single market. Where and when the member states have retained dominance over regulation and enforcement, as in insurance or property in the US, or in state aid to favoured companies or professional certifications in the EU, the results have been illiberal and economically harmful ... The alternative to a strong Brussels is not a decentralised free market and minimal government interference. It is greater political capture of economic policy-making and abuse of authority by member states and sub-national governments. Politicisation is more likely and more obstructive to market competition when done by local or member governments than when the federal authority has competence. Subsidiarity is in many cases an invitation to corruption, entrenchment of incumbents and horse-trading of handouts. Too many political veto points equals too many opportunities for extortion.

Posen, 1998, p.88

As the power for self-interested voting is diluted, policy improves – we see the worst policy at local level, better policy at national level, and the best policy at international level.

At the heart of this argument, Posen is arguing that government policy is in fact mostly obvious, and democratic voting often encourages only ill-advised, self-interested decision making.

Even some conventional thinkers have lost faith in democracy for Africa. In the late nineteenth century, the European imperial powers engaged in a major territorial scramble and occupied most of the continent of Africa, creating many colonial nation states, and leaving only two independent nations. The colonial governments were, of course, completely undemocratic as far as black representation was concerned.

In the 1950s, Tunisia was the first colony to win independence and Zimbabwe, in 1980, was the last. However, in South Africa and Zimbabwe the large white population developed a system of second-class citizenship for other races. This system followed the example of the Jim Crow Laws in the USA that circumvented having to give black people the power to vote in southern states, introduced after the abolition of slavery and repealed in 1965. As a result, the white South Africans were able to retain control until an equitable settlement was forced upon them by the prospect of civil war in 1994.

Since the end of colonisation Africa has failed to develop, and in many case the standards of living are thought to be lower than those in colonial days.

Despite democracy, constant tribal conflict, corruption and poor policy decisions have dogged the continent. More recently, the advantages South Africa gained by having more sophisticated management of their country until 1994 appear to be coming apart. Remarkably, it appears that an authoritarian government of educated colonialists, set only upon exploiting the region for profit with little or no regard for the local people, offers the uneducated Africans a higher standard of living than democracy. Hence some are welcoming China's recent increasing involvement in Africa.

Liberal authoritarianism has its roots in the idea that economic policy today is well understood by experts (but not by the masses). From this follows the idea that it should concentrate on improving economic efficiency using economic expertise and it should interfere as little as possible with national moral preferences. Indeed, frequent referendums for soft issues would help endear the public to authoritarian economic policy. For example: should euthanasia be legalised? Let the people decide. Should the names of sex offenders be published? Economists do not care. Should the UK host the Olympics? Give the people the numbers and let them choose. However: should the government be allowed to use compulsory purchase orders to knock down 500,000 existing homes and build something new? Ask for public input, but let the policy experts decide. Should we build nuclear plants? Leave this one entirely to the scientists and the economists – it is an important issue and public opinion here is worthless.

In fairness, this idea of moral democracy and economic authoritarianism is more complex. Consider health care. Political gridlock in the USA, until Obama, has left health care to the market and the situation is clearly economically undesirable with sixteen per cent of GDP (the highest in the world) going on care, despite twenty-five per cent of the population having no insurance. Universal health care looks like the best policy option even on economic grounds, so at least this decision is easy.

Now, turning to the UK: Margaret Thatcher spent approximately six per cent of the UK's GDP on health care before Tony Blair raised that to eight per cent, much to the satisfaction of most voters. How should the rate be set in our liberal oligarchy? An economist could calculate the best spend by optimising GDP. Given access to antibiotics, death and incapacity levels plunge, therefore pushing growth upwards. However, many more expensive treatments are much less likely to be productive. Clearly this is the wrong metric – it is a moral issue as well. However, handing the emotional masses the decision could drive the level irrationally high (the odds of winning the lottery are pointlessly small but seventy per cent of the UK public like to play; they simply do not mind that statistic). It is a very hard problem because we cannot get at the utility curves for income versus heath easily – which is what the experts would try to target, according to the constitution. Nevertheless, it is far more likely to be solved by a panel of experts and some experimentation than it is by popular political representatives.

Russia has achieved an authoritarian democracy by controlling the media. It is an interesting system because in the event of real incompetence, North-Korea-style, no amount of manipulation would prevent the government being ejected. In the meantime, however, the government massages public opinion in an intelligent direction, and it can also lift the public. For example, in the USA the *Financial Times* reported that thirty per cent of Americans believe, to some extent, in a September 11th CIA conspiracy theory. If this were the consequence of a free press, perhaps Plato would encourage us to find ways to constrain it. The complaint against the Russia system today is that media censorship may have been used to suppress even reasoned debate of government failure. Liberal authoritarian models do not allow this. Control of the masses might be acceptable, but intelligent dissent must be allowed.

SPATIAL ALTERNATIVES TO THE SYSTEM OF DEMOCRATIC STATES

By now it should be clear that democracy is not a one-country regime, nor a characteristic of single states. We have seen Held's ideas on cosmopolitan democracy. We will now consider some spatial alternatives.

A few examples will suffice. The simplest spatial definition of a democracy is that decisions are taken by those who live in an area or zone, and that these decisions then apply to that area (zone). The hypothetical opposite to this is only possible on an infinite land surface: namely, that every possible use of a zone is allocated a sufficiently large territory to allow effective existence of that zone. Or, in social terms, that every possible form of society is allocated sufficient territory to exist. But the planet's surface is finite, which must therefore preclude some form of territorial allocation.

The conventional definition of a state, learned by most students, is that a state consists of a territory, a government that controls all or part of it and its population. At its simplest, the extent to which that population controls the government determines the degree of democracy. Democracy concerns specific territory: here again is the symbiosis of democracy and the nation state. In a world of nations, a democratic regime governs a historically constituted people inhabiting a specific territory – a classic nation state. Exceptions to that principle are very rare. In July 2000, a convention in Prague proposed European Union recognition of the Roma (a subgroup of the Romani people who live primarily in Central and Eastern Europe), as a non-territorial nation, with their own Parliament. However, this is so completely contrary to the standard pattern of one parliament, for one nation, on one territory, that recognition is unlikely. Recognition of a non-national territory, as such, is even more unlikely.

Now let us consider a definition of a post-democratic state: a state is a territory with a purpose.

If the purpose of a territory is fixed before it has a population, obviously there can be no democratic process. Any suggestion of this type is treated with deep suspicion among liberal political theorists.

Three formal characteristics define the spatial order of a post-democratic world.

- State formation is free and multiple.
- States formed do not necessarily have an initial population.
- The population migrates to occupy states formed.

In other words, the transition to post-democratic space involves the migration of the population of the earth, to achieve a maximum of possible states, or at least a plurality of states.

The main obstacle to such a migration is not economic feasibility, or the transport system, but political resistance. Ignoring that issue, and assuming such a migration, what kind of states could be formed?

The least productive grounds for state formation are the irreconcilable ethical universalisms. It would be possible to partition countries with abortion controversies (Poland or Ireland, for example) into two states: one where abortion is legal, one where it is not. However, very few people would be satisfied with this: they regard it as a moral issue, concerning in principle the whole world. On the issue of abortion, there is no ethical or cultural relativism, and there is no territorial solution to the problem of conflicting universal beliefs. State formation on this basis could only be a form of territorial clarification, an illustration of the ethical divide.

A second category of possible states allows for evasion of moral wrong or injustice. This category includes forms of 'refuge states' – in effect, an extension of the principle of asylum, to state formation by victims of injustice. If no existing state offers asylum protection, a new state offers the only effective guarantee of protection from discrimination, persecution, injustice, racism and oppression. There is already one state that claims refuge from persecution as legitimation for its formation: Israel. However, Israel has never used that as the only justification of its existence – it relies instead on the more usual claim to a national homeland for a specific people.

A third type of possible state is founded on non-universal ideologies or beliefs. As an example, it is possible to imagine state formation on the basis of existing political parties. In the electoral geography of Western Europe, some regions have long-term political preferences, over centuries. (Political geographers in France have been the most successful in tracing these regional preferences.) Even medium-term concentrations of support for political parties, over one generation approximately, could serve as a basis for state formation. In practice, there are legitimate objections to using political parties as the basis for division of territory. They would collectively gain a near-monopoly of territory, but their active membership is rarely more than one per cent or two per cent of the population.

A fourth category relates to certain semi-political historical preferences, usually ignored in political theory. Many people have a preferred 'Golden Age' related to their political views. For European Christian Democrats, it is often the Catholic Middle Ages, for classic liberals, the free-trade era of the early nineteenth century. If people wish to return to the past in this way – in whole or in part – they could be given territory to do so. State formation, based on the reconstruction of a preferred past, is a feasible way of dividing territory – 'nostalgia states'. For instance, when the territorial integrity of Italy seemed under threat during the last twenty years, proposals for the reconstitution of the Papal States surfaced. The Italian nation state has proved more durable than expected, but the political consequences of a revived papal state are interesting. Traditionalist Catholics from all over Europe would gain a 'homeland' to which they could migrate.

These first four categories are related to familiar issues in political theory, but they are far from exclusive. There are many other possible bases of state formation. Among existing nation states it is possible to find differences in social organisation and constitutional tradition. But these form the tip of a huge iceberg.

Many options of this kind are so far apart that they could not be accommodated in the same state. A modern nation state assumes some underlying cultural unity or shared basic values: 'multicultural' might work, but not 'multi-constitutional'.

This is an indicative list of the types of option involved.

- Social organisation: is society hierarchical or egalitarian? Is the family treated as the basic unit of society? Is the educational and workplace tradition hereditary or meritocratic?

- Legal systems: are there universal laws, or separate group laws and courts (such as existed in many colonial territories)?

- Economic structure: is there a central bank and is there a single currency? Are there any banks and other modern financial institutions? Is there a free market?

- Organisation of production: is it competitive-entrepreneurial, or centrally planned, or organised by some form of non-competitive organisations?

- Taxation: is there a unitary tax system? Is control of expenditure centralised or can the individual influence it? Does the tax system allow conscientious objection to, for instance, military expenditure?

- Military organisation: is there any armed force at all? Is there a centralised army, or a citizen militia?

- Ownership and property rights: is there any restraint on transfer and use of property? Is wealth systematically redistributed?

- Constitutional structure: is the state centralised, federal, or confederal? Is there any separation of powers? Is there any separation of church and state?

- Public administration: is it bureaucratic, interventionist, arbitrative or traditionalist in style?

- Parliamentary and electoral systems: is there a parliament? Does it have more than one chamber? Which electoral system is used?

- External relations: is the state pragmatic or idealist in its dealings with other states? Does it recognise other states? Does it trade – or strive for autarky?

The reservoir of territorial alternatives to democracy is vast!

Again, many of these options are related to familiar political controversies. However, an entirely different factor would probably be the main driver of new state formation, in a post-democratic world. It is a factor generally ignored in state theory and political geography: technology. The common view is that technology is a unit, developing in a linear fashion through history.

This picture of unity is false: there are technologies, in the plural. Technologies contradict each other, they are opposed to each other and they compete with each other. And in principle, each technology requires its own state, to guarantee its existence.

In existing nation states, there is a tendency to standardise not only national culture and language, but also technology. This tendency will, in the long term, produce a world order of national technologies, parallel to the world order of nation states. There is no guarantee that these national technologies will differ among themselves: they might be only superficially different. The number of nation states in any case limits them. In the long term, that will limit or block technological change. Technological state formation does for a 'dissident' technology what the technology cannot do itself – secede.

Energy technologies in Europe are a good example. The trend at present is to coordinate national policies involving a mix of technologies – coal, natural gas, oil, solar energy, wind and nuclear energy. In reality, the mix is dominated by some technologies, and others are marginalised.

Creating a plurality of states, to guarantee a plurality of energy technologies, would produce a totally different Europe. It would be a continent divided into the states of Carbonia, Methania, Petrolia, Solaria, Aeolia and Nuclearia, among others. Such possible states, with a specific technology as their core value, are alien to conventional political theory – yet this list is only one possible division. There are many technologies, and many possible combinations.

MODERNITY AS A NON-CONVERGENT FORCE

John Gray (1998, 2007) is a major critic of endism. He attacks the confident, post-Cold War view of the world that over time we would all converge around modernity, democracy and affluence, where countries were judged by how far down this road they had travelled.

He argues in fact that some have not moved at all and some have decided to go in the opposite direction. To Gray, the historical inevitablism of the eighties and nineties lies in ruins, and modernity is not a convergent force. It will produce different outcomes in different societies.

Determinism is the ideology that has produced a number of corpses, whether it is the economic determinism of Marx, the biological determinism of Nazism or the religious determinism of Christianity and Islam.

The technocratic idea that the Internet is a globally unifying force is simply nonsense; it is just as likely to produce division and conflict.

The Fukuyama idea that history will end with global liberal democracy is patently not proving to be the case.

For Gray, the ideology of globalisation itself is now at an end. The free market it requires is not the culturally neutral balm it was taken to be, but a distinct Western system, which to others may seem absurd, brutal, illogical or blasphemous.

What evidence is there of the encroachment of Western liberal democracy into the Arab world? Looking at the developments in the Middle East and the economic collapse in the Western world in October 2008, is it too difficult to understand that from the mix of - isms in their lenses, they do not believe it or want it? From the perspective of Jerusalem or Gaza, the end of history looks more like the bang of chaos than the whimper of liberal democracy.

From a different perspective Robert Kagan (2009) describes the collapse of the delusion that the fall of communism heralded the neo-Hegelian 'end of history' and the neo-Kantian idea of a 'world transformed'.

He argues that Americans deluded themselves that commerce would be the only form of future competition and Europeans foolishly imagined that the world would be irresistibly attracted to the EU's vision of pooled sovereignty, human rights law and supranational institutions.

Instead, there has been a reversion to powerful nation states vying for dominance with the various autocratic powers especially asserting themselves on the back of their new-found economic power.

In the Chinese case this involved their savers assuming huge tranches of American debt to finance a consumer boom. In addition, Kagan observes that 'Africa is teeming with Chinese from Sudan to Zimbabwe', and China is giving considerable support for Pakistan.

In Russia, Putin has used gas and oil wealth to bully neighbours and increase defence spending by twenty per cent annually for the past four years. He has also sold large amounts of military hardware to China.

Iran is also fully aware of American intention to construct a broad Sunni coalition from Egypt to the Gulf.

Thus Kagan concludes that we are back to what Lord Palmerston called a world where there are no friends, just interests and as Kagan's book title suggests, *The Return of History and the End of Dreams*.

AGONISTIC PLURALISM

First, where does agonism derive from?

> Agonism implies a deep respect and concern for the other; indeed, the Greek *agon* refers most directly to an athletic contest oriented not merely toward victory or defeat, but emphasising the importance of the struggle itself – a struggle that cannot exist without the opponent. Victory through forfeit or default, or over an unworthy opponent, comes up short compared to a defeat at the hands of a worthy opponent – a defeat that still brings honour. An agonistic discourse will therefore be one marked not merely by conflict but, just as importantly, by mutual admiration.
>
> Chambers, 2001, p.35

Agonism is a political theory that emphasises the potentially positive aspects of political conflict. It accepts a permanent place for such conflict, but seeks to show how we might accept and channel it positively.

Agonists are sceptical about the capacity of politics to eliminate, overcome or circumvent deep divisions within our society – of class, culture, gender, ideology and so on. They argue that the theories that have been the backbone of political theory for the past thirty years are essentially optimistic about the possibility of finding a harmonious and peaceful pattern of political and social cooperation.

Agonists believe this optimism is unjustified and, hence, reorientate political theory to another question: how should we deal with irreducible difference? In the view of agonists, traditional viewpoints that keep their eyes fixed on forms of utopian cooperation have failed to respond usefully to the messiness of contemporary political practice.

Thus, agonism can be seen as a response to the perceived failures of strands of idealism and materialism to accord with reality, and to provide useful responses to contemporary problems.

> Democratic theory needs to acknowledge the ineradicability of antagonism and the impossibility of achieving a fully inclusive rational consensus.

> Mouffe, 2000, p.165

Agonism is avowedly pluralist in its political outlook. It sees political tensions as having an essential place in society, but believes that they should be approached discursively, not in an attempt to eliminate 'the other'.

Agonists believe that we should design democracy so as to optimise the opportunity for people to express their disagreements. However, they also maintain we should not assume that conflict could be eliminated, given sufficient time for deliberation and rational agreement. In other words, conflict has a non-rational or emotional component. These two positions mean that they are opposed to aspects of deliberative theories of democracy, because it gives a rationalist picture of the aspirations of democracy.

> I use the concept of agonistic pluralism to present a new way to think about democracy which is different from the traditional liberal conception of democracy as a negotiation among interests and is also different from the model which is currently being developed by people like Jurgen Habermas and John Rawls. While they have many differences, Rawls and Habermas have in common the idea that the aim of the democratic society is the creation of a consensus, and that consensus is possible if people are only able to leave aside their particular interests and think as rational beings. However, while we desire an end to conflict, if we want people to be free, we must always allow for the possibility that conflict may appear and to provide an arena where differences can be confronted. The democratic process should supply that arena.

> Mouffe, 2000, p.27

COMPLEXITY ECONOMICS

Complexity economics is the application of complexity science to the problems of economics. It is one of the four Cs of a new paradigm surfacing in the field of economics. The four Cs are complexity, chaos, catastrophe and cybernetics. This new mode of economic thought rejects traditional assumptions that imply the economy is a closed system that eventually reaches an equilibrium. Instead, it views economies as open complex adaptive systems with endogenous evolution. Complex systems do not necessarily settle to equilibrium – even ideal deterministic models may exhibit chaos, which is distinct from both random (non-deterministic) and analytic behaviour.

The table below illustrates the differences between the complexity perspective and classical economics. Beinhocker (2007) proposes five concepts that distinguish complexity economics from traditional economics. The first five categories are Beinhocker's synthesis; the last four are from W. Brian Arthur as reprinted in David Colander's *The Complexity Vision*.

	Complexity Economics	Traditional Economics
Dynamic	Open, dynamic, non-linear systems, far from equilibrium	Closed, static, linear systems in equilibrium
Agents	Modelled individually; use inductive rules of thumb to make decisions; have incomplete information; are subject to errors and biases; learn to adapt over time; heterogeneous agents	Modelled collectively; use complex deductive calculations to make decisions; have complete information; make no errors and have no biases; have no need for learning or adaptation (are already perfect), mostly homogeneous agents

Networks	Explicitly model bi-lateral interactions between individual agents; networks of relationships change over time	Assume agents only interact indirectly through market mechanisms (e.g. auctions)
Emergence	No distinction between micro/macro economics; macro patterns are emergent result of micro level behaviours and interactions.	Micro- and macroeconomics remain separate disciplines
Evolution	The evolutionary process of differentiation, selection and amplification provides the system with novelty and is responsible for its growth in order and complexity	No mechanism for endogenously creating novelty, or growth in order and complexity
Technology	Technology fluid, endogenous to the system	Technology as given or selected on economic basis
Preferences	Formulation of preferences becomes central; individuals not necessarily selfish	Preferences given; individuals selfish
Origins from Physical Sciences	Based on Biology (structure, pattern, self-organised, life cycle)	Based on nineteenth-century physics (equilibrium, stability, deterministic dynamics)
Elements	Patterns and Possibilities	Price and Quantity

If you accept the arguments of complexity economics, this has considerable implications for politics and policy. It does in fact have the potential to make the historical framing of politics obsolete.

Beinhocker (2007) argues that the Left–Right framing of issues is now redundant. He argues that history has clearly not ended as witnessed, for example, by the mobs on the streets of Seattle protesting at the 1999 World Trade Organisation meeting.

He concedes that there is a centrist consensus that agrees that markets and states each have a role to play in society. However, there is now an intellectual vacuum – if the two poles symbolised by Marx and Smith are both wrong, then where is the new coherent framework to replace them? The so-called 'third way' (Giddens, 2000) is no more than a set of political tactics for winning elections from the middle ground rather than a truly new economic paradigm.

Complexity economics has the potential to fill this vacuum. The fundamental question is how best to evolve rather than Left versus Right.

CONCLUSION

Let us start by suggesting that it is questionable as to whether democratic liberalism seems to be an example of historical determinism as rigid as Marx, Christianity or Islam.

Please do not take the word 'rigid' in a critical sense but merely in that it is conveying a historical story with a beginning and an end. The idea that global liberal democracy will be the end of history is clearly debatable.

Whereas endists see history as the unfolding of an inevitable narrative, those who argue for the 'myth of end' see it as chaos, a random directionless tale of chance and uncertainty.

Summary

Is politics all about obtaining power over people to converge on a desirable and inevitable end? Or are there different and ongoing battles throughout time so that the human race will always be 'regressing, progressing or mired' with no end in sight?

The essentially utopian nature of religious philosophies and Marxism makes their position clear as endist philosophies. The notion that mankind has progressed through a series of primitive stages of consciousness on his path to the present, and that these stages corresponded to concrete forms of social organisation, such as tribal, slave-owning, theocratic and finally democratic-egalitarian societies, has become inseparable from the modern understanding of man. We may be in the process of witnessing the end of history as such: that is, the end point of mankind's ideological evolution and the universalisation of Western liberal democracy as the final form of human government.

The claims with regard to the end of history are implausible. We cannot rule out the possibility of new ideologies with mass mobilising potential that are capable of legitimating new regimes, benevolent or authoritarian. History is not closed and the very form and shape of democracy will remain contested for generations to come.

The next twenty years might see a spectacular growth in the number of protectorates. A general recolonisation – unthinkable during the Cold War – is now a medium-term possibility.

In the face of these momentous developments, the model of democratic autonomy has to be rethought in relation to a series of overlapping local, regional and global structures and processes. Doing so leads to the cosmopolitan model of democracy.

We lived under the illusion that economic success required political liberalisation. All the optimism of the 1990s rested on this assumption. Now it appears that the causality is less certain. Autocratic governments can sustain economic growth, and indeed their economic success helps them sustain their autocracy. This means, if nothing else, that we must be ready for a world in which powerful autocracies endure and perhaps even thrive. The reservoir of territorial alternatives to democracy is vast.

The historical inevitablism of the eighties and nineties lies in ruins, and modernity is not a convergent force. It will produce different outcomes in different societies.

Agonists believe that we should design democracy so as to optimise the opportunity for people to express their disagreements. However, they also maintain we should not assume that conflict could be eliminated, given sufficient time for deliberation and rational agreement.

Complexity economics argues that the fundamental question is not Left versus Right; it is how best to evolve.

Reader's Notes:

12

Conclusion: Your/My Political Philosophy

Hegemony has to be not just well-intentioned but also prudent and smart in its exercise of power.

Francis Fukuyama

I don't know whether this world has a meaning that transcends it. But I know that I cannot know that meaning and that it is impossible for me just now to know it. What can a meaning outside my condition mean to me? I can understand only in human terms ... I do not want to found anything on the incomprehensible. I want to know whether I can live with what I know and with that alone.

Albert Camus

Well, it's time to go to the opticians for your fitting. Notice I did not say 'final' fitting as I hope you have realised an enquiring and thoughtful mind will always be making some modifications to the composition of the lenses.

This is what I hope you have achieved.

Generally:

- an understanding as to what political philosophy is all about
- the beginnings of your own personal political philosophy
- a greater sense of confidence in your ability to articulate how you think the way you do about political theory.

Specifically, a greater understanding of:

- the political philosophy behind the way you vote
- how religious beliefs and political philosophy interrelate
- the relevance of Marxist ideas today
- the effectiveness of democracy and possible alternatives
- the ways forward for global capitalism bearing in mind the need for social cohesion and environmental conservation
- the importance of individual conscience
- the idea that we possibly live in a world of tragic contingencies without historical inevitability.

Finally, what about the six statements that you were initially asked to agree or disagree with that were to do with the three basic questions of political philosophy.

What have you got written down? Try to write something now, summarising your views.

After some fifty years mulling it over, here is my current attempt. My effort must of course be longer than yours because I must try as best I can to explain things in a way that you can clearly understand. 'If you can't say it clearly, you don't understand it yourself.' (John Searle).

My personal political philosophy is guided by the fact that from an early age I have always been attracted to both existentialism and humanism.

I first became interested in political philosophy in the fifties and sixties (my teens and twenties) when existentialism was very much in vogue. In some ways it is now somewhat dated, but in others it still provides for me the most acceptable answers to key questions with regard to the inherent difficulties of freedom and free will.

My early reading led me to realise that Milton's Satan in *Paradise Lost* and Goethe's Mephisto in *Faust* are the literary embodiments of free will. Both of these characters represent the existential ideal: they accept their fates, however absurd, in return for a form of freedom.

In *Paradise Lost*, Satan states 'The mind is its own place, and in itself / Can make a Heaven of Hell, a Hell of Heaven.' He is surely saying any individual can create their own heaven or hell on earth in the way they live their life.

At the start of F W Murnau's film *Faust* (1926), there is an unleashing of the forces of darkness, the evil dead, circling the earth. The Devil and God confront one another. 'The earth is mine!' Mephisto says. His opponent counters, 'Man belongs to God.'

Man is a battleground, with two grand adversaries claiming ownership, a sly metaphor for humanity's lack of self-determination. According to Murnau, it is irrelevant whether God or the Devil wins, because in either case man (Faust), loses. Religion, superstition and mythology are determining man's nature, depriving him of the free will that is his due.

Exploring this further led to existentialism, the first book I read being *The Myth of Sisyphus* by Camus. I was fascinated by his statement

> There is but one truly serious philosophical problem and that is suicide. Judging whether or not life is or is not worth living amounts to answering the fundamental question of philosophy. All the rest ... come afterwards.

> Camus, *The Myth of Sisyphus*, p.3

In this essay, Camus introduces his philosophy of the absurd: man's futile search for meaning, unity and clarity in the face of an unintelligible world devoid of God and eternity. Essentially the absurd is the meaningless routine in everyday life that arises when man and the world come face to face, and man 'feels an alien, a stranger ... this divorce between man and his life, the actor and his setting, is properly the feeling of absurdity' (p.6).

Camus writes 'there are but two methods of thought' for overcoming the absurd: 'the method of La Palisse and the method of Don Quixote' (p.4).

Either it is the method of fighting what is worth fighting, or the method of creating something to fight solely for the purpose of overcoming.

Does the realisation of the absurd require suicide? Camus

answers no: it requires revolt. The only way to escape the absurd is to remain aware of it and actively choose. In short, just to keep doing.

Integrating Camus's absurd with the myth of Sisyphus is obvious; the routine of pushing a rock up a hill only to have it fall ad infinitum is the most basic model of the absurd. The endless system of promotions, supposedly a realisation of the American Dream, is no different than Sisyphus's rock. Every day people struggle to provide themselves with food, shelter, and a few personal possessions, all the while convincing themselves that this is meaningful. However, rarely are those personal possessions meaningful, much less the food and shelter enjoyed. None of those things reflect a life of purpose and conscious action, but a vicious cycle filling their life with the absurd.

The absurd must be accepted and freedom of thought and action chosen over the mindlessness of the absurd.

Camus is suggesting that our instinct for life is much stronger than our reasons for suicide and if asked for the reasons why we do not choose suicide, he suggested two types of answer.

- First those (Kafka and Kierkegaarde) who propose taking 'a leap of faith', by placing their hopes in a God beyond this world.

- Second, those, like myself, who believe that such meaning as there is in human existence is found or imposed by humans themselves; no purpose for mankind is imposed from outside.

This latter route is the more difficult to follow but I found in existentialism the most meaningful explanation as to the implications of this.

Which brings us to the relevant ideas of Jean-Paul Sartre. I will start with extracts from a first-person lecture given by James Haught in 1991 at the University of Charleston.

Good evening. My name is Jean-Paul Sartre ... I want to assure you that, regardless of what you've heard, my life had a beneficial goal: I sought to help people understand the reality of their

229

individual lives amid the world's chaos and madness and to impress upon them the importance of struggling to improve the human condition.

My message was simple: we are born into an unfathomable existence that has no discernible cosmic or divine purpose – a life often absurd or horrible – and the only valid values are the ones we create for ourselves.

Existence – the reality that engulfs us – is the heart of my philosophy of existentialism. Existence is all there is and we must look at it with the clinical eye of a scientist.

Human behaviour is a bizarre jumble of affection and hostility, greed and generosity, violence and gentleness. The Chinese concept of the yin and yang – good and evil mixed in each personality – correctly describes the human psyche. The world abounds with love and with horror. People are capable of terrible cruelties to each other. Your modern America has 23,000 murders a year and 100,000 rapes, mostly for no logical reason. 'Hell is other people' is a key line in one of my plays.

Meanwhile, random luck governs much of life. Chance gives some people wealth or intellect or health, while others are born to misery and early death. By sheer accident some are privileged Americans and some are starving Ethiopians. In the Third World 40,000 children die of malnourishment every day and the prosperous northern world doesn't even notice.

There is no grand order of life. There is no God putting people on Earth as a testing place, consigning the wicked to hell and the righteous to heaven. Such supernatural beliefs are infantile – and the fact that billions of people hold them and worldwide churches promulgate them merely shows the super-stition of the species. (Over the centuries, millions of people have killed each other for their religious beliefs and performed human sacrifices to non-existent gods. What further proof is needed of the insanity lurking like a monster within our kind?)

On a more logical plane, many people believe there is a 'human nature', a universal essence that makes us crave kindness and renounce cruelty. But we existentialists disagree. We think people simply are born as biological creatures and subsequent conditioning by family and culture shapes each person's nature. 'Existence precedes essence' is a fundamental principle of our philosophy.

The universe is indifferent to people like you and me. There is no 'right' and 'wrong' apart from human needs. If southern whites lynch a black in a tree, the tree doesn't care. If 10,000

Macedonians in full battle array massacre occupants of a Greek city under the Mediterranean sun – or if America's 'smart' bombs kill 200,000 Iraqis – the sun continues to shine on both the killers and the killed. Nature doesn't care.

Yet 'right' and 'wrong' are crucial human contrivances – agreed-upon rules to prevent pain and enhance life. What we do may not matter to the universe, but it matters to our fellows.

Since we are born into a world that has no god dictating the rules, nor even a biological essence governing behaviour, every person is utterly alone in choosing how to live. 'Man is condemned to be free' is my phrase for this situation. Despite all the conditioning influences that shape us, it finally is up to each individual alone to decide his or her actions. Even when we ask others to guide us we are making a personal choice. 'Radical freedom' is a label applied to this condition. 'There is no reality except in action,' I often contended. And we cannot escape the consequences of our actions…

Despite all the uncertainty and futility of life, every person must develop individual integrity and strive to improve the lot of humanity. There are no divine or universal laws, yet we must adopt private values and pursue them. This is the only 'authentic' life.

Now let us examine these ideas in greater detail.

Sartre said in 1946, 'Existentialism is a humanism' because it expresses the power of human beings to make freely willed choices, independent of the influence of religion. Most of the following is taken from Sartre's 'Existentialism and Humanism', which is a somewhat scandalous public lecture delivered to an enthusiastic Parisian crowd on 28 October 1945. Also used are his publications 'Existentialism is a Humanism' and 'Being and Nothingness'. Sartre produced three slogans to summarise his key ideas.

1 Existence precedes essence. Or, if you will, he says we must begin from the subjective. It is not at all obvious at first how this amounts to the same thing.

2 Each man is responsible for all men. (What can this mean for someone who rejects all moral absolutes?)

3 Man is condemned to be free.

Existence Precedes Essence

When Sartre states 'Existence precedes essence' (thus reversing the usual way philosophers have thought about existence and essence), he does not mean that it is true all the time. He only means to say that sometimes it is so.

In the case of a paper knife, for example, essence does precede existence. In other words, the paper knife was first designed, and then produced. The plan was there first, and then the thing itself was made in accordance with that plan. Now of course, the paper knife is an artefact. Therefore, for artefacts in general, essence precedes existence.

He goes on, if God exists, and if (as he is traditionally conceived) God is the creator of the whole of reality, then it follows that the whole world and everything in it is a kind of divine artefact. It was designed by God, and then created in accordance with that pre-existing divine plan.

If God exists, then essence precedes existence for everything in the world. If essence precedes existence for everything in the world, then God exists (or something just like God).

Note: the two statements above together mean that it goes both ways: God exists if and only if essence precedes existence for everything in the world.

Of course, as Sartre says, we all know God does not exist.

In conclusion, there is at least one being for which essence does not precede existence, the human being. Rather, it is the other way around: existence precedes essence.

Therefore:

1 there is no pre-established nature or essence that sets any limits on what I can be or do

2 there are many alternatives open to me, many possibilities for me to choose among

3 I am free to do whatever I will with myself.

In short, Sartre's argument amounts to saying that man is free if and only if God does not exist.

If God exists and knows what we are going to do before we do it, then how can human beings have free will any more? If Sartre is right, and I think he is, the problem of reconciling divine foreknowledge with human free will is insoluble.

God does not exist, then. Man is not prefabricated. On the contrary: 'Man makes himself.'

For Sartre, this fact fundamentally alters our way of thinking about human beings. Our essence comes at the end of our lives, not at the beginning.

Only when it is all over can one say, 'This is who I really am, this is what it is to be me.'

Thus, for Sartre, living your life is like writing a novel, like creating a work of art. Before it is done, it does not make any sense to ask what it 'really' is, whether it is satisfactory or not. Those questions have answers only when it is completed.

In effect, what Sartre is doing is rejecting any kind of notion of a 'personality' deep down inside one, a 'real self' hidden by the more or less false 'public' self. There is a corollary of this: if human beings are free to choose what to make of themselves, then they are also responsible for what they become.

This 'responsibility' is not a question of having to answer to some absolute moral standards. Rather the point is that, if you do not like the outcome of your choices, if you do not like who you turn out to be, you have no one to blame but yourself.

I find the notion of freedom is a scary thing. We do not like the idea that we are responsible for things and that if people are evil, thieves or cowards or whatever, they are that way because they choose to be.

In addition, we do not have the option of not playing the game; we must choose. Even if we choose to commit suicide, we are responsible for that choice. So we are in a situation where we must choose, and yet have nothing at all to guide us, no imposed code of morals. If someone makes a decision on the basis of a certain ethical or religious system, say, then he is responsible for choosing that system.

EACH MAN IS RESPONSIBLE FOR ALL MEN

The idea here is based on a combination of two notions. Firstly, actions are statements of values. They are ethical statements. It does not really matter what we say our values are; actions speak louder than words.

Secondly, the principle of generalisation in ethics is the idea that ethics is not a matter of individuals. Ethical principles are general, and of a form to apply to everyone in a particular set of circumstances.

Now, put the two points together. When I choose, when I act, I am in effect making a claim about values, about ethics. And all such claims are general in form. It follows, therefore, that whenever I act, I am in effect 'legislating' morality for all mankind. Other people may not obey my rules, may not agree with my values, but that is not the point. So every man ought to say 'Am I really a man who has the right to act in such a manner that humanity regulates itself by what I do?' (Sartre, *Existentialism Is a Humanism*, p.352).

Sartre is a relativist in the sense that he thinks there are no moral absolutes. But it in no sense follows from this that we cannot argue about values. We can try to persuade one another. All that follows is that there are no absolutes about these things. Arguments about morals then become like arguments about aesthetics. They are a matter of taste. Sartre himself makes this comparison on page 364. If you do not like Thelonious Monk and I do, I can try to get you to see it my way. I can say, 'Listen to what he does to rhythms. Listen to how he uses the sustain pedal and some tricky fingering to give the effect of bent notes on a piano.' And you can say, 'Yes, but those awful minor seconds that assault the ear!' And so on. There is something to argue about here, and sometimes such arguments can be won. But not by appealing to some absolutely authoritative canons of aesthetic beauty!

When Sartre states, 'we are unable ever to choose the worse,' he is taking us back to the Socratic paradox, where Socrates argued that no one knowingly and deliberately chooses to do evil. Here is his reasoning.

What is evil is in the end bad for me, in the sense that it will frustrate my ultimate desire for happiness. Evil harms the evildoer. If that were so, then why on earth would anyone ever choose to do evil, if he knows it is going to harm him?

Perhaps in some long-term sense you do know that what you are doing is going to harm you. In that case, you can choose to do it anyway only by allowing yourself to be distracted from what you know, by allowing yourself to get momentarily confused by the attractive aspects.

Take, for example, smoking. Imagine you are trying to give up smoking, and you know full well all the awful things it does to you. You know all that, but there is a pack of cigarettes on the table, beckoning to you. And so what happens? You begin to make excuses. Well, maybe just one.

In short, according to this Socratic view (which many people find very plausible), evildoing arises only out of confusion and ignorance.

Now, if you hold this view, then knowledge is obviously going to be an important thing. The more you know, the less evil you will do by mistake, and the less harm you will do to yourself. This was the Socratic position. And, in it, we see the origin of the ethical emphasis on knowledge. Knowledge takes on a kind of moral importance. There is urgency about education. Only by giving people knowledge can we be sure to do away with as much evil as possible.

We know what happens to this emphasis historically. It led to an overemphasis on intellect, to rationalism and the Enlightenment. So perhaps it strikes you as odd to find Sartre, the existentialist, saying, 'we are unable ever to choose the worse', thereby appearing to affirm the importance of knowledge, the confidence in reason, against which the entire existentialist movement is reacting!

But there is a difference. The Socratic view said that no one knowingly does evil. Sartre's claim is that no one ever chooses evil, with no mention of knowledge.

The point is this: for Socrates, there may very well be a difference between what you think is evil and is going to harm you and what really is evil and is going to harm you. For the Greeks, there were absolutes about these things. Human nature is a certain way; there is something we can be mistaken about here, and knowledge is an important factor in the picture.

For Sartre, on the contrary, there are no absolutes about

values. There is no human nature in advance. And since there are no absolutes about these things, there is nothing to be mistaken about. Knowledge is simply not a factor in Sartre's set-up. His point is thus not based on an appeal to enlightened self-interest, as Socrates' point is. For Sartre, it is rather a matter of an analysis of the very process of making choices and decisions.

For him, the reason one can never choose the worse is that, in the very process of choosing, one sets up values in such a way that this choice becomes the right one.

MAN IS CONDEMNED TO BE FREE

I said that for Sartre we must choose something or other. Even if we choose to commit suicide, that is a choice. We cannot avoid making choices.

The point is that, although I am free to choose whatever I want, I am not free not to choose! For Sartre, there is brute fact about this. We exist; we are responsible for our choices. But we are not responsible for the fact that we are responsible. No one asked me whether I wanted to exist.

This is the notion summed up in the statement 'Man is condemned to be free.'

As Sartre says on p.353:

> Condemned, because he did not create himself, yet is nevertheless at liberty, and from the moment that he is thrown into this world he is responsible for everything he does.

In *Existentialism Is a Humanism*, this is what Sartre calls the human condition. The human condition is the realm of 'brute fact' over which we have no control. He later calls it not 'the human condition' but 'facticity'.

In *Being and Nothingness*, he tries to forge a whole new concept of human freedom. Perhaps the best metaphor to use to understand his picture of human freedom is the common picture of 'the fork in the road'. The fork in the road represents a choice among various alternatives. When I get to this point in the road, I can choose to go any way I want (even backwards, I suppose). The choices are limitless. But I start from here. I am not free to choose to start from somewhere else.

The notion of the human 'condition' or 'facticity', then, is roughly the notion of the context in terms of which I exercise my freedom. Freedom is never just freedom in the abstract; it is always freedom to choose in a certain context. I am free to do whatever I want in these circumstances. But I am not free not to start from these circumstances. Knowing what existentialism is, however, is a small problem, as I have discovered, compared to trying to live the life it recommends. Theory is all well and good, but in the end it's actions that count. I cannot agree more with Gary Cox (2009) when he states that existentialism is not so much

> ...a philosophical theory worked out in every single detail, so much as an ideal to aspire to through sheer unrelenting will power and bloody-mindedness, a life of maximum responsibility and minimum excuses.

Cox illustrates very well the problem of bad faith or self-evasion with examples taken from Sartre's Being and Nothingness (2003). I particularly liked his explanation as to the dilemma faced by many homosexuals. To avoid bad faith

> ...he has to accept that he chooses his conduct. He could have chosen to behave differently but he didn't. He is responsible for his conduct and to be authentic he has to take responsibility for his own conduct. He has to accept that it is a part of himself and always will be. He has to own it.

With regard to the individual and society and social change, I am aware of the vast lacunae between on the one hand, Jon Elster who in his book *Explaining Social Behaviour*, (Cambridge, 2007) argues that the elementary unit of human life is individual human action with social change arising as a result of the action and interaction of individuals, and, on the other, those going back to Emile Durkheim, (1858–1917) who saw society as the source of social meaning in contrast to God. Society was a reality sui generis and capable of bringing about social change. Or as modern philosopher Simon Blackburn puts it:

> Culture gives Canada one quarter of the murder rate of the USA and a few centuries – far too short a period for natural selection to take place – changed bloodthirsty Vikings into today's peaceful Scandinavians.

To me the essential point is the recognition that there is a two-way interaction between the individual and society that is constantly varying over time, space and context.

Therefore one's individual essence and society may change as a consequence of choices made, while subject at all times to the social pressure existing at the moment the choice was made.

> Humans and our world are interconnected: neither causes the other, instead we shape and are shaped by our environment.

> Merleau-Ponty, 1945

Humanism provides me with the elements of the good life:

> Individual liberty, the pursuit of knowledge, the cultivation of pleasures that do not harm others, the satisfactions of art, personal relationships, and a sense of belonging to the human community.

> Grayling, 2007

This is an excellent general statement but more specifically Todorov in his book *The Imperfect Garden: the Legacy of Humanism* explains a good society as one based on secular ethics with three irreducible values:

> I must be the source of my action, you must be its goal, they all belong to the same human race. These three characteristics (which Kant called three 'formulas of one and the same law') (Fondements, II, 303) are not always found together … But only the uniting of the three constitutes humanist thought.

> Todorov, 2002, p.30

The autonomy of the I.

Liberty. The autonomy of the subject. Freedom of action, the absence of physical coercion.

> Man has the unique capacity to detach himself from his own being, the individual is at once a living being like others and the consciousness of that being, which allows him to detach himself from it … such is the basis of human liberty.

The finality of the YOU.

Fraternity. Treating others as if they are our brothers i.e. making others the goal of our affections and acts. The acceptance of the particular human being other than self as the ultimate goal of our actions. Altruism: man has no right to exist for his own sake; service to others is the only justification for existence.

The universality of the THEY.

Equality. The unity of the human race. Recognition of the equal dignity of everyone. This does double duty both as one value among others and as a means of legitimising the three core values.

> One can wish that all human beings were autonomous, that they were all treated as ends in themselves, or provided with the same dignity.

These values square well with existentialism and are to be seen as interacting and constraining on one another, e.g. my freedom should not be at the expense of your freedom or dignity and my autonomy should not be at the expense of the equality and fraternity (the freedom of my fist stops at the cheek of my neighbour, said John Stuart Mill) of my community.

Hence the society has the capability to become democratic and contractarian.

> Humanism … envisages men in their current imperfection and does not imagine that this state of things can change; it accepts with Montaigne, the idea that the garden remains forever imperfect.
>
> Todorov

Hopefully all of you will not be saying 'I knew it' at this moment as this would suggest that, while writing this book, I have not been as successful as I have really tried to be in rising above my own perceptions of political reality.

And if you are still wondering where I came on the Political Compass test, I came in the same spot in the bottom left as Gandhi and the Dalai Lama!

Clearly everyone's effort will be different as everyone's lenses are different. What matters though is that it sums up accurately the mix of -isms through which you perceive reality and what it is to lead a good life and that this gives you self-confidence. I am happy with my lenses but I have no right to try to impose them on you. However, it is good for me to try to help you to find the best for you, so long as I act in an honest way.

Not all your choices will work out best for you, but you will at least have the reassurance that the choice was made from within to give what is to you a consistent philosophy.

As I stated at the start, I am not interested in advocating any particular mix other than the one that you are happy with and that hopefully I have helped you to develop.

Finally of course you cannot stop at this point, as the lively mind will continually be reflecting on changes in society and their possible implications for your philosophy.

Also, do not forget that there are many ways in which the end of the first decade of the new century marks the end of one era and the beginning of another.

I started by arguing that this is a particularly opportune moment to produce this book as 'The party is definitely over. And the present decade has acquired its permanent character as a historical pivot defined by the nightmares of 9/11 and the panic of 2008–09' (Andersen, April 2009).

If I have grasped your interest and you are wondering what next, might I suggest the 2009 Reith lecturer Michael Sandel (1996, 1998, 2009) and the writings of Phillip Blond.

First, Sandel. What follows is taken from the 2009 Reith lectures, which have as their theme 'A New Politics of the Common Good', and are available on the Internet. As well as being thought-provoking, he is an excellent lecturer.

Sandel sees his obligations as a philosopher as being continuous with his responsibilities as a citizen. For him, political philosophy is engaged or it is nothing.

The responsibility of political philosophy that tries to engage with practice is to be clear, or at least accessible – clear enough that its arguments and concerns can be accessible to a non-academic public. Otherwise, it's not possible really for political philosophers to generate debate that could possibly challenge existing understandings.

He argues that political philosophers must intervene in the debates themselves.

Public philosophy is set apart from academic political philosophy, in that it means not only to be about prevailing practices and assumptions, but also to address them … To address fellow citizens about them and to try to provoke discussion and critical reflection among the public generally. So that political philosophy isn't only about public things, but engages public things and, if it's successful, reorients the way people relate to politics and the public realm.

Sandel is highly critical of economics that, he argues, is excessively pessimistic about human beings, conceiving of them as little more than bundles of preferences and desires. This was a picture it inherited from utilitarianism, for which all moral and political principles are justified to the extent that they promote the greatest happiness of the greatest number.

His first book, *Liberalism and the Limits of Justice* (1982), based on his Oxford thesis, was a full-frontal attack on the version of liberalism set out in John Rawls' *A Theory of Justice*. He has deep misgivings about the Rawlsian model, which seems to him to make the surrendering of the moral and religious convictions that people hold most dear a condition of access to the public sphere.

The effects of emptying public life of moral and religious discourse, he believes, have been disastrous.

It's contributed to a moral vacuum that has been filled by narrow, intolerant moralisms. It has allowed the Christian right to have more appeal than it might otherwise have had, precisely because the field was cleared.

241

Sandel's argument is that political progressives, of whom he is one, should actively engage people's deepest beliefs, rather than ignore them. Sandel thinks that Obama, for one, has recognised this.

> He is trying to articulate a politics of the common good and, unlike a lot of politicians, particularly those to the left of centre, he does not shy away from engaging with moral and spiritual language. He has brought moral and religious sensibilities back into politics, against a background in which such themes have been monopolised by the Christian right. Progressives have reacted, not by engaging the Christian right, but by trying to keep morality and religion out of politics altogether.

Sandel's challenge is to the whole architecture of neoliberalism, arguing that a particular conception of the individual is being challenged in the current economic crisis. His arguments are an uncomfortable reminder of what we lost when we threw in our lot with a vision of politics as little more than the pursuit of economic growth and the protection of individual choice.

Secondly, the ideas of Phillip Blond who, in 2009, launched a think tank, ResPublica (see on Internet) with the support of David Cameron, the leader of the Conservative party in the UK.

The following section is largely taken from a Prospect article (28 February 2009) entitled 'The Rise of the Red Tories'. I would recommend very strongly that you read the whole article.

Blond is convinced that:

> We're in the middle of a paradigm shift ... We are witnessing the end of the neoliberal project – just as thirty years ago we saw the end of Keynesianism. We're in a shift of comparable proportions. The interesting question is what comes next.

The one thing we do not want is the 'cartel-driven capitalism' and 'loads-of-money ideology' of recent years. He argues that what ought to come next is something he calls communitarian civic conservatism – or 'Red Toryism', a term borrowed from Canadian politics. Two more -isms for you.

'The current political consensus,' he writes, 'is left-liberal in culture and right-liberal in economics. And this is precisely the wrong place to be.'

He agrees with Cameron that we do live in a broken society, as recently highlighted by Ian Duncan Smith, but argues that it wasn't only 'the dead hand of the welfare state that caused the bonds and attachments of civil association (the "old mutualism of the working class" and so on) to give way; late-modern capitalism's "perennial gale of creative destruction" (to use Joseph Schumpeter's phrase) has played its part, too.' (Derbyshire, 2009)

The driver for a new capitalism must come from a revival of 'community and reciprocal values'. Ordinary people have been crowded out from wealth and entrepreneurship by a libertarian understanding of a free market.

Blond argues that slashing the powers of large public and private concerns is essential to helping the less well off. The power should be handed over to social enterprise or community interest companies modelled on the John Lewis Partnership in England, where employees have a stake in the business.

Blond's Red Tory thesis, therefore, is that the Conservatives can, and should, meet this challenge. They need to recognise that neoliberalism, or 'free-market fundamentalism', has created 'private-sector monopolies' (high-street behemoths such as Tesco) that are every bit as corrosive of the 'intermediary structures of a civilised life' as the state monopolies of the old, Keynesian dispensation.

Blond calls for a 'new communitarian settlement', involving what he terms the 'relocalisation of the economy' and the 'recapitalisation of the poor'. To this end, he recommends, among other policy measures, an extension of the Post Office's retail banking function and the establishment of local investment trusts that would offer finance to people without assets.

In any case, he thinks the left has got Cameron wrong.

I think he is in deadly earnest. And I don't think it's cover for another agenda. The left wants to believe it's Thatcherism Mark II, but it isn't. The left is still far too mired in the old politics, and it's the right who are making the running. The reason my article has had such an effect is that no one can doubt it's progressive. And I believe that Cameron is committed to it.

He points to the Conservative leader's speech at Davos, in which he repudiated the 'old economic orthodoxy' and argued for a 'popular capitalism', or 'capitalism with a conscience', to replace 'markets without morality'.

One left-of-centre politician who does take Cameron and Blond seriously is Jon Cruddas, the MP for Dagenham, and another speaker at Blond's coronation as the Conservative party's philosopher-king. 'We, Labour, ignore Blond's work at our peril,' Cruddas said.

> There's a fault line running through the history of conservatism, between liberal-economic conservatism and a richer, more paternalistic tradition. Phillip's trying to rehabilitate the second one. What it does is allow the Conservatives to use a different language, a discourse about our obligations to others that is much richer than the Thatcherite brutality built around a notion of atomised economic exchange.

A central feature of his Toryism is a critique of 'liberalism', a term capacious enough in his hands to apply to the cultural libertarian-ism of the 1960s as well as to the great philosophers of the liberal tradition, such as Locke or Mill. According to Blond, what the post-1968 'politics of desire' shares with those liberal titans, and in fact also with the Thatcherite or neoliberal model of rational economic behaviour, is a certain idea of individual human beings.

In the liberal view, at least as Blond characterises it, the defence of individual freedom, in its most extreme form, demands of each man that 'he refuse the dictates of any other'. In other words, liberal autonomy entails the repudiation of society, and no vision of the common good can be derived from liberal principles. The atomised dystopia of twenty-first-century Britain, the 'broken society' overseen by a highly centralised bureaucratic state, turns out to have been the historic bequest of Locke and Mill.

Finally Blond is a committed Christian so we must presume he is an 'endist' and that he is perhaps looking for a new form of capitalism where the poor have not been crowded out from wealth and entrepreneurship by a libertarian notion of free markets.

This is contentious, to say the least.

One final thought, on a lighter note, when Sen (2005) told his grandfather that he was an atheist, he received an excited response and was told that this was excellent news, as he had joined the Lokayata tradition of Hinduism.

So if ever there is a time to enter the world of political philosophy, this is it.

Welcome.

Bibliography

BOOKS & ARTICLES

Aghion, P and P Howitt, *Endogeneous Growth Theory*, Massachusetts, MIT Press, 1998

Akerlof, G and R Shiller, *Animal Spirits: How Human Psychology Drives the Economy, and Why It Matters for Global Capitalism*, New Jersey, Princeton University Press, 2009

Albertazzi, D and D McDonnell, *Twenty-First Century Populism: the Spectre of Western European Democracy*, Hampshire, Palgrave Macmillan, 2008

Althusser, L, 'Ideology and Ideological State Apparatuses' in *Lenin and Philosophy and Other Essays*, translated by B Brewster, New York and London, Monthly Review Press, 1971

Andersen, K, 'That Was Then and This Is Now', *Time* magazine, New York, 2009, vol. 173, no. 14

Arendt, H, *On Violence*, New York, Harcourt Brace & Co, 1970

Aristotle, *The Politics*, London, Penguin Classics, 1981

Arrow, K, S Bowles and S Durlauf [eds], *Meritocracy and Economic Inequality*, New Jersey, Princeton University Press, 2000

Arthur, W Brian, S Durlauf and D Lane, 'Introduction: Process and Emergence in the Economy', in *The Economy as an Evolving Complex System II*, Reading, Massachusetts, Addison-Wesley, 1997

Baker, D, *Plunder and Blunder: The Rise and Fall of the Bubble Economy*, Sausalito, California, PoliPoint Press, 2009

Barkley, T, 'Protectionism on Rise in 17 of the G20 – World Bank Report Real Time Economics: Economic Insight and Analysis' from *The Wall Street Journal*, New York, 2009

Barry, B, *Culture and Equality*, Cambridge, Polity Press, 2001

Bartky, S, *Femininity and Domination: Studies in the Phenomenology of Oppression*, New York, Routledge, 1990

——, *Sympathy and Solidarity and Other Essays*, New York, New Jersey, Rowman and Littlefield, 2002

de Beauvoir, Simone, *The Ethics of Ambiguity*, Citadel Press, 2000

——, *The Second Sex*, New York, Vintage Books, 1974

Beck, U, *The Cosmopolitan Vision*, Cambridge, Polity Press, 2006

Beetham, D, *Democracy*, Oxford, Oneworld Publications, 2005

Beinhocker, E, *The Origin of Wealth: Evolution, Complexity, and the Radical Remaking of Economics*, Boston, Massachusetts, Harvard Business School Press, 2006

Bergesen, A, *The Sayyid Qutb Reader: Selected Writings on Politics, Religion and Society*, New York and London, Routledge, 2007

Berlin, I, *Liberty: Revised and Expanded Edition of 'Four Essays on Liberty'*, Oxford, Oxford University Press, 2002

Besson, S and J Marti [eds] *Deliberative Democracy and its Discontents*, Hampshire, Ashgate Publishing Limited, 2006

Bhagwati, J, *Protectionism*, Massachusetts, MIT Press, 1989

Blackburn, Simon, *The Big Questions: Philosophy*, Quercus, 2009

——, *Truth: A Guide for the Perplexed*, UK, Allen Lane, 2005

de Bonald, L, *The True and Only Wealth of Nations: Essays on Family, Economy and Society*, Naples, Florida, Sapienta Press of Ave Maria University, 2006

——, *Recherches Philosophiques sure les premier objets des connaissance morales, Oeuvres de M de Bonald*, Paris, Leclere, 1843

Bordo, S, *Unbearable Weight: Feminism, Western Culture and the Body*, Berkeley, California, University of California Press, 1993

Bowles, S, *Microeconomics: Behavior, Institutions and Evolution*, New Jersey, Princeton University Press, 2004

Buchanan, J and G Tullock, *The Calculus of Consent*, Ann Arbor, University of Michigan Press, 1962

Bullock, A, *The Humanist Tradition in the West*, London, W W Norton & Co. Ltd, 1985

Camus, A, *The Myth of Sisyphus*, London, Penguin, 1975

——, *The Outsider*, London, Penguin, 2000

Canovan, M, *Populism*, London, Longmans, 1981

Chirot, D, *Why Some Wars Become Genocidal and Others Don't*, Jackson School of International Studies, University of Washington, 2002

Clarke, J, *Viewpoint: The End of the Neo-cons?*, BBC, 13 January 2009

Clinton, H, *It Takes a Village*, New York, Simon & Schuster Ltd, 2008

Colander, D, *The Complexity Vision and the Teaching of Economics*, Cheltenham, Elgar, 2000

Cole, J, *Engaging the Muslim World*, New York, Palgrave Macmillan, 2009

Constant, B, *Political Writings*, Cambridge, Cambridge University Press, 1988

Cooter, R and T Ulen, *Law and Economics: 5th Edition*, Reading, Massachusetts, Addison-Wesley/Longman, 2007

Cotterrell, R, *Emile Durkheim: Law in a Moral Domain*, California, Stanford University Press, 1999

Cox, Gary, *How to Be an Existentialist*, London, Continuum, 2009

——, *The Sartre Dictionary*, London, Continuum, 2008

Curry, P, *Ecological Ethics: An Introduction*, Cambridge, Polity Press, 2005

Dahl, Robert, *Democracy and Its Critics*, Connecticut, Yale University Press, 1991

——, 'The Concept of Power, Behavioral Science 2', 1957, pp.201–15

——, *Who Governs: Democracy and Power in an American City: Second Edition*, Connecticut, Yale University Press, 2005

Dalton, D, *Power over People: Classical and Modern Political Theory*, Chantilly, Virginia, The Teaching Company, 1991

d'Ancona, M, '2010: The Day that Changed Politics Forever', *The Sunday Telegraph*, 9 May 2010

Davies, N, *Dark Heart: The Shocking Truth about Hidden Britain*, London, Chatto and Windus, 1997

Dawkins, Richard, *The God Delusion*, London, Transworld Publishers, 2006

——, *The Selfish Gene*, Oxford, Oxford University Press, 1976

Day, R H, *An Introduction to Macroeconomic Dynamics*, Massachusetts, MIT Press, 1999

Delanty, G, 'The Foundations of Social Theory', in *The New Blackwell Introduction to Social Theory*, Oxford, Blackwell, 2007

Derbyshire, J, 'Cameron's Philosopher King', *New Statesman*, 19 February 2009

Domhoff, G W, *State Autonomy or Class Dominance*, New York, Hawthorne, 1996

——, *Who Rules America? Challenges to Corporate and Class Dominance*, New York, McGraw-Hill, 2010

Downs, A, *An Economic Theory of Democracy*, Cambridge/York, Cambridge University Press, 1957

Durkheim, E, *Rules of Sociological Method*, New York, The Free Press, 1982

Eatwell, R and A Wright, *Contemporary Political Ideologies*, London, Continuum, 1999

Eisenstein, Z, 'Developing a Theory of Capitalist Patriarchy' in *Capitalist Patriarchy and the Case for Socialist Feminism*, New York, Monthly Review Press, 1979

Elliot, M, *The Road to Ruin Time*, 2009, vol. 173, no. 14

Faraj, Muhammad Adb al Salam, *The Neglected Duty*, translated by Johannes Jansen, New York, Macmillan Publishing, November 1986

Feingold, R, 'Representative Democracy versus Corporate Democracy: How Soft Money Erodes the Principle of One Person One Vote', in *Harvard Journal on Legislation*, Cambridge, Massachusetts, 1988, vol. 35, no. 2, pp.377–86

Fernandes, E, *Holy Warriors*, London, Portobello Books, 2009

——, 'Sharia Law UK' in *The Mail on Sunday*, 5 July 2009

Foucault, Michel, Hubert Dreyfus and Paul Rabinow 'Afterword: the Subject and Power' in *Beyond Structuralism and Hermeneutics: 2nd edition*, Chicago, University of Chicago Press, 1983

Foucault, Michel, *Discipline and Punish: the Birth of the Prison*, translated by Alan Sheridan, New York, Vintage, 1977

——, *The History of Sexuality, Volume 1: An Introduction,* translated by Robert Hurley, New York, Vintage, 1979

——, 'Two Lectures' in Colin Gordon [ed.], *Power/Knowledge: Selected Interviews and Other Writings 1972–1977*, New York, Pantheon, 1980

Frayn, M, *The Human Touch: Our Part in the Creation of the Universe*, London, Faber and Faber, 2006

Freedman, L, *A Choice of Enemies: America Confronts the Middle East*, London, Weidenfeld and Nicolson, 2009

Friedman, B, *Moral Consequences of Economic Growth*, New York, Knopf Borzoi, 2005

Friedman M and R, *Free to Choose*, New York, 1980

Fromkin, D, *In the Time of the Americans: FDR, Truman, Eisenhower, Marshall, MacArthur: the Generation that Changed America's Role in the World*, New York, Knopf Borzoi, 1995

Fukuyama, F, *After the Neocons: America at the Crossroads*, London, Profile Books, 2006

——, 'After NeoConservatism', *New York Times*, 19 February 2006

——, *The End of History and the Last Man*, New York, The Free Press, 1992

Gamble, A, *Hayek*, Cambridge, Polity Press, 1996

Gates, Bill, 'How to Fix Capitalism', *Time* magazine, New York, 2008

Geroski, P A and P Gregg, 'Coping with the Recession' in *National Institute Economic Review*, November 1993, 146, pp.64–75

——, *Coping with Recession – UK Company Performance in Adversity*, Cambridge University Press, 1997

Giddens, A, *The Third Way and Its Critics*, Malden, Massachusetts, Polity Press, 2000

Gieben, B, *Study Guide for Models of Democracy*, Cambridge, Polity Press, 2006

Gill, R and J Porter, *Moral Action and Christian Ethics*, Cambridge, Cambridge University Press, 1999

Gintis, H and S Bowles, *Moral Sentiments and Material Interests*, Massachusetts, MIT Press, 2005

Goldberg, J, *Liberal Fascism*, London, Penguin, 2008

Goodin, R and P Pettit [eds], *Contemporary Political Philosophy*, Oxford, Blackwell, 1997

Gray, J, *False Dawn: the Delusions of Global Capitalism*, London, Allen Lane, 1998

——, *Straw Dogs*, London, Allen Lane, 2002

Grayling, A C, *What is Good?*, London, Phoenix, 2007

Habermas, J, *Legitimation Crisis*, London, Heineman, 1976

Habermas, J and John Viertel, *Theory and Practice*, Cambridge, Polity Press, 1988

Halper S and J Clark, *America Alone: the Neoconservatives and the Global Order*, Cambridge, Cambridge University Press, 2004

Hartsock, N, *Money, Sex and Power: Toward a Feminist Historical Materialism*, Boston, Northeastern University Press, 1983

——, 'Foucault on Power: A Theory for Women?' in *Feminism/Postmodernism*, New York, 1990

Hayek, F A, *Hayek on Hayek: An Autobiographical Dialogue*, London, Liberty Fund Inc., 2008

——, *The Road to Serfdom: Text and Documents – The Definitive Edition*, University of Chicago Press, Chicago, 2007

——, *The Use of Knowledge in Society*, reprinted from the American Economic Review, vol. 35, no. 4, September, 1945, pp.519–530

Hedges, C, *American Fascists: the Christian Right and the War on America*, London, Jonathan Cape, 2008

Heidegger, Martin, *Being and Time*, London, Blackwell, 1993

Held, D, *Cosmopolitanism/Anti-Capitalism*, Cambridge, Polity Press, 2007

——, *Models of Democracy*, Cambridge, Polity Press, 2006

Held, V, *Feminist Morality: Transforming Culture, Society and Politics*, Chicago, University of Chicago Press, 1993

Hoagland, S, *Lesbian Ethics: Toward a New Value*, Palo Alto, CA, Institute of Lesbian Studies, 1988

Hobbes, Thomas, *Leviathan* (1641), New York, Penguin, 1985

Hodgson, G, *The World Turned Right Side Up: A History of the Conservative Ascendancy in America*, Boston, Houghton Mifflin, 1996

Hoffman, B, *Inside Terrorism*, New York, Columbia University Press, 2006

Holmes, S, *The Anatomy of Antiliberalism*, Cambridge, Massachusetts, Harvard University Press, 1993

Hong, H [ed.], *Kierkegaard Søren: Journals and Papers*, Bloomington, IN, Indiana University Press, 1976

Hume, D, *An Enquiry Concerning the Principles of Morals*, Oxford, Oxford University Press, 1998

——, *Of Suicide*, London, Penguin Great Ideas, 2005

Ibrahim, R, *The Al-Qaeda Reader*, London, Broadway, 2007

Kafka, Franz, *The Trial*, translated by Willa and Edwin Muir, revised and with additional material translated by E M Butler, New York, Schocken Books, 1995

Kagan, R, *The Return of History and the End of Dreams*, New York, Atlantic Press, 2009

Kahneman, D and A Tversky [eds], *Choices, Values and Frames*, New York, Cambridge University Press, 2000

Kant, Immanuel, *Logic*, translated by R S Hartman and W Schwarz, Indianapolis, 1984

Kay, J, *The Truth about Markets: Their Genius, Their Limits, Their Follies*, Allen Lane, London, 2000

Keen, S, *Debunking Economics: the Naked Emperor of the Social Sciences*, London, Zed Books, 2001

Kelly, S and M Allison, *The Complexity Advantage*, New York, McGraw Hill, 1999

Kierkegaard, S, *Concluding Unscientific Postscript*, Cambridge, Cambridge University Press, 2009

Kinsley, M, *Creative Capitalism*, London and New York, Simon & Schuster, 2010

Klein, N, *The Shock Doctrine*, London, Penguin, 2008

Kley, R, *Hayek's Social and Political Thought*, Oxford, Oxford University Press, 1994

Kristol, I, *Neoconservatism: the Autobiography of an Idea*, Chicago, Illinois, Ivan R Dee, 1995

Kristol, I and Lawrence Kaplan, *War Over Iraq: Saddam's Tyranny and America's Mission*, San Francisco, CA, Encounter Books, 2003

Kristol, W, *The Weekly Standard: a Reader: 1995–2005*, New York, Harper Perennial, 2006

Kuttner, R, *Everything for Sale: the Virtues and Limits of Markets*, New York, Alfred A Knopf, 1997

——, *Obama's Challenge: America's Economic Crisis and the Power of a Transformative Presidency*, Vermont, Chelsea Green, 2008

Kymlicka, W, *Contemporary Political Philosophy: 2nd edition*, Oxford, Oxford University Press, 2001

Lerman, A, 'Europe's Heart of Darkness', *The Guardian*, 4 June 2009

Levi, A, *Renaissance and Reformation: the Intellectual Genesis*, London, Yale University Press, 2002

Libet, B, *Mind Time: The Temporal Factor in Consciousness*, Harvard, Harvard University Press, 2004

Lipsey, R and K Lancaster, 'The General Theory of Second Best', in *The Review of Economic Studies*, London, 1956–1957, vol. 24, no. 1, pp.11–32

Lo, A and A MacKinley, *A Non-Random Walk Down Wall Street*, New Jersey, Princeton University Press, 1999

Lukes, Steven [ed.], *'Introduction' in Power*, Oxford, Blackwell, 1986

——, *Power: a Radical View*, London, Macmillan, 1974

——, *Power: a Radical View: 2nd expanded edition*, London, Macmillan, 2005

Machiavelli, N, *The Prince*, London, Penguin Classics, 1961

MacShane, D, 'A Lesson from Germany', *New Statesman*, 11 September 2009

——, 'Ten Lessons for the Left from Europe', *The Guardian*, 8 June 2008

Marx, K, *Das Kapital*, London, Lawrence and Wishart, 1970

Maslow, A H, *Motivation and Personality*, New York, Harper, 1954

Matravers, D C and J E Pike [eds.], *Debates in Contemporary Political Philosophy*, London, Routledge, 2002

McCulloch, G, *Using Sartre: An Analytical Introduction to Earlier Sartrean Themes*, London, Routledge, 1994

Mendell, M and D Salée, *The Legacy of Karl Polanyi: Market, State, and Society at the End of the Twentieth Century*, London, St Martin's Press, 1991

Merleau-Ponty, M, *Phenomenology of Perception*, translated by Colin Smith, New York, Humanities Press and London, Routledge & Kegan Paul, 2002

——, *The Structure of Behaviour*, translated by Alden Fisher, Boston, Beacon Press, 1963 and London, Methuen, 1965

Mill, J S, *Utilitarianism*, Oxford, Oxford University Press, 1998

Miller, Debra, *Illegal Immigration*, San Diego, California, Reference Point Press, 2007

Milliband, R, *The State in Capitalist Society*, London, Weidenfeld and Nicolson, 1969

de Montesquieu, Charles, *The Spirit of the Laws*, New York, Cosimo, 2007

Moore, C, *Keith Joseph Memorial Lecture Centre for Policy Studies*, 10 January 2008

Mouffe, C, *On the Political*, Abingdon, New York, Routledge, 2005

Mouffe, C and E Laclau, *Hegemony and Socialist Strategy: Towards a Radical Democratic Politics*, London and New York, Verso, 1985

Mulhall, S and A Swift, *Liberals and Communitarians: 2nd edition*, Oxford, Blackwell, 2000

Murdoch, Iris, *Sartre: Romantic Rationalist*, London, Fontana, 1968

Nicholson, Linda [ed.], 'Foucault on Power: a Theory for Women?' in *Feminism/Postmodernism*, New York, Routledge, 1990

Nietzsche, F, *Ecce Homo: How One Becomes What One Is*, London, Penguin, 2004

North, D, *Institutions, Institutional Change and Economic Performance*, New Jersey, Princeton University Press, 1990

Norton, A, *Leo Strauss and the Politics of American Empire*, London, Yale University Press, 2004

Novick, P, *The Holocaust in American Life*, New York, Houghton Mifflin, 2000

Nozick, R, *Anarchy State and Utopia*, Maldan, Massachusetts, Blackwell, 1974

Offe, C, *Disorganized Capitalism*, Cambridge, Polity Press, 1985

O'Hear, A, *After Progress*, London, Bloomsbury, 1999

Okin, Susan Moller, *Justice, Gender and the Family*, New York, Basic Books, 1989

Outram, D, *The Enlightenment*, Cambridge, Cambridge University Press, 1995

Paine, T, *The Rights of Man*, New York, Penguin, 1984

Panza, C and G Gale, *Existentialism for Dummies*, London, Wiley-Blackwell, 2008

Parsons, T, *The Structure of Social Action*, New York, Free Press, 1967

Pateman, Carole, *The Sexual Contract*, Stanford, Stanford University Press, 1988

Peters, R, *Hobbes*, London, Penguin, 1956

Phillips, A, *Engendering Democracy*, Cambridge, Polity Press, 1991

——, *Which Equalities Matter?*, Cambridge, Polity Press, 1999

Pinker, S, *The Blank State: the Modern Denial of Human Nature*, London, Penguin Press, 2002

Plato, *The Laws*, London, Penguin, 1970

——, *The Republic*, London, Penguin, 1974

Podhoretz, J, *Bush Country: How Dubya Became a Great President while Driving Liberals Insane*, New York, St Martin's Griffin, 2004

Podhoretz, N, 'The Case for Bombing Iran', *The Wall Street Journal*, New York, 30 May 2007

Popper, K, *Conjectures and Refutations*, London, Routledge Classics, 2002

——, *The Logic of Scientific Discovery*, London, Routledge Classics, 2002

Poulantzas, N, *State Power Socialism*, London, NLB, 1978

Prahalad, C K, *The Fortune at the Bottom of the Pyramid: Eradicating Poverty Through Profits*, University of Pennsylvania Press, 2004

Putnam, R D, *Bowling Alone: the Collapse and Revival of American Community*, New York, Simon and Schuster, 2000

Qiao, Shi, *New Perspectives Quarterly*, 1997, vol. 13, no. 3

Qutb, S, *Milestones*, Chicago, Illinois, Kazi Publications, 2007

Ravenhill, J [ed.], *Global Political Economy*, Oxford, Oxford University Press, 2005

Rawls, J, *A Theory of Justice*, Cambridge, Massachusetts, Harvard University Press, 1971 and 1996

——, *Political Liberalism*, Columbia University Press, 1993

Rees-Mogg, W, 'This Man has Thrown Us into a Black Hole', *The Mail on Sunday*, 15 July 2009

——, 'Who Would Want to Vote for Weimar?', *The Mail on Sunday*, 7 February 2010

Regan, T, *The Case for Animal Rights*, New Jersey, Prentice Hall, 1983

Rhoads, S, *The Economists View of the World: Government, Markets and Public Policy*, Cambridge, Cambridge University Press, 1985

Richardson, H S, *Democratic Autonomy*, Oxford, Oxford University Press, 2003

Roth, G and W Schluchter, *Max Weber's Vision of History*, California, University California Press, 1979

Rothbard, M, *For a New Liberty*, Auburn, Alabama, Von Mies Institute, 2006

——, *The Betrayal of the American Right*, Auburn, Alabama, Von Mies Institute, 2007

——, *The Irrepressible Rothbard*, Burlingame, CA, Center for Libertarian Studies, 2000

Rothkopf, D, *Superclass: the Global Power Elite and the World They Are Making*, New York, Little Brown, 2008

Rousseau, J-J, *Discourse on the Origin of Inequality*, Amazon Kindle book, 2006

——, *The Collected Writings*, New England, University Press of New England, 1990

Roy, O, *Globalized Islam: The Search for a New Ummah*, New York, Columbia University Press, 2004

Sachs, J, *Commonwealth Economics for a Crowded Planet*, New York, Penguin, 2008

de Sade, D A F, *La Philosophie dans le Boudoir*, Paris, J-J Pauvert, 1968

Safranski, R, *Nietzsche: a Philosophical Biography*, London, W W Norton & Co., 2002

Sageman, M, *Understanding Terror Networks*, Philadelphia, University of Pennsylvania Press, 2004

Sandel, M, *Democracy's Discontent: America in Search of a Public Philosophy*, Cambridge, Massachusetts, Harvard University Press, 1996

——, *Justice: What's the Right Thing to Do?* Cambridge University Press, 2009

——, *Liberalism and the Limits of Justice*, second edition, Cambridge University Press, 1998

Sartre, J-P, *Being and Nothingness: An Essay in Phenomenological Ontology,* London, Routledge, 2003

——, *Existentialism and Humanism*, London, Methuen, 2002

——, *Existentialism and Humanism*, New Edition, London, MSG House, June 1977

——, *Existentialism Is a Humanism*, Yale University Press, July 2007

Schmitt, C, *The Concept of the Political* (1932), University of Chicago Press, 2006

Schopenhauer, *The World as Will and Representations*, translated by E F J Payne, Dover, 1958, available online

Schumpeter, J, *Capitalism, Socialism and Democracy*, London, Routledge, 1994

——, *Capitalism, Socialism and Democracy*, London, Allen and Unwin, 1976

Sedley, D, *Creationism and Its Critics in Antiquity*, Berkeley, California, University of California Press, 2008

Sells, M, 'Understanding, Not Indoctrination', *The Washington Post*, 8 August 2002

Sen, A, *The Argumentative Indian*, London, Allen Lane, 2005

Shiller, R J, *Irrational Exuberance*, Princeton University Press, 2006

Simon, R J [ed.], *The Blackwell Guide to Social and Political Philosophy*, Malden, Massachusetts, Blackwell, 2002

Skocpol, Theda, *Diminished Democracy: From Membership to Management in American Civil Life*, Oklahoma, University of Oklahoma Press, 2003

Smith, A, D D Raphael and A L Macfie [eds], *The Theory of Moral Sentiments*, Oxford, Clarendon Press, 1976

Smith, A, R H Campbell, A S Skinner and W B Todd [eds], *The Wealth of Nations*, Oxford, Clarendon Press, 1976

Smith, J, 'Islam and Christianity' in *Encyclopedia of Christianity*, Oxford, Oxford University Press, 2005

Soros, G, *Soros on Soros*, New York, John Wiley, 1995

Stelzer, I [ed.], *The NeoCon Reader*, New York, Grove Press, 2005

Stiglitz, J, *Globalization and Its Discontents*, New York, WW Norton & Co, 2002

Summers, L and Caroline Freund [eds], 'Regionalism and the World Trading System' in *The WTO and Reciprocal Preferential Trading Agreements*, Cheltenham, Glos, Edward Elgar Publishing, 2007, pp.421–427

Tanner, M, *Nietzsche*, Oxford, Oxford University Press, 1994

Tawney, R H, *Religion and the Rise of Capitalism*, London, Hesperides Press, 2006

Teilhard de Chardin, P, *The Nature of Man*, London, Hesperides Press, 1969

Thaler, R H, *The Winner's Curse: Paradoxes and Anomalies of Economic Life*, Princeton University Press, 1992

de Tocqueville, A, *Democracy in America*, New York, Everymans Library, 1994

Todorov, T, *The Imperfect Garden: the Legacy of Humanism*, Princeton University Press, 2002

Tomalin, C, *Mary Wollstonecraft*, London, Penguin, 1985

Valantasis, R, *The Making of the Self: Ancient and Modern Asceticism*, Cambridge, James Clarke & Co, 2008

Vestal, T M, *Ethiopia: A Post-Cold War African State*, Wesport, Connecticut, Greenwood, 1999

Vietor, R H K, *Contrived Competition: Regulation and Deregulation in America*, Cambridge, Mass, Harvard University Press, 1994

——, *How Countries Compete: Strategy, Structure, and Government in the Global Economy*, Boston, Harvard Business School Press, 2007

Warnock, Mary, *Existentialism*, Oxford, Oxford University Press, 1992

Wartenberg, Thomas [ed.], 'Five Faces of Oppression' in *Rethinking Power*, Albany, New York, SUNY Press, 1992

——, *Inclusion and Democracy*, Oxford, Oxford University Press, 2000

Weber, Max, *Economy and Society: an Outline of Interpretive Sociology*, translated by Ephraim Fischoff et al, Berkeley, California, University of California Press, 1978

————, *The Protestant Ethic and the Spirit of Capitalism*, New York, Penguin, 2002

Wheen, F, *Karl Marx*, Fontana, New York, Fourth Estate, 1999

Willets, D, *The Pinch: How the Baby Boomers Took their Children's Future – And Why they Should Give it Back*, London, Atlantic Books, 2010

Williams, G [ed.], *John Stuart Mill on Politics and Society*, London, Fontana, 1976

Winter-Ebmer and S Raphael, *Identifying the Effect of Unemployment on Crime*, San Diego, University of California, 1998

Wright, R, *Non Zero: the Logic of Human Destiny*, New York, Pantheon Books, 2000

Wright Mills, C, *The Power Elite*, New York, Oxford University Press, 1956

Wrong, D H, *Power: Its Forms, Bases and Uses*, Edison, New Jersey, Transaction Publishers, 1995

Young, I M, 'Five Faces of Oppression' in *Rethinking Power*, ed. Thomas Wartenberg, Albany, NY, SUNY Press, 1992

————, *Inclusion and Democracy*, Oxford, Oxford University Press, 2000

————, *Justice and the Politics of Difference*, New Jersey, Princeton University Press, 1990

————, *Throwing Like a Girl and Other Essays in Feminist Philosophy and Social Theory*, Bloomington, Indiana, Indiana University Press, 1990

INTERNET

A Liberty Library, www.well.com/conf/liberty/home.html

All about Libertarianism

Blond, P, 'The Rise of the Red Tories', Prospect, www.city.ac.uk/social

'Bush: U.S. at War with "Islamic Fascists" ', CNN.com, www.cnn.com/2006/POLITICS/08/10/washington.terror.plot/index.html, 10 August 2006

Chu, B, 'Chinese Liberalism vs. Western Authoritarianism', http://thechinadesk.blogspot.com/2007/09/chinese-liberalism-vs-western.html, September 2007

Cole, Juan, 'Informed Comment: Thoughts on the Middle East, History, and Religion', www.juancole.com

Couch, K and R Fairlie, 'Last Hired, First Fired? Black-White Unemployment and the Business Cycle', http://ideas.repec.org/p/uct/uconnp/2005–50.html Working papers: 2005–50, http://ideas.repec.org/s/uct/uconnp.html, University of Connecticut, Department of Economics, November 2005

Dillow, C, 'Don't Bank on a Caring, Sharing Recession', *Times Online*, http://www.timesonline.co.uk/tol/comment/columnists/guest_contributors/article5511646.ece, 14 January 2009

Dobson, James, 'Letter from 2012 in Obama's America' (PDF), Focus on the Family Action, 23 October 2008

Engelhardt, T, The World according to Tomdispatch.com, www.Tomdispatch.com

Ertelt, Steven, 'James Dobson Mourns Obama Victory, Forecasts Significant Abortion Promotion', http://www.lifenews.com/nat4557.html, 7 November 2008

Eikmeier, D, 'Qutbism, An Ideology of Islamic-Fascism 2007', http://www.carlisle.army.mil/usawc/parameters/07spring/eikmeier.pdf

Gill, N S, 'A Little Etymology', www.About.comAncient/Classical History

Haught, J, 'My Name is Jean-Paul Sartre', lecture at University of Charleston, 20 November 1991, http://www.holysmoke.org/haught/sartre.html

——, 'To Question is to Answer', http//:holysmoke.org/haughty/index.html

Hooper, W, 'Not the End of History? Democracy & Various Heretical Arguments for Liberal Authoritarianism 2008', www.willyhoops.com/democracy-authoritarianism.htm

Internet Encyclopaedia of Philosophy. http://www.iep.utm.edu/p/polphil.htm

Jefferson, T, 'The Jefferson Bible', http://www.angelfire.com/co/JeffersonBible/

Johnson, Paul, 'The Myth of American Isolationism – Reinterpreting the Past', Foreign Affairs, http://www.foreignaffairs.com/articles/50987/paul-johnson/the-myth-of-american-isolationism-reinterpreting-the-past, May/June 1995

Kagan, R, 'The End of the End of History: Why the Twenty-First Century will look like the Nineteenth', *The New Republic*, http://www.carnegieendowment.org/publications/index.cfm?fa=view&id=20030, 23 April 2008

Kant, Immanuel, 'Observations on the Feeling of the Beautiful and Sublime', translated by John T Goldthwait, University of California Press, http://en.wikipedia.org/wiki/Observations_on_the_Feeling_of_the_Beautiful_and_Sublime, 2003

Keele, 'Guide to Political Thought and Ideology', www.keele.ac.uk/depts/por/ptbase.htm

Kimber, Richard, 'Political Thought', www.psr.keele.ac.uk/thought.htm

Krastev, I, *The New Europe: Respectable Populism, Clockwork Liberalism*, Open Democracy, http://www.opendemocracy.net/democracy-europe_constitution/new_europe_3376.jsp, 21 March 2006

Marx/Engels Archive, http://csf.colorado.edu/psn/marx

Maslow, A H, 'A Theory of Human Motivation', *Psychological Review*, 1943, 50 (4), 370–96, http://psychclassics.yorku.ca/Maslow/motivation.htm

Mayer, C, 'Labour Pains' in *Time*, http://www.time.com/time/magazine/article/0,9171,1904081,00.html, 23 June 2009

Mazzoleni, O, *Moral Integrity and Reputation of Politicians as Perceived by Supporters of Anti-Establishment Parties. A Comparison between Switzerland and Italy*, http://www.esri.salford.ac.uk/esri/resources/uploads/File/Conferences/CorruptionMarch07/Mazzoleni%20-%20Paper.doc, 2007

Prepared for the Workshop 'Corruption and Democracy in Europe: Public Opinion and Social Representations', University of Salford, 29–31 March 2007

McDonald, Henry, 'Ulster Police Defend Response to Attacks on Romanians', *Guardian.co.uk*, http://www.guardian.co.uk/uk/2009/jun/19/belfast-romanians-race-attack, June 2009

Muhlberger, S, Chronology of Modern Democracy compiled for the World History of Democracy site, www.nipissingu.ca/department/history/muhlberger/histdem/, 2004

Political Compass, www.politicalcompass.org

Political Philosophy: Internet Resources, http://people.brandeis.edu/~teuber/polphil.html [Takes you into hundreds of interesting sites]

Posen, A, 'Do Better Institutions Make Better Policy? Review', http://ideas.repec.org/a/bla/intfin/v1y1998i1p173–205.html, *International Finance*, http://ideas.repec.org/s/bla/intfin.html, Blackwell Publishing, vol. I, pp.173 and 205, October 1998

Sayyeed, Abdul-Ala Maududi, 'Jihad in Islam' (Lahore, Pakistan: Islamic Publications), pp. 8, 9, and 24, http://www.islamistwatch.org/texts/maududi/maududi.html

Spade, Paul Vincent, Jean-Paul Sartre quotes from Internet site: pvspade.com/sartre/pdf

Stanford Encyclopaedia of Philosophy, http://plato.stanford.edu

Qutb, Sayyid, *In the Shade of the Quran*, translated by A A Shamis Riyadh, Saudi Arabia: WAMYInternational, www.youngmuslims.ca/online_library/tafsir/syed_qutb/, June 1995

Qutb, Sayyid, *Milestones*, http://www.youngmuslims.ca/online_library/books/milestones/hold/index_2.asp, American Trust Publications, December 1991

Treanor, P, 'Liberalism, Market, Ethics', http://web.inter.nl.net/users/Paul.Treanor/index.html#lib

van der Veen, Wilma, Website, stmarys.ca/~evanderveen/wvdv/

Wikipedia, www.wikipedia.org – Over 15,000 articles just on political philosophy, over 200,000 on politics. Read cautiously.

Winter-Ebmer, R and S Raphael, 'Identifying the Effect of Unemployment on Crime', http://ideas.repec.org/p/cdl/ucsdec/98–19.html, University of California at San Diego, Economics Working Paper Series 98–19, Department of Economics, UC San Diego, 1998 http://ideas.repec.org/s/cdl/ucsdec.html

Printed in Great Britain
by Amazon

79264365R00154